IMPRESARIO

IMPRESARIO

A MEMOIR BY *S. Hurok*

IN COLLABORATION WITH *Ruth Goode*

GREENWOOD PRESS, PUBLISHERS
WESTPORT, CONNECTICUT

Library of Congress Cataloging in Publication Data

Hurok, Solomon, 1888-1974.
 Impresario.

 Reprint of the ed. published by Random House,
New York.
 1. Hurok, Solomon, 1888-1974. 2. Impresarios--
Correspondence, reminiscences, etc. I. Goode,
Ruth, joint author. II. Title.
ML429.H87A3 1975   780'.92'4 [B]   75-8838
ISBN 0-8371-8125-9

Originally published in 1946 by Random House, New York

Reprinted with the permission of Random House, Inc.

Reprinted in 1975 by Greenwood Press,
a division of Williamhouse-Regency Inc.

Library of Congress Catalog Card Number 75-8838

ISBN 0-8371-8125-9

Printed in the United States of America

To my wife

EMMA

and my daughter

RUTH

CONTENTS

List of Illustrations

LIST OF ILLUSTRATIONS

Illustrations following Page 196

My gratitude goes in full measure to the many artists, colleagues, critics, newspaper men and women, some of whose names appear in these pages, and to the unnumbered good people, down to and including the chef at Fouquet's, who have helped to make my first thirty years as an impresario so richly satisfying.

I make my deepest obeisance, however, to those who quietly and almost anonymously have walked beside me during some of these years: to Mae Frohman, my good right hand, who has held me back by the coattails from many a brink and spurred me to climb to new heights, sharing my crises no less than my triumphs; to soft-speaking, sharp-thinking Marks Levine, whose wisdom it has been my privilege to enjoy for a decade and a half; to Gerald Goode, the demon head of my publicity department for fifteen years, with whom even my disagreements were electrifying; to my present publicity man, Barry Hyams, and to my entire office staff; to L. E. Behymer who traveled 3,000 miles, at the beginning of my Hippodrome era, to call on me at my desk space in 220 West 42nd Street and see what I was made of; to the managers from coast to coast whose names are too many to mention here though never too many for me to remember and cherish. With their help I look forward to another thirty years of adventure in the world of good entertainment.

S. HUROK

IMPRESARIO

Overture

I AM A HERO-WORSHIPER. I belong to that fraternity who crowd into the aisles, run down to the platform and stand agape, eyes turned upward, until the last encore. I am one of that clamorous throng that rudely wedges its way into dressing rooms after each performance. I am star-struck!

All my life has been devoted to the pursuit of artists. When, with Charles B. Dillingham's urgent fist prodding the small of my back, I bent speechless over the hand of Anna Pavlova for the first time, I was an acolyte adoring at a hallowed shrine.

When I heard Feodor Ivanovitch Chaliapin present me to Jules Massenet with those magic words, "This is my American manager," I took flight to the special heaven reserved for fools and hero-worshipers. It mattered hardly at all that the great basso was telling an outrageous lie, that he was having his little joke at my expense. It made little difference, at that moment, that I had spent all but my last cent to make the trip to Paris, that Chaliapin had told me only an hour before that he had no use for an American manager because he did not have the slightest intention of ever returning to America. But whatever Feodor Ivanovitch might think, I was his American manager, if for no other reason than that, a creature obsessed, I would move mountains, wrestle whirlwinds and sit out a war and a revolution until his little joke became truth.

3

And I was still a hero-worshiper years later when Chaliapin brandished his throat spray and his laryngoscope before my eyes and the canceled concert dates rained about my unhappy head like hail. To me Chaliapin was then and ever will be a great man, a hero, though his malingering pushed me to the edge of bankruptcy.

I have had enough such tests in my life to prove that my case is incurable. Chaliapin with his cancellations, with his demand for $3,000 a concert—$4,000 if the concert was in the Hippodrome —was not the severest of my ordeals. Not even the various Russian Ballets which have succeeded each other regularly for a decade in my esteem—and the public's—have strained my fanatic zeal to the breaking point.

Temperament spooned by the smoking ladleful out of an international pot—Russian and English temperament, Swedish and Irish and Balkan and Californian and Dutch-Javanese temperament—all different, yet all alike in one aspect: they are all hot enough to singe the eyebrows off a manager. My eyebrows always grow back, though not, alas, my hair.

The premier dancer who offered a choice of duelling weapons to a maître de ballet; the amorous intrigue that ended with a stabbing in a hotel corridor between midnight and dawn; the merger—my dearest dream—that was sealed by hamburgers and coffee at the St. Regis in New York at three A.M. and blew up in a London courtroom—these have accelerated my pulse rate, but were mere lively incidents on a calendar whose next day always promises livelier ones.

Temperament has never frightened me. Temperament is a hero-worshiper's bread and caviar. A serene spirit like Marian Anderson's is all too rare. An impresario's day is incomplete without at least one of these: a wire from a violinist in Florida who won't fill a sold-out concert date in Canada because it's snowing there; a call from Omaha that two leading dancers have run away to get married—or divorced, it's the same thing; an attack of nerves that sets the wires humming from Houston; or a train missed because a godlike Hindu dancer won't leave without his stack of movie-fan magazines.

Temperament creates problems—to patch up the schism or to leave it, to tell the press or to kill the story, and always the problem of how to keep the show going on.

But temperament is still my caviar. It is very expensive caviar, to be sure, and one must know how to enjoy it without getting indigestion. Bread I could have earned in almost any other business, but caviar is irresistible. I have had to learn how to cure a singer's cold on concert night without medicine; how to stop a duel with an aspirin tablet; how to avert a murder with a yo-yo top; how to concoct a love philtre out of a Coca-Cola.

Yet with one artist all ingenuity failed. Isadora Duncan, the Olympian in the red tunic with a bottle of champagne in her hand, bested me in every encounter. Nothing, nobody could tame Isadora.

The veteran hero-worshiper sees yet never believes that idols are made of clay. Goddess that she was, Isadora's frailties too were on an Olympian scale. Moderation was a word without any meaning whatever to her. She had no conception of money—mine, yours or her own; she was incapable equally of unkindness or tact; she breakfasted on port, dined on whisky and supped on champagne. Still I adored Isadora, and I adore her still. She kissed me good-bye when we parted, and I walked in a dream back to my hotel.

When, after Isadora's departure, I found myself not only alive but flexing my wits for the next bout with temperament, I knew that I was doomed. I could never escape my fate. I was chained forever, hitched wagonlike to the stars.

I have asked myself, how does such a thing come about? How

5

does a normal, healthy child grow up to become a hero-worshiper, a genius-tamer, an impresario?

I think this might never have been my fate if I had not been born in Russia. Old Russia, like New Russia, was a land of artists, and like New Russia, it cherished its artists. The Imperial Opera and the Imperial Ballet were filled with men and women who had been born into direst poverty, who had dipped an education, a profession, a munificent living out of the bottomless coffers of the Czar only by virtue of their talent. And the people of Old Russia, like those of New Russia, adored their artists, petted their artists, begrudged their artists nothing.

When I was a boy in the Ukrainian town of Pogar not far from Kharkov, I breathed air spiced with the incense of artist-adoration.

A lad in a remote provincial town, the son of a hardware and tobacco merchant, brought up to the paternal business—could I have been farther from the shining world of the theatre, the opera, the ballet if I had been born on the moon?

Yet, though I had never heard an opera, I had heard of the opera. I had heard of the handsome giant with the incredibly wonderful voice, the basso Chaliapin. As little boys in America collect pictures of baseball players, of prize fighters—and in wartime, of war planes—so I collected pictures of artists. And at the head of my collection was Chaliapin.

The artists of Russia have been my jewels, my pride—and my undoing. I have had my ups and my downs. And I fell to the depths in every case because I have flung discretion to the winds and plunged on something Russian. In the very year which saw me climb the first Alpine height of my career—the year in which Pavlova, Duncan and Chaliapin were all under my proud management—the stones I had laboriously laid one atop another were being pried from under me by my losses on the Russian Opera Company.

I reached a peak with the Russian Pavlova and hit bottom with the Russian Chaliapin. I was climbing out of the pit a few years later only to stumble again with the Russian Habimah Theatre. I was waiting for Mary Wigman to arrive and start me on a new ascent to security when I spent almost my last penny on a Russian Gypsy troupe.

When I announced my intention of bringing over the first Russian Ballet company, Nikita Balieff, the moon-faced ringmaster of Chauve-Souris, exploded: "Look at you! You're a happy man —you have a company of puppets [the Piccoli]. Wooden dolls act and sing and dance for you. They make money and they don't make trouble. And, you fool, you want a Russian Ballet!"

The first year of the Ballet in this country almost convinced me he was right.

But I would not have missed any of them. I still seek another Chaliapin, though I must brush swooning maidens out of his path, doctor his colds, and break the back of my bank account on his fees. Or another Escudero, to divert in the act of maiming an offending stage carpenter. Or another Isadora, though she bare her bosom and lecture Bostonians on the sin of secret lust.

In retrospect such frightening moments are wrapped in a golden aura. I could not be convinced that I am still alive if I did not expect each day would bring more of them.

CHAPTER ONE

On My Way

*I*N MY BOYHOOD the names of Gomel and Mogilev were familiar. They were near-by towns where the folk of Pogar had relatives and business connections, where they went to visit. Kharkov was as familiar, and far more glamorous; it was to our South Ukrainian town what Indianapolis is to the corn and hog farmers of Indiana.

Pogar was a town of no importance. It did not even break the headlines when the Red Army came roaring back across the South Ukraine, sweeping the Nazis once more out of Kharkov, battering through at Smolensk. Even when Gomel and Mogilev enjoyed their brief illumination in the news, little Pogar was only one of the dozen or hundred "populated places" liberated in one day.

To me, looking back over the years and the miles, Pogar has its own tender moment. It was, after all, the place where everything began, including my life.

Pogar had a population of about five thousand souls, mostly merchants and tradesmen serving the surrounding farms. Produce merchants came to our district from all parts of Russia to buy potatoes, onions, apples. Trade was brisk in flax and tobacco. From our gentry's huge estates these products were shipped all over Russia and even to the world beyond.

There were seven churches in Pogar, and our one synagogue. In the center of the town was the small city park, donated by a rich landowner. Lilacs bloomed in the park, and I climbed the iron fence to steal the fragrant blossoms for my sweetheart.

None of our streets was paved, and only one, the mile-long main street, was cobblestoned. In the summer evenings the folk of Pogar strolled up this street, from the pine forest that skirted one end of the town, through the town, and up a hill. The hill broke sharply down into a ravine, and there, neatly fringed by sandy beaches and with a backdrop of pines, lay our little lake. From it a stream flowed into the Desna, which flowed into the Sozh to Gomel, the Dnieper to Kiev, and thence to the Black Sea.

Easter was the beginning of life in Pogar. At Easter the afternoons were already long and beautiful, the sun already warm, and all of us boys and girls and some of the grown-up married folk would climb our hill to make the *Karavod*, taking hands in a circle and singing all the old songs. We boys would dart from the circle, down the cobbled street to see how much more of the lake's ice had broken and melted away, how much farther the water had spread— and then back again up the hill to join the singing. But we could not stay long. Every minute, it seemed to us, the sun grew perceptibly warmer, the ice receded farther, the summer and swimming and days of good fun drew closer. There were still weeks of alternate frost and mud between Easter and summer, and the sap was yet to rise and be gathered from the maple trees, but once Easter had come, summer was in the air.

Later the apple orchards bloomed, and the lilacs in the city park. And then at last came the long light evenings, the moonlit nights when we rowed on the lake until nearly dawn, singing to our accordions and balalaikas. I too played the balalaika, badly.

In summer the students were home from the universities; our main street was festive with their uniforms, and there was new life in Pogar. Some spent their vacations hunting and idling, but the intellectuals got up amateur theatricals, lectures, discussion

9

groups. The quiet town awoke to find itself bubbling with secret revolutionary fervor.

And then, too soon, the sad time came again. The days grew cool, the sunlight thinner and briefer, and the uniformed students, like the bright birds, were gone, leaving our main street drab and commonplace. The heavy rains poured down, turning the roads to mud. Ruts froze hub-deep so that one walked as over sharp stones. The streets thawed and froze and thawed and froze again, and boards were laid down so the people could walk, and we never went out without our galoshes.

Today my life functions at its peak as summer ends; there is the bustling frenzy of another new season getting under way. And yet I cannot see the summer die without that nameless melancholy, that tender regretful longing which is in the marrow of my bones.

But with the first snow those melancholy vapors vanished, swept away by the sharp dry cold, heady as dry champagne. The trees, the shabby little houses were deep in white, glittering with a clean beauty that was blinding in the sun and other-worldly in the moonlight. We had great nights in our little town in the winter. That cheap and foolish little town was heaven.

Christmas was best. Christmas was the high and happy time, the gaudy frosting on the cake of the year. The tinselly trees, the presents, the visiting back and forth from house to house, from town to town, from farm to village, the eating and drinking. It went on for one, two, even three weeks when New Year's came late. I can still remember the feel of the clean, cold, wrinkled cheeks I had to kiss, the prick of frozen whiskers as the old men kissed me, first on one side, then on the other. The market overflowed with food, with smoked meats and wooden tubs of fresh caviar, pressed caviar, red caviar, with fish and herring by the barrels.

The market was not far from my father's store. My father had some tobacco plantations, some as near as seven, some as far as thirty-five miles from town. But he also did a wholesale and retail business in iron, steel, paints, window glass and assorted hardware.

The bookkeeping in our store was done very simply. There was a big empty wall, and when a peasant or a builder came in and made a purchase, my father took a piece of chalk and wrote on the wall, "Ivan Stepanovitch owes us 180 rubles." Sometimes the list was very long. "Gregor Fyodorovitch," the wall said, "owes us 500 rubles; Piotr Igorovitch owes us 680 rubles," and so on. And when Piotr Igorovitch came in to buy a new saw, and my father would ask him for something on account, he would say, "Me? I don't owe you any money. Look at the wall!" And sure enough, there would be no trace of Piotr Igorovitch's name or the amount of his debt on the wall.

My father, who was not the shrewdest of businessmen, never quite understood why he remembered Piotr Igorovitch's bill so clearly, and nothing about the occasion of its being paid, but he blamed his memory rather than doubt the wall. We children, however, were on to Piotr Igorovitch. We knew that while he stood in his great coat, seemingly enjoying the warmth of the big stove and waiting his turn with sleepy patience, his shoulder was slyly rubbing the chalk record of his debt off the wall. When I was about eight years old my brothers had grown up enough to be listened to in business affairs, and they abolished the wall-accounts and instituted a more conventional system of bookkeeping.

When my nostalgia gets the better of me I have only to pick up a volume of Ostrovsky's plays. There is the life of Pogar, the life of the thousands of Pogars of Old Russia, complete to the last unbuttoned button: the pompous and stupid officials, the little tradesmen, the great-hearted, good-natured, gullible Russian peasant whose patience and fortitude were the chains of his

11

bondage then, but are the weapons with which he is restoring his land today.

In a recent short film about Russian children in wartime the teacher was reading to the little ones. The story she read was about young Ivan, who followed a Red Army soldier all the way to his village and then called the police to arrest the soldier, a Nazi in a stolen uniform.

"Tell me, Ivan," demanded the spy, before he was led away to be shot. "My uniform is perfect, I speak Russian as well as you —how did you know I was not a Red Army man?"

"I followed you for a long time," Ivan replied. "The sun was shining, the birds chirping, everything was beautiful. And you were not singing. So I knew you could not be a Russian."

To be born in Russia is to be born singing. I was playing the balalaika when I was eight. There was not a worse balalaika player in Pogar, perhaps not in all the Ukraine, but still I played. And what were we doing those lovely long summer nights, on the lake, on the way home when the early dawn was already pointing a finger into the eastern sky? We were singing three-part choruses.

I used to visit my married sister who lived on one of the tobacco plantations. There was a water mill near by, where the peasants came to have their grain ground. At night I would steal out of my room and go down to the mill.

The farmers might have to stay two days, three days, waiting their turn with the miller. They would put their small bony horses out to pasture, open their bundles of bread, herring, cucumber, fat pork, and sit under the trees by the mill stream, eating and telling stories of Russia in their youth, of the Polish war. The younger men sat around their fires, listening sometimes, but mostly they would sing. There were always two or three balalaikas and accordions, never any lack of rich baritones, ringing tenors, and at least one earth-shaking basso.

Farther off a boy would be feeding his tethered horses, singing to the sound of his companion's wooden flute. From still another quarter a shepherd's pipe wailed in a thin minor key. And as I crept sleepily home into my bed, early in the morning, the girls would pass under my window on their way to the fields, singing.

When I left Russia to make my fortune, whatever my confused aspirations, I carried the singing of Russia with me. The magnificence of the New World dazzled me, the splendor of its opportunities fired me with ambition, but I was appalled by a land which did not sing. I always felt that where a nation, a community, even two people get together and sing, they cannot think or do evil. It was this lack of a people's music in America, together with my unquenchable Russian enthusiasm for artists, which combined to push me into the world of music.

In Pogar I was a bad boy. Not only did I steal lilacs from the city park, I also sneaked up on the women bathing in the lake. I was a very bad boy in school. I showed a really remarkable resourcefulness in finding ways not to do my lessons. Pogar was too small for me.

I begged my father to take me on his next buying trip to Nizhny-Novgorod. This is the ancient storied town, now called Gorki, where for as long as there has been a land of Russia, the great fair went on for three months during the summer. When I was thirteen my father at last took me there, and showed me Moscow, too, on the way. Before those domes and steeples, the great squares and the busy bustling streets—all of them paved, too!—I lost all heart for Pogar.

The next year, at fourteen, I was already a shrewd buyer, good at driving a bargain, and I went out to buy merchandise for our business. My horizon expanded. I made friends in the cities where my buying trips took me, began to go to revolutionary meetings, and became an inconspicuous figure in the little revolutionary movement of Pogar.

In 1904 my father sent me to Ekaterinoslav on business. One

night some friends took me to the iron works of the city, to hear a speaker. He was a stocky man with a long beard, a bushel of hair, flowing mustache, and he was dressed as a merchant. But he did not talk like a merchant. What he said seared the mind with words of flame. Six months later I learned that I had listened to Maxim Gorki that night.

Russia blew wide open the next October. It was the fateful 1905. On the fourteenth there was the general strike, and the constitution was given to the people. Later it was taken away.

Back in Pogar I announced that I could no longer stay at home. My father gave me 1000 rubles and sent me to Kharkov to learn the hardware business in the big city. I was to work for our brokers, Panamarov and Rudzov.

But I had much more ambitious plans. After a week in Kharkov, I returned to another small town near Pogar to visit a sweetheart, and then I was off.

Of my 1000-ruble capital I still had 900. I went to Brest-Litovsk, which did a thriving trade in smuggling emigrants out of Russia. It was a Friday afternoon.

In Brest-Litovsk one could do no business until Saturday night. Then we each paid our 350 rubles to the black-market emigration operator and were sent out of Russia, huddled on the hard benches of a third-class train. We crossed the Russian border, but at the threshold of the great Austro-Hungarian Empire we were turned back.

The black-market operator tried again. We were taken to the eastern edge of Germany. To those whose memories of the map of Europe do not go back before 1914 this is all very confusing, but it will help to remember that there was no Poland then except in the hearts of Polish patriots, that the Czar, the King of Prussia, and the Empress of Austria had long before divided Poland among them like three greedy beggars with a tasty *pirojki* pie; the three well-fed empires met and glared at each other across lines which

14

they had drawn on the prostrate body of Poland a century before.

At the German border, in the dead of night, carrying all our belongings above our heads, we waded across a chilly, shallow lake. When we stepped ashore we stood dripping on the inhospitable soil of the Kaiser.

The immigration officials at the border town of Mislevitch put us through de-lousing steam baths and health examinations and then shipped us to Hamburg, to dump us into barracks, where we lived for three weeks, sleeping in our clothes on the hard wooden floor, our scanty possessions for a pillow. In the morning thin coffee was poured out for us, and rolls handed around. In the evening big kettles of unsavory soup were carried in.

I suppose that barracks still stands, unless, like many other symbols of an ugly past, it has been blasted by the bombs of the United Nations. I know it still stood in 1931 because in that year I was in Hamburg to meet Yasha Yushny, the genial master of ceremonies of the little Russian revue, *The Bluebird*. The show was neither a great contribution to theatrical history nor a good financial enterprise, but it gave me my wife, Emma, and I am amply rewarded.

From the Kaiser's excellent hotel our group of immigrants, swelled now to a considerable number from other lands of Eastern and Central Europe, were at last ferried across Hamburg's busy harbor to a broad-beamed tub called the *Graf Wildersee*, and poured into the hold. I slept miserably in a hammock on that rocking, pitching little 6,000-ton washtub, in air reeking of tar, herring and unwashed, seasick humanity, for twenty-three nights. And then I stepped ashore at Castle Garden.

On that morning in May, 1906, I looked at New York for the first time. Tired, ill-fed, bulky with my two heavy hampers of clothes and my goose-feather pillow, I put regret behind me and thought about my next step. I had relatives in Brooklyn, and relatives in Philadelphia. Brooklyn was nearer; perhaps that was

15

why I chose Philadelphia. Wasn't it, after all, the city of Independence Hall, the Liberty Bell, and especially Benjamin Franklin? I arrived in New York with three rubles in my pocket. When I exchanged this I had $1.50. But I needed $2.25 for the fare to Philadelphia. It cost me 50 cents to get to Brooklyn and find a relative of a Pogar friend, to borrow the additional sum, which, with my expenses, now came to $1.25. He was a plumber's helper earning $3.50 a week. It took him a good day and a half to get together $1.25 for me. I had 10 cents left for carfare from Broad Street station and I walked to save the dime. It was a long walk, a hot day, and I still carried all my belongings. I fell into my relatives' house, a very weary and disenchanted young man.

I peddled notions in Philadelphia, with indifferent success. The impatient housewives couldn't understand a word of my sales talk. I progressed to a can factory, a pie bakery, an ice-cream factory. I was a conductor on a street car, very briefly—the dispatcher soon found out I was letting people off at the wrong corners.

I washed soda bottles for a dollar a day, but found it unprofitable work and quit. My most interesting job in Philadelphia was bundling newspapers on Saturday night for the Sunday edition of the old Philadelphia *Press*, because Linton Martin was a reporter on the *Press* and used to take a bunch of us shabby boys home to his apartment and play *Tristan und Isolde* on the piano for us at 3 A.M. Martin later became music critic of the *Inquirer*, and my good friend.

In the end I went back to hardware, working for Metzger and Son on South Street, selling hardware, paint and glass.

By November I was rich. I was earning six or seven dollars a week. I bought myself a new suit for eight dollars and took the train for New York to see some friends from home. I went down to Brooklyn Bridge, to Park Row, where the newspaper offices were. I watched the editions being thrown on the newsstands, heard the newsboys shouting, drank in the bustle, the rattling trolleys, the tinny music of a barrel organ and said to myself, "This is no village." I returned to Philadelphia, settled my affairs and hurried back to New York.

I went down to Chambers Street and offered my services to Charlie Weiland, hardware wholesaler at 147-149. He suggested a dollar a week less than I had been earning in Philadelphia, but for the opportunity of making my career in the metropolis I accepted. I went to work as a stock boy, and enrolled in night school at the Educational Alliance to improve my English.

I was on my way.

CHAPTER TWO

A Comet Named Feodor

𝓕EODOR CHALIAPIN was my personal Halley's Comet. I can remember the breathless nights in 1910 when whole families sat on the rooftops of New York with their mattresses and pillows, watching the gleaming visitor from the infinite as it swam across our sky. Little children were awakened to gaze on the shining wanderer of remote and silent spaces which would not be seen again in the lifetime of most of us.

Just such a celestial visitor was the Russian basso to me. Three times he burst upon the firmament of my world, set it afire with the brilliance which dazzled my own and many other worshipful eyes.

Unlike Halley's Comet, however, which came and went with a magnificent aloofness from human affairs, the comet named Feodor carried in his shining train both fortune and disaster for me. Except for the first time, when his distance from the last row of the gallery was still to be measured in light-years, at every encounter I could distinctly smell the odor of my own singed hair.

The name Feodor Ivanovitch Chaliapin had been familiar to me before I left his and my native land. From 1902 until after the abortive 1905 revolution, Russia was aflame. The young people, down to boys and girls of ten, hungered and thirsted for freedom.

Not a young man or young woman, who had enough education to have heard of European democracy, failed to plunge into one of the dozen, the hundred eager tasks of preparing for the day of revolution. They wrote and printed and distributed leaflets. They carried on propaganda in the factories, the university classrooms. They gathered groups of illiterates and taught them in their own homes.

Chaliapin, already famous as an artist in the Petersburg Opera, was more famous to me as one of the young men leading the burning youth of Russia toward freedom. He was a friend and comrade of Gorki and Andreyev, young revolutionary writers. His big frame and strong face were familiar to us on the postcards sold in music stores and bookshops all over Russia—"Chaliapin meets Gorki," "Chaliapin with Andreyev," the captions said.

Chaliapin was born in Kazan, a provincial town on the Volga, and he was a true son of Mother Volga, far more her child than a child of the frustrated clerk who was his father or the unhappy woman who suffered a beating regularly on the twentieth of each month, the day the elder Chaliapin received his salary and spent it on vodka.

The boy grew to manhood on Mother Volga's bosom, working as a stevedore on the river boats. It was there he met Maxim Gorki, another rebellious peasant lad, and he used to tell wonderful tales of their days and nights on the river. There were times when their only trousers were made of two wheat sacks stitched together with rope, with a rope around their skinny hips to hold them up.

He told, too, of the singing of the river men, not only the famous boatmen's song which has been so brutally tortured for American ears, but songs like "Dobinushka," an eloquent complaint against the back-breaking work of the stevedore, and unnumbered rich articulations of the hard life of the river, its longing and its beauty.

19

Chaliapin was all but self-taught, vocally. Except for a brief period with the teacher Oussatoff, he gathered up almost unconsciously the technique to enhance his enormous native genius. Probably his experience with Mamontov's famous opera company in Moscow, in which he sang leading bass roles in most of the great Russian operas, gained him much as a craftsman, but his gift for evocative detail in a characterization, his ability to sink himself in the character, particularly in *Boris Godunov*, was his own. By the time I had heard of him he had already stepped beyond the confines of Russia to be heard by the outside world, at La Scala in Milan in 1901. He spent another season there in 1904.

First Round to the Critics

When I landed in the United States I was an unnoted and unnoteworthy member of a migration of some magnitude and importance. Other young Russians, far better known than I, were also journeying across the Atlantic to America in 1905 and 1906. Poets, artists, writers poured in upon these shores, escaping the Czar's retribution. Among them was Alla Nazimova, the lovely actress who was the 1905 revolution's gift to Hollywood, and Breshkovska who later became the Grandmother of the Revolution, and Maxim Gorki.

Gorki was admitted over the objections of some sections of the press and his lectures were sold out despite the fact that he spoke in Russian, with an interpreter who read his speech afterward in English.

I followed Gorki to Philadelphia, to Boston. I was in the crowd of admirers pressed against the lecture platform at the end of each evening, happy if I could get close enough to grasp his hand and say a word of greeting in Russian.

When the Metropolitan Opera announced that Chaliapin

would sing in the season of 1906-1907, I had no intimation of any special significance in the news for me. I only knew that I would be in the top gallery for every one of his performances—and I was. I heard him sing *Mefistofele*, *The Barber of Seville*, *Don Giovanni* as often as he sang them.

The reaction of the New York critics puzzled me—and it was not the last time I was to be perplexed by them. The last time, I am sure, will be the day I read my final batch of newspapers.

With one exception, they detested him. They accused him of clowning on the revered Metropolitan stage. Only one voice rose in counterpoint to the chorus of disapproval, to articulate the delight of the public in this new and original artist.

That was Henry T. Finck, the critic of the *Evening Post*, who bravely maintained his opinion that the Russian was one of the great singing actors of all time. When Chaliapin returned in 1921 and the critics rose to unanimous rhapsodies in his favor, Finck had the exquisite satisfaction of being able to point out that he had said as much the first time, and had said it alone.

Chaliapin shocked the critics, that first time. Always impatient of convention, he created his own interpretation of the operatic character he played. In *Mefistofele* he came on the stage, his magnificent body half naked. The critics could not accept his earthy characterizations. The public could, however, and made no secret of its enthusiasm. Chaliapin had an enormous popular success.

His reputation as a man who loved to eat and drink began on that first visit. He told reporters, as he was boarding the boat at the end of his engagement, that the best thing in New York was the Castle Cave Restaurant, then a modest place on Seventh Avenue in the Twenties, owned by one Bardush.

Chaliapin did not set foot on these shores again until 1921. But Bardush was at the pier to meet him in a handsome Packard. We had a feast at the Castle Cave that night which lasted until

21

four in the morning, beginning with Bardush's famous oysters prepared over charcoal—of which Chaliapin ate three or four dozen—and continuing with enormous steaks.

That was during the Prohibition era, but Bardush brought out his finest French wines, white and red. Chaliapin had made his restaurant famous by that remark to reporters on the pier, and Bardush was bent on showing his gratitude for fifteen years of unexpected prosperity.

Bohemia in Brownsville

But that was in 1921, and many things happened to me before I sat down to feast with Feodor Chaliapin in the Castle Cave. Yet, coming out of the Metropolitan after one of those Sunday-night concerts in the winter of 1907—I went to them all—I gazed across Broadway to the office building that held Brown's Chop House of savory memory.

"Some day," I said to a friend, "I'm going to manage artists like Chaliapin, maybe even Chaliapin himself. And I'll have my office in that building."

My companion, who has since proved his solid sense by becoming a produce merchant in another city, neither laughed at me nor argued with me. He merely shrugged his shoulders and began hunting through his pockets to see if he had the carfare home.

On the whole my friends were tolerant of my ambitions. We were all alike, all afire with hopes and plans. Each of us was Columbus, sailing a frail vessel across new seas on a course known only to fate, but each of us was as sure as Columbus that he would discover the rich land at the other side of the world.

For myself, I was already impatient on that Sunday night. I had been in America since May, in New York since Thanksgiving. I had my job downtown in the hardware store on Chambers Street, at which I earned seven dollars regularly every week, and I sold enough Rogers silver on Sundays and evenings to add at least five dollars a week more to my income.

I felt, walking out of the Metropolitan Opera House in my eight-dollar suit, a complete New Yorker.

I went home and wrote a letter to Chaliapin, care of the Metropolitan Opera House, proposing myself as his manager for the next season. He did not answer.

I was becoming more and more active in the labor movement, but my activities, as I look back on them, seemed always to follow the track of my obsession with music.

While I was one of the first organizers in the campaign to send the Socialist Shipliakoff to the New York State Assembly from the Twenty-third District, I did my part by way of music. Rallies for the campaign were set to music. Benefits were concerts —by popular artists of the day, when I could persuade them; by boys of the neighborhood who hoped to be concert artists of the day after next. Mark Warnow, the successful band leader, has since reminded me of the violin concert he played for me at the Sunday School of the Labor Lyceum at 219 Sackman Street.

Brownsville in those days was a steaming microcosm of culture in the heart of Brooklyn, alive with intellectual striving and artistic hungers. It was no garden spot to the eye, with its pushcart-cluttered market streets and the frame houses in various states of upkeep which shouldered each other in the residential districts. But it was a lush garden for the mind. In South America, Cuba, Mexico, in the capitals of Europe I have met musicians, artists and writers who first budded in Brownsville.

In meeting rooms above the crowded stores the air shook with furiously happy argument, spiced with the odors from the delicatessen downstairs—a peculiarly fortunate arrangement considering how intellectual activity always sharpens the appetite. And the argument continued through the adjournment for a hot pastrami sandwich with dill pickle and unnumbered glasses of tea.

There was never any lack of audience for speakers, for concerts, and I was kept busy supplying the artists and organizing the events. Elsewhere in New York in those days music was not big business. Concerts offering artists of world renown, two or three of them in a joint appearance, failed to sell out the thousand seats in the old Steinway Hall on Fourteenth Street.

But music thrived in Brownsville. So, having tried my managerial wings on our local talent and what smaller artists the Wolfson Musical Bureau—my first contact in the business world of music—could swing my way, I began to have bigger ideas.

Perhaps that is understatement. What I hatched, lying awake one restless night, was the biggest idea of all. I would get Efrem Zimbalist!

The name Zimbalist, in the year 1911, could only be written in capitals. The stripling from Russia was the sensation, the lion, the darling of the music world. You did not merely say "Zimbalist"—you either whispered it in awe or shouted it in wild acclaim. His coming had been heralded by rhapsodic reports of his European triumphs; his debut in Boston had set the music world to quivering with ecstasy. For me to dare to ask Zimbalist to play his violin in Brownsville was pure brass. Brownsville had a word for it: we called it *chutzpah*.

Trembling a little at my own foolhardiness, I invaded the sacred precincts of Carnegie Hall and called upon the prodigy's manager, Loudon Charlton. Charlton listened politely to my proposition, which was of itself a surprise. For I not only wanted Zimbalist to play at Brownsville's New Palm Garden for the benefit of the Socialist Party; I wanted him to play at a bargain rate, besides!

Charlton did not throw me out of his offices. He sent me to Zimbalist. The young man was staying with his mother at the Park Chambers on Sixth Avenue and 56th Street.

This was a moment for me. For the first time I sat and talked, face to face, as manager to artist, with a Big Name. Thirty years ago Zimbalist was a delicate-featured young man with curly black hair and a gentle, open face. He listened to me with sympathetic courtesy. When I left him I had a contract in my pocket. The contract specified $750 for the concert—it was not good business for an artist to cut his fee—but Zimbalist had agreed to deduct $250 and call it a personal donation to the Socialist Party.

The concert was a sensational success. Brownsville was enriched by a great musical event and the Socialist Party by a tidy sum for its treasury.

As for me . . . Now I could write to Chaliapin again. Still no answer.

How to Found a Musical Society

By now I was married for the first time—my sweetheart from the town near Pogar had followed me to America. I was a man with a position in the community. But Brownsville, like Pogar, was small. I had long been dreaming of managing a concert in Carnegie Hall. If Zimbalist would play for me in the New Palm Gardens, why not in Carnegie?

With all my brashness, I could not yet imagine, in type on window cards and three-sheets, the words S. HUROK PRESENTS.

I had a friend and partner, since deceased, whose name was Goldberg. We put the first two letters of each of our names together, coupled them with Beethoven's own prefix as a symbol of our aspirations, and thus was born the Van Hugo Musical Society.

The Van Hugo Musical Society presented Efrem Zimbalist in a concert in Carnegie Hall. The house was packed, and there were two hundred fifty fervent Zimbalist admirers on the stage. With a prudence which has not always been my characteristic,

25

I had not given up my hardware job. I was an impresario only evenings, Sundays and holidays, and also during lunch hours, when I went down to the newspaper offices to place the advertisements for my first real concert venture.

My boss, the store manager, was a Mr. Fred Dietz, a music lover who played the flute and held chamber-music sessions in his parlor at home. I invited him to the concert.

"Wonderful!" he exclaimed, gazing over the full house. "I suppose those people on the platform are your Society?"

"Yes, of course," I answered blithely.

My first success was sweet, as sweet and heady as first love. The curly-haired boy with the violin had not finished his first encore before I was planning the details of another appearance for him on the same stage.

This time I did not write Chaliapin. I cabled him.

Not long after I received a cable in reply.

"MEET ME GRAND HOTEL PARIS CHALIAPIN," it said.

After the first wild excitement subsided and I could feel the crumpled cablegram in my pocket without a furiously pounding pulse, I realized that I faced a first-class dilemma.

There was in my bank account a little money, the capital I had painfully built up to finance my infant concert business. Yet, Chaliapin had called. Could I ignore that summons?

Secretly I arranged my papers and prepared for the trip. I told my wife I was going to California. And I embarked on the old S.S. *Lafayette*, not third, but second class as befitted a rising impresario.

Impresario in Paris

The journey was a haze of impatience, of which I remember only that I landed at Le Havre, took the train for Paris, left my bag at the Continental and went at once to the Grand Hotel.

Chaliapin was not in.

With an hour or so to kill, I never thought of going to the Louvre, the Tuileries, Napoleon's Tomb, or making any of the proper pilgrimages of a visitor to Paris. At home I had begun to meet artists—Mme. Melba, Eugene Ysaye—and I remembered that Ysaye's secretary had invited me to look him up when I was in Paris. At the time I had thought the invitation was one I could put in the future file. But here I was in Paris! I went to Ysaye's hotel.

The Belgian violinist remembered me and was more than cordial. In the end he invited me to join him and some friends at dinner that night. I accepted, and went back to the Grand Hotel.

I sent word up to Chaliapin's suite from the lobby, and was told that I could go up. All at once the moment I had dreamed of for so long was upon me. I stood in the presence of the great man, feeling like Jack face to face with the giant, a giant in a big baggy English tweed suit with gray eyes drilling holes into my pretended assurance.

He looked at me from under the eaves of his brows and shrugged.

"I did not think you would look like this," he rumbled ominously.

"How . . ." My voice stuck, and I had to begin again. "How did you think I would look?"

"Oh—an old man. Long beard. Hunchback, perhaps."

He stood looking down at me from his six feet four inches, and under that amused gaze I could feel myself shrinking to pygmy size. I began to talk very fast. I outlined my plan of presenting him in New York, Chicago, San Francisco. A grand concert tour! A wonderful presentation! A fabulous success!

I talked on and on and at last the words ran out and I stopped talking. I stood waiting, ready to produce contract and fountain pen.

27

I waited the longest moment of my life, while he looked me up and down, up and down, up and down.

Then he said, "I will never go to the United States again."

He said it with a finality that left me without breath. "Then why—why did you cable me to meet you in Paris?" I stuttered at last.

"Ah—I wanted to see the man who had the effrontery to write to me for four years."

I said nothing—I couldn't have said a word to save my life. But my face must have betrayed my dismay, my utter deflation. His eyes gleamed and his rugged face broke into festoons of laugh wrinkles.

"Cheer up, my friend. Come, I'll take you to dinner at the home of a friend. You'll hear his new opera."

I explained haltingly that I had already accepted an invitation to dine with Ysaye.

"Why, then Ysaye shall come too, and his friends."

He went to the telephone and called up his host, and the roaring in my head quieted enough for me to gather that he was talking to Jules Massenet.

"I will bring with me my American manager," Chaliapin said to the venerable composer, and looked at me without a flicker on his poker face.

They played and sang until dawn. The opera was *Don Quixote* which Massenet had composed for Chaliapin, and which he later sang for the first time in Monte Carlo. I sat, modest and unnoticed, bathed in the radiance of men whose gifts were wine to me that night, and would be bread and butter to me on nights to come.

In the morning I descended to earth with the realization that my business in Paris had come to nothing. Chaliapin had dismissed me with a basso roar of laughter. I stayed in Paris only until the next boat left for New York. I arrived back home with about $170 of my little capital left.

Labor Lyceum to Hippodrome

When I returned from my ill-fated hegira I plunged into community work in Brownsville. The labor movement was taking over the building called the New Palm Garden and transforming it into a Labor Lyceum, the first, I believe, in the East. The new venture needed a director.

The job of running the Labor Lyceum appealed to me. Public service has rewards which cannot be deposited in the bank. I have always liked people, and I had, especially in those days, the horse-power to be riding in a dozen different directions at once.

As director of the Labor Lyceum I needed all my energies and more. I managed meeting rooms, trade-union offices, banquets and testimonial dinners, debates and lectures and rallies. Every local organization had its dinner, its ball, its forum. We raised money for orphan homes, for political campaigns, for the relief of strikers. When the Amalgamated Clothing Workers had their big strike there was no reserve in the treasury and we went from house to house collecting contributions for the soup kitchens.

One morning early I was routed out of my bed to find the fire engines banked three deep against the building. When the firemen left there was only a shell. We raised money and built ourselves a new Labor Lyceum.

In 1916 I felt I had done my job and was ready to go on. I tendered my resignation, was the blushing guest of honor at a testimonial dinner, and set forth again on the career of impresario.

In my new offices—my very first—at 220 West 42nd Street the Van Hugo Musical Society was reborn. I was bent on bringing music to the people.

I had had success with the Zimbalist concerts—there had been two of them, the second a farewell performance when he was going to London to marry the lovely soprano, Alma Gluck. The

29

charming romance warmed the hearts of the public for many years. The Gluck-Zimbalist concerts were a recurrent valentine of the music season.

I had had successful concerts in the Brooklyn Academy of Music, and in Philadelphia, of artists I had bought from other managers.

I had also organized a series of concerts—Music for the Masses was the way I thought of the venture—at the Fourteenth Regiment Armory in Brooklyn, and that was catastrophic. Half of the artists failed to appear, and the public did not come at all. I lost my own money and some that was not my own, and I slept badly for some time after that.

Often I had walked along Sixth Avenue and always, on the block between 43rd and 44th Streets, my feet had slowed. There stood that Colosseum of a latter-day Rome, where Toto, the clown, made you laugh and beautiful mermaids sank into crystalline pools before your bemused eyes, where Anna Pavlova followed a juggling act and a trained-animal act followed Anna Pavlova; that glittering, tinsel, rococo palace of fantasy and farce, of burlesque and beauty, the Hippodrome!

A wire fence surrounds that space today, guarding an entirely realistic paved parking lot. But on the day the wreckers began tearing down the Hippodrome I stood among the crowd of side-walk superintendents, and maybe some of that glamorous old plaster dust got into my eyes, because when I turned away and began walking uptown to my office my eyes unexpectedly stung.

The Hippodrome with its 4,700 seats, plus 280 in the pit when no orchestra was required, a stage that held 1,000, and room for 400 standees, was the place I had dreamed about. The Hippodrome was to be the temple in which simple people would enter into the mysteries of great music performed by great musicians. At the Hippodrome I could afford to give them the best at a two-dollar top.

I signed a contract with the Hippodrome management for a series of Sunday concerts.

The "Hurok Audience" Is Born

The problem was not to find the artists. They kindled at the thought of so many hundreds of eager listeners. Nor was it a problem to find the audience—from Brownsville to the Bronx there were a million potential music lovers.

The problem was to bring the audience to the artist. For of those million music lovers many had not stirred out of their little neighborhoods since the day they were brought there from Castle Garden in their rumpled suits and tight Sunday shoes by the relative who had taken them from the ungentle hands of the immigration inspectors.

There began to appear in the newspapers a series of very strange advertisements. The line, SEATS NOW AT THE BOX OFFICE, would have been Greek to my audience. What I did was to sell seats at a dozen neighborhood box offices.

There was a drug store in Harlem and a drug store in Brooklyn, a jewelry store in the Bronx. In Brownsville there were seats at Levinson's Music Store, 1737 Pitkin Avenue, and on East Broadway it was Katz's Music Store at Number 183. Trade unions and organizations bought blocks of seats at half price.

As the date drew closer the advertisements became more complicated. Now they told not only where to buy tickets, but how to get to the Hippodrome. In the foreign-language papers especially, the directions were specific. The reader was advised what trolley, what El to take, how many blocks to walk, when to turn right and when left.

The people came. They came by trolley, by El, walked the correct number of blocks, turned to the right or the left, and they got there. They carried in their hands the fragment of crumpled newspaper in Russian or Yiddish, in Italian or German or Spanish, and they followed the directions like a precept from the Bible. For thousands of them it was the first time they had been on Broadway, the first time, indeed, that they had seen the busy heart of the city which was their home.

They bought seats or they stood on line for standing room all the way to Fifth Avenue; the line was three blocks long.

They were timid at first, self-conscious and unsure. Then they were excited, and then they were transported. The artists, too, were beside themselves. Such audiences they had never known before.

These were good days, wonderful days for me. I was an impresario. I was presenting Tetrazzini, Schumann-Heink, Titta Ruffo, Eugene Ysaye, Mischa Elman, the greatest artists of the day. And I was presenting them to the people at prices the people could afford.

Music has been my obsession, but it has been the obsession of many men and women. Yet in this country it has been an expensive commodity for the most part. The supply of low-priced seats for concert and opera is consistently insufficient for the demand.

Having loved music and known poverty, having stood on the lines of would-be standees and been turned away when the space was filled, having wormed my way into the Metropolitan by devious means, going in by the stage door when the front doors were closed to me, and even being thrown out on occasion, I had this special twist in my musical obsession. I had talked, dreamed, eaten and drunk Music for the Masses since I had come to America. And now Music for the Masses had come true.

I felt vindicated beyond all my hopes. The *Morning Telegraph* took to writing regularly about what it named "The Hurok audience." It was really to them that, years later, the *New York Times* paid tribute when it credited me with having done more for music than the phonograph.

32

So these were wonderful days for me. I had all this—and I had heaven too, or the promise of it. For it was in this period that I met Anna Pavlova.

Once More, Chaliapin

Chaliapin had told me that he would never return to the United States. But "never" is a big word for anyone to use. Meanwhile a world war had changed the face of Europe, and a revolution had changed the face of Russia even more. The ten days that shook the world shook Feodor Ivanovitch Chaliapin too.

He had sung a season of Russian Opera for Sir Thomas Beecham in London just before the pistol shot at Sarajevo touched off the explosion. Sir Thomas had imported virtually the whole Leningrad Opera, and the season was a fabulous success every way but financially. The English music lovers enjoyed a rare feast and Beecham's Pills paid the check.

Even in the midst of this love feast of Russian music, Chaliapin misbehaved. It was, as always with Feodor Ivanovitch, a matter of money. He was the highest-paid artist in Russia, with a salary of 37,500 rubles a year from the Imperial Opera House. Sir Thomas paid him £250 a performance for the season of Russian Opera at the Drury Lane Theatre. Chaliapin had a house in Moscow, a house in St. Petersburg, an estate at Yaroslavl. He was a rich man.

And it came as a shock, always, when this big man with the lusty big voice, the big warm personality, the zest for good eating and good drinking and good talk, the magnetism of a handsome, vigorous and virile male—that a man so big in every way could be so small about money.

Many years later, in a hotel room in Chicago, Chaliapin and I talked about this parsimony. We had gone to his hotel from the Russian Opera performance of *Boris Godunov*, had eaten a good hearty supper and drunk about a gallon of wine between us. It was very late. We were sprawling in our chairs, our dinner jackets flung on the sofa, our ties undone and our collars limp enough to be comfortable.

Out of this mellow mood I suddenly blurted, "Fe'd'r Ivanich, how does it happen that a man like you is so attached to a kopek?"

"Salomon"— He shook his heavy head from side to side like a lion in the zoo. —"you are right. It is not nice. In Petersburg I used to go to the English Club. There was an *isvostchik*, Anton, who drove me there. I would say, 'Anton, wait for me.' And Anton would pull up his collar and wait for me, all night in the freezing cold of Petersburg in winter. One night it was raining, an icy rain. I lost 5,000 rubles in the club, spent perhaps 500 more on champagne. When I came out at three in the morning Anton was waiting for me.

"He tucked me in under the fur rugs, tender as a mother, and drove me home. At my door I said, 'Anton, how much?'

" 'How should I know how much, Fe'd'r Ivanich? Say, a ruble.'

" 'A ruble! You——! For you, twenty-five kopeks is plenty!'

"And I threw the twenty-five kopeks in his face and went into my house.

"In my warm room, with the thick rugs and the big soft bed piled up with comforters, I looked at my face in the mirror and I said, 'You good-for-nothing Chaliapin! Tonight you squandered 5,000 rubles on cards, 500 rubles on champagne. And this old man, with a wife and children to feed, sat waiting for you all night in the icy rain, tired, his bones aching—perhaps even catching pneumonia, so that you, Chaliapin, should not stand one moment in the rain waiting for a droshky. And when he asked you for one ruble, what did you do?' What did I do!

"But I must tell you another story. In 1913 I went to Kazan to see Gorki to help me with my book. In my boyhood there had been a great tenor from Kazan—a handsome, dashing fellow with a beautiful voice. He had had racing stables, and a phaeton. I was one of the crowd of youngsters who had followed him around, worshiping him, aping his clothes, his mannerisms.

"Well, when I came to Kazan the people stood outside my hotel waiting to shake my hand. I washed the train dust from my face, made myself clean, and then I opened the door. They stood in line, and one came—an old man, shabby, ill, half deaf, leaning on a cane. I looked at him. It was that tenor!

"I took his bony trembling hand and I was frightened. I said, 'How is this? You were a rich man, with your racing stables, your fast carriage, your beautiful suits and fur coats . . .'

"He said, 'All gone, spent, lost at cards, on champagne.'

"'But you are not forgotten! You have your reputation! You give lessons, at least?' He shook his head. 'How do you live then?' 'I manage . . .'

"Salomon, I gave him a couple of hundred rubles. But I was frightened. And now, whenever I am stingy, it is because I think of that tenor. I think how my father beat my mother black and blue—for a *pitak*, a nickel.

"But, Salomon, next time you see me do a mean thing—you pull me by the coat and you tell me, 'Chaliapin, you stingy so-and-so, you are forgetting again!'"

Needless to say, I never pulled Feodor Ivanovitch by the coat, nor called him a stingy so-and-so. I knew another truth about him: that he could be as big-hearted as he was stingy. There was a morning in Chicago when I told him I had to leave at once for New York.

"Why must you rush away? Stay here with me—let someone else attend to it."

I couldn't, and at his urging I confessed why I couldn't. I was already beginning to suffer from declining finances.

"How much do you need? Here, I'll write a check and you only have to send it. Then you can stay."

I did not take his money, but I have never forgotten that he offered it.

To go back to London and the Beecham season of Russian Opera, there was at least one scandal. The story, inspired perhaps by Chaliapin's reputation, was that he refused to contribute his performance to a benefit for the musicians, and the orchestra went on strike. He told me that the company went on strike because the singers refused to be paid in paper; they wanted gold. Still, it was a great, unforgettable season.

That was virtually the last that Europe knew of any music but the sound of cannon for four years, and that was the last it saw of Chaliapin until 1921.

Basso with a Cold

In that year the Soviet Government gave him permission to go abroad to give concerts for the relief of sufferers from the ghastly famine. He went to Riga, and he went to London, where his first concert in Royal Albert Hall was a scene of almost hysterical welcome.

I had never resigned myself to the impossibility of bringing Chaliapin to America under my management. As soon as the shooting was over I had begun negotiations again, this time through the Russian Red Cross and Lunacharski, Commissar of Education. My efforts finally aroused Chaliapin's interest. From Riga I had a cable from him, asking me to state my proposition.

Meanwhile in London, Freddy Gaisberg, of the Gramophone Company, was working along the same lines. Freddy wanted Chaliapin in America to make recordings. He cabled Coppicus of the Metropolitan Musical Bureau that Chaliapin could now be approached.

Coppicus, knowing I had been negotiating, called me in. There was no sense in our competing for Chaliapin. Why not make a joint offer? We did, and Feodor Ivanovitch was presently on a boat, headed for a land he had sworn he would never visit again.

Chaliapin left Russia with nothing but the clothes he wore—and had worn since before the Revolution—his costumes, and a patched and shiny dress suit. He replenished his wardrobe somewhat in London, but when he stepped off the boat in New York in October he still had no warm overcoat.

But he had a valet, a little gnomish creature called Nikolai who scurried after the big man like an organ-grinder's monkey on a leash. And—Chaliapin also had a cold.

We had planned to present him at the Manhattan Opera House and we were going to make a big thing of it. We had engaged the violinist Stopock and a lady pianist, a Miss Boshko, as musical support in addition to his accompanist Berdichevsky. Miss Boshko was Chaliapin's own recommendation.

The first concert was postponed. The second concert was postponed. The third concert was postponed.

It was true, Chaliapin's cold persisted. But when the fourth date drew near I was frantically worried. Four weeks had gone by since his arrival. The public, which we had built up to a state of acute anticipation, was becoming impatient. There was beginning to be a doubt whether Chaliapin would ever sing a concert at the Manhattan Opera House. I vowed he would sing this concert if he had to be carried on the stage on a litter.

We gathered in his rooms at the Weylin before concert time that evening. Little Stopock was there, and lame Berdichevsky, and Miss Boshko. And Freddy Gaisberg and myself. And, of course, Nikolai.

We stood around in a state of gloom so thick you could beat it with a spoon. Huge Chaliapin sat on the edge of a little boudoir chair, his laryngoscope in one large limp hand. His face was set.

"I cannot sing," he said for the twentieth time. "I will not sing."

37

We had each in turn looked down his throat. We had each encouraged, urged, pleaded, and fallen silent before that grim face. Now Nikolai spoke.

"Fe'd'r Ivanitch, you sing the concert. God will help you."

This was a spark to the fuse. Chaliapin stood up, towering over the little gnome in a sizzling rage.

"God!" he roared. "What has God to do with my throat?"

Nikolai cringed. We all cringed. The glum silence blanketed us again.

I did not have at my command that night the technique I learned later. It was a reasonably sure way of curing Chaliapin's colds, and Dale Carnegie thought so well of it that he has told the story in his lectures and in his book. Later in our association, when Chaliapin found on the eve of a concert that he could not sing, I was in the habit of dropping everything and rushing to his side, dripping sympathy.

"Fe'd'r Ivanich, what a pity! Do you feel very bad? What does the doctor say? Of course you must not sing tonight! I'll cancel the concert—don't let such a trifle worry you—it will only cost you a couple of thousand dollars. . . ." But before I could pick up the telephone to cancel the concert, Feodor Ivanovitch's cold was miraculously much better.

But that night I did not know the magic of that method, and I would probably not have dared to use it if I had. Yet my stammering appeal on behalf of the public, his admirers, sitting in the concert hall, waiting to hear him and doomed to be disappointed for the fourth time—or perhaps the danger that they might lose interest in him altogether—had its effect.

Whatever the compulsion, he got to his feet at last and muttered, "We will go to the hall."

The hope that rose in all of us was premature. In his dressing room he sank heavily into a chair again.

"No, I cannot sing."

I was distraught. The house was solid to the doors. Bursts of staccato applause indicated the exhausted patience of the audience.

I went out to the front of the house and hurried down the aisle to the seat where I knew Anna Pavlova would be. She came backstage with me to the dressing room.

If it had not been for her tender persuasions, Chaliapin would not have sung that night. She flung her slender arms around his massive shoulders and tears poured from her eyes—and from his.

"All right, Aniuta, all right," he said. "But let someone go out and tell them I have a cold—otherwise I cannot."

I will never forget that concert. It was pitiful. If I had it to do again today, I would have prevailed on him not to sing.

It was pitiful, and it was comic. First my good friend Freddy, short, wearing glasses—an admirable fellow, but not on the glamorous side—made his little speech. Mr. Chaliapin was not in good voice, he said. He had had a persistent cold. But he did not wish to disappoint his audience. He would sing.

Then Miss Boshko walked out on the stage and played a piano solo.

Then came the procession. First Feodor Ivanovitch, six feet four inches tall, a mountain of a man, strode to the piano. Behind him came Berdichevsky the accompanist, limping on his wooden leg. Next, carrying his fiddle, little Stopock, who looked—perhaps I malign a fine musician, but I say in that parade he looked—barely five feet tall. And last came Nikolai, the dwarf, scurrying in at the tail end, carrying the Master's music.

Standing in the wings, I said to myself, "The gang's all here," and waited for the laugh. But somehow there was no laugh. I blessed that audience, as I have had reason to bless audiences since.

There was no laugh. On the contrary, there was an ovation. The public gave its tribute to an artist, no matter how he might perform that night. At last he put up his hand for quiet, and his great

39

voice spoke, telling them the number of the song he would sing first.

This was his custom. Chaliapin could not be held to a program. He would sing only what he felt like singing when the time came to sing. So we distributed programs in which were printed translations of his complete repertoire—a hundred-odd songs and arias— and before he sang he would boom out the number of the song in the program. Then he would wait while the pages rustled all over the hall, until he was satisfied that every last listener had had time to read the words. He could not sing, he said, to people who had not the vaguest notion what he was singing about.

Tonight he went through the ritual. He waited, Berdichevsky waited, Stopock waited, Nikolai waited. Then, when the moment seemed right to him, he nodded his leonine head. Berdichevsky's fingers moved over the keyboard, Stopock raised his bow arm, and the Master opened his mouth to sing.

What came therefrom would be called anything but singing. His tortured vocal cords made sounds approximating music as closely as the caw of a crow resembles the full-throated baying of a great Dane.

He sang a half dozen songs at most, and then he was through. The audience was probably too dazed to protest. Whatever the reason, they filed out quietly. That was Chaliapin's first American concert.

Grand-Opera Temperament

Freddy Gaisberg and I bundled him off to Jamesburg, New Jersey, where a little Russian lady managed a retreat—Shostak's was the name. Morris Gest was there, I remember. The country was restful, the company congenial, the cooking excellent. By the time November 21st came around, he was ready for his great *Boris Godunov* at the Metropolitan.

If Chaliapin remembered his reception by the critics in 1907, he gave no sign. Gatti-Casazza greeted him with voluble, tearful embraces—Gatti had been the director at La Scala when Chaliapin had sung there. He ushered Feodor Ivanovitch into Caruso's dressing room. Chaliapin gave way to a moment of emotion in that room. Caruso had died only a few months before, in August.

Rehearsals went on schedule. Chaliapin was on his best behavior. And the performance, Chaliapin's first in fifteen years— it could not have been my imagination, for I have been present at many memorable nights at the Metropolitan in my life—the very walls of the glamorous old house seemed to quiver with excitement.

That was a great *Boris*. Chaliapin's kingly bearing and the potent instrument of his voice were only half the magic. The other half was Chaliapin the actor, forgetful of self, immersed in the person of the tragic Czar.

The impact of his performance stunned the audience. The critics went away still shuddering at his magnificent madness, to pour eloquent tribute on his name like flooding streams in the spring.

They had delicately reserved judgment after the disastrous concert at the Manhattan Opera House. There was no need for any kind of reserve after *Boris*. And Henry Finck of the *Evening Post*, who alone did not have to sup on his own words of 1907, modestly enjoyed the rewards of his sound critical judgment.

As for Chaliapin, the reception of *Boris* had an effect we might have anticipated. He took his praises graciously, in stride. But he became once more the bad boy of music. His first outburst came the next season, when rehearsals began for *Faust*.

Chaliapin had never liked to sing *Faust*. He preferred the musically inferior Boito version of the story, *Mefistofele*. When that kindly patriarch, the venerable composer Glazounov, came to this

41

country under my management, I once talked with him about this, and he gave his diagnosis of Chaliapin's aversion to the Goethe-Gounod opera.

"Chaliapin and other artists who are the greatest interpreters of certain roles," Alexander Constantinovitch said, "win their great fame when the composer is weaker than they. Which are Chaliapin's most memorable performances? The *Mefistofele* of Boito, the *Don Quixote* of Massenet, even Moussorgsky's *Boris* are all lesser music than Gounod. And the combination of Gounod and Goethe—there is hardly a tenor or soprano or baritone who can dominate that combination. In *Faust* the music and the poetry will always be greater than any artist."

Whatever the reason, Feodor Ivanovitch always sought excuses to avoid singing *Faust*. I had begged him to do it in French, but he protested he had not done it in a long time, was not sure of the text. Why could he not do *Mefistofele* in Italian, instead?

But *Faust* it was to be, this season at the Metropolitan. And dress rehearsal was called for ten in the morning. Chaliapin, who normally went to bed at four or five A.M., found it irksome to get up so early, but the rules for musicians, chorus, stagehands are written in stone, and rehearsal time cannot be changed for anyone.

He arrived in a foul temper. He stepped out on the stage in his velvet coat, walked about while the cast and chorus stood in respectful silence, the conductor held his baton, the violins poised their bows.

Then he blurted in French, in a loud voice, "Do you call this a temple of music? This is no temple, it's a stable!"

There was a concerted gasp, and then a silence. Gatti rose abruptly from his seat in the auditorium, his face white in the light from the stage, and muttering in Italian, stalked out to his office. Chaliapin turned and strolled, his hands still in his pockets, off the stage.

Madame Alda followed him to his dressing room. A charming gentle person, a wise woman as well as a fine artist, Frances Alda is one of the few singers I know who lived with modest grace while she was a prima donna of the Metropolitan, and can still live graciously without having to give music lessons, now after so many years in retirement.

As Gatti's wife, she was deeply hurt by Chaliapin's rudeness. "How could you do that to Gatti," she asked him, "before the whole company?"

Chaliapin shrugged. "It was the way I felt," he said. He put on his hat and coat, kissed her hand while she stood there stunned by his indifference, and went out nonchalantly to return to his suite at the Majestic Hotel.

I walked around the block a few times and then I went into the Opera House again. I found Gatti in his office.

Chaliapin was nervous, I said. His first *Faust* at the Metropolitan—surely the maestro, who had been party to so many scenes, who had nursed the temperament of so many great artists, surely he would understand. And, I lied cheerfully, Chaliapin was sorry, so sorry.

Gatti growled at me in Italian and turned away.

I hurried out and took a taxi to the Majestic. There I went through the same performance. Gatti was sorry, so sorry. And really, it was such a little matter for which to lose $3,000 "right out of your own pocket, Fe'd'r Ivanitch." Fe'd'r Ivanitch promptly put on his coat and hat again and we went down to find a taxi.

Once, walking in Central Park long after midnight, I saw a little man leading a great Saint Bernard dog on a leash. I felt just like that, bringing Chaliapin into Gatti's office.

At the door my courage failed me. I had no wish to be faced with any embarrassing questions about who had apologized to whom. I stood back while he went in first.

They fell into each other's arms. And the rehearsal went forward as scheduled.

The next time it was *The Barber of Seville*, and Chaliapin simply did not show up for rehearsal at all. He was sick, he said on the telephone. Gatti was almost in tears. He had assembled such a fine cast, spent so much money to give his friend Chaliapin every advantage.

Elvira de Hidalgo, I remember, was to sing Rosina, and Papi was conducting.

"How can he do this to me?" Gatti wailed. "He is my friend for twenty years, and I would do everything for him!"

This time I did not lift a finger to bring Chaliapin around. I thought it would be a lesson to him to lose the $3,000 for the performance. Alas, it was no lesson.

Another season, in Chicago, I had to play peace-maker again. This time Giacomo Spadoni, now the chorus master of the Metropolitan, was his victim. At a rehearsal of Boito's *Mefistofele*, Spadoni either did or did not give a cue and Chaliapin, a master of invective in any language, flung a word at him in Italian. It was an unforgivable insult, and it had been delivered in front of the entire company, musicians, technicians, stagehands, and the management.

Herbert Johnson, director of the Chicago Opera, would not go to Chaliapin to demand an apology. George Polacco, the musical director, declined with equal vehemence the office of telling the great Chaliapin he had done wrong. Again it was up to me.

So I went to Feodor Ivanovitch and said how sorry Spadoni was, and I went to Spadoni and said how sorry Chaliapin was, and the quarrel wound up in a monstrous feast in Chaliapin's apartment on Lake Shore Drive that night, for which Spadoni brought the wine and faithful Nikolai prepared a wonderful *schi*.

The party lasted until past four in the morning. Some time during the night I went into the music room and put a recording

on the Ampico. I sat there swaying over the pedals and the "loud"
and "soft" keys, and Edith Mason, the Chicago soprano, later
with the Metropolitan, who was Polacco's wife at the time, stood
in the doorway and caroled: "Listen to him! No wonder he's such
a successful impresario! Listen to the way he can play the piano!"
That's a fair measure of how much wine we drank that night.

BORIS in Chicago

The next season I presented a *Boris* of my own of which I was
forgivably proud. That was in Chicago, where I was offering the
Russian Opera Company in a full season of Russian opera, the first
such season in America.

It was the only performance of *Boris* to be given in this country
all in Russian; at the Metropolitan Chaliapin sang in Russian
and the rest of the cast in Italian. With Chaliapin supervising
the settings, the costumes, the music, it was as authentic a production, as faithful to Moussorgsky's music and to the Russia
which nourished him and Chaliapin, as could be achieved.

The settings were designed by Anchutin, whose pretty daughter Leda grew up to become a ballerina and to marry the fine dancer
André Eglevsky. I bought a handsome Persian chair for the Coro-
nation Scene.

And as a special touch of sentiment, the entire Russian Opera
Company gathered on the stage after the first-act curtain and
presented Chaliapin with the bread and salt of welcome in the
ancient Russian ceremony; the bread on a silver tray wrapped
in a hand-sewn white napkin.

The performance was quite late in starting, because Chaliapin
had to go over every detail once more. And the second-act curtain
did not go up for so long a time that it seemed forever.

From my favorite spot at the back of the house I became aware
of the growing restlessness of the audience. They had gone out

and smoked their cigarettes in the lobby and exchanged greetings with their friends, and had come back and settled themselves in their seats, and still the curtain did not rise on the second act. I looked at my watch. The intermission was already thirty-five minutes long.

I hurried backstage.

"What's the matter with you? Why doesn't the curtain go up? The audience . . ."

Without a word the stage manager led me onto the stage. There stood Chaliapin on the set, pen-knife in hand, laboriously carving out designs in the window for greater authenticity.

When the next intermission stretched to twenty-five minutes, to thirty minutes, I went backstage again. This time I found him kneeling on the stage, the handsome Persian throne lying ignominiously on its back, while with a saw he had borrowed from the stage carpenter he sawed an inch off each of its legs. The chair was too high, he explained, industriously sawing away.

And as he sawed, I could literally feel the money running out of my pocket. For in the theatre the witching hour of eleven-thirty changes everything. Stagehands, musicians must be paid overtime. And with those intermissions, the great opera, long to begin with, ran on well past midnight.

Chaliapin's fanaticism for detail had already put the entire opera season hopelessly in the red before the curtain had ever gone up. Rehearsal time stretched on interminably, and the bill for the big orchestra grew heavier and heavier, while he corrected the conductor in his tempi, the artists in their every inflection.

Over our bottle of wine one night after a performance I asked him why he did this. "Why is every word so important to you, Fe'd'r Ivanitch? Why must you demand from every artist such perfection in every detail? Will you never be satisfied?"

"No," he roared. "Because on one word may hang the mean-

ing of a whole character, or of a whole mood. Why, if I say a
speech this way, the audience will think the man I speak of is,
alive, while if I say it another way, they will be sure he is dead!
No, Salomon, an artist who does not insist on perfection is no
artist!"

And could I say, in the face of this noble credo, that his worship of perfection was driving me into bankruptcy?

So we played *Boris* three times a week for four weeks in the
Auditorium, a great *Boris*, inspired by a great man. Whatever I
say about Chaliapin, I do not believe there has been or will be
an artist of his caliber in our time or in our children's time. His
hands, expressive as a ballet dancer's, beautiful as sculpture, always held a pencil—as he talked he wrote or sketched. I picked
up menus, scraps of paper with his sketches on them and had
them framed. Those who never saw him can regret it all their
lives. For me to have been so close to him and his family was
worth many times the anguished hours he cost me, to say nothing
of the cash. The great days and great nights I spent with Chaliapin
I shall never see again.

Chaliapin was always an actor, on and off the stage. There was
already a legend growing up about his romantic escapades and
his readiness with his fists. In Chicago a story had broken into
the newspapers about his attentions to a lady member of the
opera company, which had caused a lively bout with a fellow
artist courting the same lady.

Another newspaper story told of Chaliapin quarreling with still
another artist, and getting his nose broken. This story went all
over the world, even reaching his secretary in Russia, who cabled
anxiously to know what had happened.

Chaliapin's version was that he had been misunderstood by
dolts who knew nothing of opera in general and *Boris* in particular.
He had merely been rehearsing the Palace Scene, showing the
tenor who sang the role of Prince Shouisky how the mad Czar

cuffed and cursed the Prince. He cabled his secretary that if he, Chaliapin, had had his nose broken, there would have been news of a tenor's funeral the next day.

Chaliapin sang another concert at the Manhattan Opera House the first season, and made a short tour. I took him down to William Street one day to meet the late Arthur Brisbane, whose column about him appeared on the front pages of Hearst papers throughout the country.

I took him to the office of Herbert Hoover's American Relief committee in a downtown skyscraper, where he ordered packages of food to be sent to his family and friends at home. They showed us photographs, heartbreaking scenes of starvation in the Volga district where he was born. Chaliapin turned away to the window, where he stood looking out over the city, his eyes filled with tears.

But his tenderness of heart never interfered in matters of money. When I asked him to sing a Sunday concert at the Hippodrome for the two-dollar-top audience, he demurred. His contract called for a fee of $3,000 a concert. But the Hippodrome was so big, he said. He would have to have $4,000.

I have been asked by my colleagues in the music business how I expected to pay Chaliapin $3,000 a concert and come out with a whole skin.

I was not thinking of my skin, whole or otherwise. If Chaliapin had asked for $30,000 a concert I would have given the proposal my serious attention. It seemed to me then that the public would pay any amount to see and hear that great artist, as I would myself. I was younger than I am now, and I was an incurable hero-worshiper, as I have said before.

I am no less a hero-worshiper today, although I find it harder to discover heroes worthy of my adoration. But I have learned not to curb my own enthusiasm, but to use other measuring rods for the public.

In those days I wrote contracts the way a certain school of sentimental poets used to write verses: If the poet was melancholy, rain was not rain, it was nature weeping; if he was glad, the sun smiled and the little brooks gurgled with joy.

I have come to understand that little brooks gurgle with water, not joy, and that there is just so much money in the public's pocket which it will spend for music—sometimes a little more, often a little less, but always within an upper limit.

But when Chaliapin was in question I did not see the ceiling even after I had hit my head against it.

What Was in the Trunks?

The day of his departure, we sat talking in his hotel while little Nikolai went ahead with a representative from my office to show the customs officials that the costumes, which had been brought into the country under bond, were properly being taken out again. My man telephoned me, very much upset, from the pier.

"This Nikolai," he said, "won't open the trunks."

My hair—I still had hair in those days—stood on end. What, besides the costumes which had been properly declared, was in those trunks?

I hurried to the dock.

There sat Nikolai the gnome, perched on a trunk, his ugly little face covered with a green pallor, beads of sweat on his forehead, while a whole battery of customs officials glowered at him. He gave me a look to wring the hardest heart.

"Please, Mr. Hurok, don't make me open the trunks. I will be in a terrible trouble!"

"It's the law, Nikolai. You must open them," I told him.

He moaned softly all the time he was finding the right key out of a huge bunch, and fitting it to the lock, and it took him forever.

At last there was a click, and two customs men leaped for the lid and flung it back.

There, among the velvets and satins glittering with embroidery and glass gems—there we found, not diamonds, not silver and gold, but some fifty cakes of American soap and several dozen hotel and Pullman towels. Nikolai had collected them with a squirrel's slyness from every hotel and every train throughout the tour.

The next season, Chaliapin took out of Russia some of the Gobelin tapestries and fine rugs from his Leningrad house, with the knowledge and consent of the Soviet Government.

Mrs. Hurok and I visited that house in Leningrad in the summer of 1938—Chaliapin had died in Paris that April. The house was occupied then by his faithful friend and secretary, Isai Grigorievitch Dvorischin, a merry soul who had always been able to make Chaliapin laugh.

Isai had been a member of the chorus of the Petrograd Opera. In 1938 he was Assistant Regisseur of the Mariinsky Theatre where the Opera was housed.

He showed me through Chaliapin's home, through the storied theatre, and at every step he paused to tell me some memory, tender or laughable, of the Master.

"Here was Chaliapin's dressing room—here he sat to put on his make-up—here he stood in the wings, waiting for his cue on the opening night of . . ." For Isai my tour was a holy pilgrimage to a dozen little shrines cherished in his heart.

When we parted tears sprang suddenly into his eyes. "Feodor Ivanovitch died with the belief that I had forsaken him," he said. "It was not true. I was always his friend, and shall always be his friend. You believe me, don't you?"

I believed him, for a man never had a more devoted, self-abnegating friend than Isai Grigorievitch was to Chaliapin. As I left him I thought of another friend, a man of a stature equal to Chaliapin's own, with whom his brushes in later life had been stormy. That was Maxim Gorki.

Chaliapin and Gorki

The years of the Revolution left their mark on Chaliapin's mind. Naturally he suffered. Even the new Russia, which has cherished its artists as no other country in the history of man, could not provide comfort for him in those terrible days. After the years of exhausting war, of civil war, of counter-revolution in which the armies of the Allies, including our own, played a shameful part after World War I—and all this on top of generations of grinding poverty under the Czars—the wonder is not that Russians suffered, but that they survived.

Years later when the splendid Habimah, the Moscow Hebrew Art Theatre, came over under my management, I heard tales of meals made of potatoes fried in castor oil, because the human body requires fats to function and there was no other kind to be had.

So it was not surprising that Chaliapin, concerned for the nourishment of his family, often took his payment for singing in a few pounds of flour or potatoes, or a ham if there was one to be found.

Chaliapin had the intellectual capacity to understand the Revolution. He was a man of amazing powers, and from his youth had been surrounded by the greatest intellects, first of Russia, then of Europe and America. He had a surprising grasp of branches of man's knowledge; he could discuss medicine with you like a doctor.

Later, he occasionally voiced his irritations with the Revolution in newspaper interviews. His sentiments were for the most part exaggerated and misquoted, but Maxim Gorki could not forgive him.

51

They had not spoken to each other for many years when one day, with Chaliapin beside me, I knocked on the door of Gorki's suite in the Adlon Hotel in Berlin.

I had heard that Gorki was at the Adlon en route from Paris to Moscow. Hero-worshiper that I was, unable to bear it that two of my favorite heroes were at odds, I had called Gorki. They had quarreled, I felt, as married people quarrel, still loving each other, and I was certain they wanted to be friends again.

I asked Gorki if I might bring Chaliapin to see him.

"Where is that fool?" Gorki roared into my ear. It was all the invitation I needed.

At my knock, the door flew open. Chaliapin stepped in and enveloped Gorki in his arms like a huge bear.

Thus they greeted each other. How they parted I cannot say, for I stayed only six to eight hours and then left them together, in a welter of tears and vodka. But I heard this much.

Chaliapin said, "Well, I'll see you soon in Moscow."

Gorki peered up at the big man, a sidewise, skeptical gaze. "I don't know when you'll be in Moscow. But I know that no one can envy me enough. I am going home, to my own land, the land of my birth. You—can do what you like."

The year before Chaliapin died I was in Moscow, and I carried away with me a message for Chaliapin from Premier Stalin.

Nemirovitch-Dantchenko, the brilliant stage director and administrative head of the Moscow Art Theatre, and also organizer of the Musical Studio, presented me to the great man of the Soviets one night at the theatre, in an intermission of Bulgakov's *The White Guard*. In those days, before the treason trials, Stalin was not inaccessible, especially not to artists of the music and theatre world, and their managers. He went constantly to the theatre, the ballet, the opera, and it was in the lounge next to Stanislavsky's office, reserved for high Government officials and their guests, that I stood, among a dozen Soviet celebrities, in Stalin's presence.

Nemirovitch-Dantchenko presented me as Chaliapin's American manager.

"What is Chaliapin doing?" Stalin asked. "Why doesn't he come to Moscow?"

"I suppose," Nemirovitch-Dantchenko offered, "he needs quite a lot of money to live these days. He makes money abroad."

"We'll give him money, if it is money he needs," Stalin said.

"Well, then, there's the matter of housing. He has a large family, you know." The housing shortage in Moscow was one of the favorite subjects for feature stories in the European and American press in those days.

"We'll give him a house in Moscow. We'll give him a house in the country, too. Just tell him to come home."

I gave the message to Marie Valentinovna, Madame Chaliapin, whom I met in Paris. Chaliapin was in Baden-Baden, and since this was 1936, I would not set foot in Hitler's Reich. Chaliapin did not live to accept the invitation.

The Clan Chaliapin—a Census

I should like to stop and set down here the vital statistics of Chaliapin's family. The legend is that he had as many as twenty wives, and the estimated number of his children ranges from twenty-five upward.

Certainly he was a man of overwhelming personal magnetism. While he was under my management I was constantly brushing languishing maidens out of his path. Once at least, to my knowledge, he had to call the police to disengage him from a clinging female who was making a scene in his hotel in New York.

It may come as a shock, therefore, that his record as a family man was not in any way uncommon.

His first wife was Iola Ignatievna, an Italian dancer. She once told me that she had come to this country in 1894 in the course of her professional travels, to dance at the old Academy of Music on 14th Street.

Iola's children are Kira, whom I met in Moscow; Tanya; Lydia; Boris, who, as I write, is in New York, and Feodor, who is in Hollywood. Iola was a good wife and a good mother. She went to the Soviet Union some years ago to visit Kira and remained there. According to the last reports she is there still.

Marie Valentinovna, an Esthonian, was his second wife, a charming, cultured woman. She brought to the household two children by her first husband, Edward and Stella, and bore Chaliapin three daughters: Marfa, Maria and Daska.

Two wives, eight children, two step-children—that is all. I have known both of the fine women who bore Chaliapin's name and all of the children, and I can swear on the Book that this was his family before the law.

I took Chaliapin on concert tour, and I took him on tour in *The Barber of Seville*. Every performance was a hazard, every time he sang a triumph for me.

It was on tour that I learned the technique for getting him onto the stage that Dale Carnegie admired. But even that method was only about fifty per cent efficient.

I still wake up at night shuddering, to realize that I have been dreaming about Chaliapin and his laryngoscope. Whenever that dreadful little instrument came out of his luggage I knew another cancellation was hanging over my head.

It required years to repair the hole burned in my fortunes by the passing of that blazing comet named Feodor. But I have never forgotten that in Chaliapin I was privileged to know one of the rare creatures of this world. I paid a high price for the privilege, but I valued it highly.

One of his colleagues asked him, "Why do you bother to

sing Don Basilio in *The Barber of Seville?* It is such a small part."

His answer is one I have quoted to many an artist since.

"To a great artist," he said, "there is no such thing as a small part. And to a small artist, there are no big parts."

CHAPTER THREE

The Incomparable

*P*AVLOVA WAS DANCING at the Hippodrome. Along with the trained elephants and the acrobats, the Chinese jugglers and the nymphs who vanished in the disappearing tank, Pavlova was dancing to the music of Tchaikovsky.

Where Pavlova was, there was I. I was standing, as always, at the back of the house, watching her exquisitely poignant figure far away on the huge stage, a miniature, from where I stood, like a figure seen through the wrong end of the telescope. I might as well have been looking through a telescope, and she might as well have been on Mars, for all the hope I had of ever spanning the infinity between us.

And at the very moment that it seemed intolerable any longer to worship from afar, as the curtain fell slowly on the fragile statuette, a hand grasped my arm.

"I'm going back to her dressing room—come along, Sol," Dillingham said.

I had lost my awe of Charles B. Dillingham by then—we were both managers, after all—but at that moment he was God, or at the very least, Saint Peter.

The words that I would say to Anna Pavlova when I met her were ready on my tongue. I had polished and rehearsed them during the thousand times I had met her face to face in imagination. I had practiced my speech in Russian, and I had practiced it in

English, and I had never made up my mind in which language my flowery eloquence would be most effective.

She sat before her dressing table, a plain little red robe thrown over her shoulders. Dillingham's voice, presenting me, came from a million miles away.

English or Russian, Russian or English? Which should I speak? I was pilloried by the dilemma. I stood dumb, silent, stupid, blanketed by a fog in which Russian words and English words ran together and became Sanskrit and ancient Greek.

She was smiling. She put out her hand to me and, like an automaton, I bent over it. When I straightened she was speaking to Dillingham.

"Let your friend come too," she said. "It will be gay, three of us."

So I had met Pavlova, and been invited by her to supper, and I had not said a single word.

We went to Palisades Park and sat at a table in the outdoor restaurant. I have always known how to enjoy my food, but that night it lay almost untouched before me, and several times Madame reminded me that I was forgetting to eat.

She surprised me. I was astonished to see how much she ate, for one thing. I had eaten with tenors and sopranos, and their consumption had not startled me by its quantity. After all, Madame Schumann-Heink and Titta Ruffo had girth; they had waistlines to support.

Since that night at Palisades Park I have supped with ballerinas more times than I can remember, and I do not even blink at the thick steaks, the mountains of potatoes, the quarts of milk they can put away. If they eat like stevedores, I dare say the number of foot-pounds of energy they expend in a performance would at least equal a stevedore's eight-hour day.

But to see the delicate, fragile Pavlova, whose waist I could span with the fingers of my two hands, attack that two-inch steak made me gasp.

And as she ate and talked and laughed, I could not take my eyes from her face. The exquisite mask of the ballerina was gone; here was a woman! The cold, chiseled melancholy turned to sparkling animation, the great dark eyes shone, and every now and then the carved lips parted and there came forth a burst of rich, hearty laughter.

So much has been written about Pavlova: how exacting she was as artist, how charitable, how severe with her girls and how kind to them, and one conductor who was briefly her musical director devoted nearly a whole volume to proving that she had no sense of rhythm! But no one, it seems to me, has said in so many words that Anna Pavlova was a woman, with all of a woman's warmth and love of life, with a capacity for gaiety and adventure that could exhaust even my boundless energies. Despite the severity of her training in the Imperial School in Theatre Street, despite the strictness of her devotion to her work, there was nothing nun-like about her. She loved life and she should have lived it fully, if she had not been a slave to her gifts. And she lived her whole life with a profound, a tragic disappointment; she was hungry for love.

That night I had not yet discovered that she could weep, but I learned how she could laugh. She laughed at me for letting my food grow cold on my plate, and half laughing, half embarrassed, I managed to nibble a bite or two, though I had no idea what I was eating. In later years, when I had sacrificed the silhouette of youth to the pleasures of the gourmet, she would not urge me to eat. Rather, she would warn me against the rich Russian foods we both enjoyed.

"Hurokchik, your stomach!" she would remind me.

When the huge steak had disappeared, and the French fried potatoes, and the salad, and the ice cream, she pushed her chair back and said what I was to hear her say so many times in the years to come.

"Well, what shall we do now?"

It became a signal with us, like the opening phrase of a dearly loved piece of music. It set the stage for a night of light-hearted adventure.

Linking arms with Dillingham on one side and me on the other, she led us through the sights of Palisades Park. She giggled at us in the funny mirrors, shrieked on the roller coaster, danced a fox trot with me on the dance floor, and danced it very well.

After that I was a frequent visitor in her dressing room at the Hippodrome, and there were many suppers together. Her partners, Alexander Volinine and Ivan Clustine, were often with us, and we had many happy evenings.

And always I was at the performance, standing up in back. She said she knew I was there; she could hear my special brand of applause. I never could fool her, then or later when she was under my management. She always knew when I was in the house.

I remember that Dillingham production; I should remember it. It was called *The Big Show* and it was BIG. There were Powers' elephants, Mooney's horses, a trained lion act. Then came Pavlova in "The Sleeping Beauty" with Bakst's settings. And after Pavlova came the Mammoth Minstrel Show with a cast of 400—count 'em—400. Oh, the dear, dead, wonderful Hippodrome!

Pavlova had been stranded with her company in South America by the war, and she was glad to find a haven in the United States. But as soon as the armistice was signed she was ready to go. Almost the first boat to England took her home to Ivy House. I did not see her off.

In 1920 I presented Fokine and Fokina at the Hippodrome and at the Metropolitan Opera House. One night at the Hippodrome Fortune Gallo came up to me.

"Well, Hurok, I'm going to be a competitor of yours," he said. "I'm going to bring Pavlova back to America next season."

Pavlova's own lawyer Goldberger, Gallo told me, had gone to London to make the deal for him.

I was bitter. But I was determined not to be left entirely in the cold. I offered to take the New England tour, and Gallo accepted. Actually, he managed only a small part of the tour himself. He sold the Midwestern tour to managers in the Middle West.

I did not go down to meet her at the boat, but during her week at the Manhattan Opera House I went to see her three times. In Boston I began to talk about the following season. I met her in Detroit, went to Indianapolis and Chicago with her. After Chicago I had a signed contract for the next year in my pocket, and I was a happy man.

I believe I made as much on that New England tour as Gallo made on his whole sixteen weeks.

Wedding in the Newspapers

The next season began my long and unforgettable association with Pavlova. I made that entire first tour with her, and not for business reasons. At the end of that coast-to-coast tour, after the triumphs in the big cities and the struggle to put on a show in the little towns, after the uncomfortable hotels and the sleepy taxi-rides to catch early trains and the long train rides that demanded all our resourcefulness to keep ourselves and each other from boredom, I knew Pavlova.

I knew her tears as well as her laughter. I knew her stoic devotion to her work, to her company, to her audience. And I knew her unsatisfied heart.

The truth is that Pavlova was never married. I myself married her off in the press. In 1925 the newspapers printed a story I gave them, announcing for the first time that she had been married to Victor Dandre—some of them called him her accompanist—seventeen years before.

Anna Pavlova was the daughter of an unknown father and a simple woman living outside St. Petersburg. She never saw her father, although once, sitting in a park in Calgary, she told me that he was a Jew. It was virtually all she knew about him.

Her gift alone saved the young Anna from a lifetime of poverty-stricken anonymity. The shrewdness of the Czar's Government in picking jewels out of the mire of its own neglect of the people brought the little girl to the Imperial Ballet School. From there on she made her own way. She was never one of a group; always she stood alone. Even with Diaghilev she did not stay long. One season, and she was off in search of her solitary destiny.

When she was a young newcomer in the glittering world of Theatre Street in St. Petersburg, Victor Dandre came into her life. He was the son of a landowner in Poltava, a gilded youth in a position of some responsibility in the Czar's diplomatic service. Like all the young men of his class in the capital, he was a fanatic balletomane. He had been one of Preobrajenska's beaux. When Pavlova emerged from the Imperial School and began to be noticed in the Ballet, he devoted himself to her career. He arranged concerts for her, showered her with flowers and gifts.

He spent—for one of his position—vast sums of money on her, and presently it appeared that it was not all his own money. Some of it was the Czar's. When he was arrested, Pavlova came at once to his rescue. Whether she loved him then or not, she could not —being Pavlova—see him sacrificed for his devotion to her. She used her influence, of which a *prima ballerina assoluta* in St. Petersburg had a great deal, to get him out, and put him in charge of her business affairs. They left Russia together.

For Dandre it was forever. Even had he been permitted to return, his bitterness against the old regime, his inability or unwillingness to understand the new, were an effective barrier to his ever going back. For Pavlova it need not have been forever, for any regime would have embraced her, and she herself longed to return. But Dandre stood in the way.

He managed her affairs scrupulously, but without brilliance. He himself admitted that her American tours were the most profitable, and the reason was clear. His was a road-show mentality; outside the United States Pavlova was poorly presented. In this country I made sure that she had fine dancers to set her off, an augmented orchestra. I concerned myself even then, as I believe a manager must, with details of production, making certain the settings and costumes were clean and in good repair, taking pains with the quality of the stage technicians, worrying about the music and spending lavishly on advertising.

Hers was an incredible life. She toured the year round, with perhaps three or four weeks for rest in July. And of those weeks, she spent two or three taking the cure at one of the European spas. Then there was a week in Paris, occupied with painters and composers, planning her new ballets.

By August she was rehearsing again, by September she was dancing. There were four to six weeks in England, two of them at Covent Garden. Then back to the United States.

Vacation on Canvas

I remember the storm of protest with which she greeted me when I went to London to meet her in 1923. I had sent her on her famous Oriental tour in 1922-23. In those years we considered it a good idea to have an artist absent herself from her public for a season. Let the public go hungry, we used to say—whet their appetite. Today I no longer believe in that policy. The public have become fickle. If an artist is not constantly before them, they forget, they take up other idols.

She had returned from the Orient directly to London, to Ivy House, in its setting of ancient oaks, where she had planned a nice long vacation. Savely Sorine, the artist, had asked her to pose for a portrait, and she thought she could rest and pose too.

When I arrived, she was furious with Sorine.

"Six weeks!" she said. "He says he is my friend. For six weeks I did nothing but sit for him in the garden! There went my beautiful vacation—all gone in paint and canvas!"

That portrait by my friend Sorine was very much admired. It was exhibited in the Luxembourg and other distinguished galleries. The Duchess of Kent, when she was here on a visit, went with Mrs. Otto H. Kahn to the Brooklyn Museum to view it and have their pictures taken with it for the newspapers. Also Stanislavsky of the Moscow Art Theatre, with Moskvin and Kachaloff. But apart from its artistic merits, Pavlova could never forget that for it she had sacrificed her precious vacation, probably the only real vacation of her whole life.

On tour there was no rest for Pavlova, no moment without work, without the heavy burden of her company, the concern for "her girls." Her long hours at the bar, a small figure in practice tights alone on a bare stage, are a legend now. Then there were the hours she spent working with her company. Clustine, Novikoff and others staged ballets for her. Novikoff revived the wonderfully successful *Don Quixote* for her 1924-25 season, and Clustine staged an Oriental ballet which was so acrobatic that it frightened me. I persuaded her to take it out of the repertoire.

As for her own ballet, "Autumn Leaves," it had a special, a poignant significance for her. She composed it in South America in 1918. Its theme—the poet, the solitary flower of summer, the autumn wind which would ravish its beauty—was for her a reference to her girlhood days in St. Petersburg. She had loved a young man who was drowned, and it was to his memory that she dedicated the ballet. When she came off the stage after the curtain, her eyes were full of tears and she went to her dressing room without speaking to anyone.

"Autumn Leaves" was more than just another production in her enormous repertoire. When it was on the program, she always insisted on a special last-minute rehearsal of it before the curtain rose. And if it was not danced properly in performance she would keep the company afterward to correct it.

Sorine's portrait has perpetuated a Pavlova who was chaste, nun-like, remote. That is how she is remembered by those who knew her only on the stage, because it is the mask of the prima ballerina, the de-humanized romantic heroine of the white ballets. In that period of the ballet the ballerina was presented as a fairy, as an enchanted swan, as a ghost-maiden—but never as a woman. She flew rather than leapt; in her white tutu, her severe coiffure, her coldly white makeup, she moved across the stage as a creature not of this world.

But Pavlova was very much of this world. Let my readers who are too young to have seen her in the "Bacchanale" with Mordkin look at those pictures of the young Pavlova. She was a woman with fire and feeling.

A Night on Montmartre

Nor was she the prude that stories of "her girls" have made her out to be. It is true that with the members of her company she insisted on the strictest decorum. On trains the feminine contingent had its own sleeping car, and woe betide any girl who strolled into the car where the male dancers and musicians were quartered. One girl who was seen casually sitting on the edge of a male dancer's berth—it was all very innocent—was strangely absent from the company the next year. Madame refused to renew her contract.

There was no gadding about in the corridors of hotels, no running back and forth between dressing rooms in the theatre. Doors were kept closed and shades carefully drawn. It was no wonder that blue-nosed fellow-voyagers on the trans-Atlantic boats, who spent the first day out being indignant at having a ballet company on board, ended by gushing admiration for the ballerinas who were "such really well-bred, nice girls."

Madame engaged her dancers with an eye to family and breeding as well as talent; her girls came for the most part from nice families, and since they were young, she considered that their parents had entrusted them to her and held her responsible for their behavior.

But her own life was her own. While there was never a whisper about her name, she managed to live in her own way. There was an evening, a memorable evening, when we showed Pavlova the sights of Paris.

She was dancing a charity performance, and I was going to the painter Constantin Korovin's studio to see his designs for *Don Quixote*. Incidentally I looked in at the Théâtre Champs-Elysées to see Diaghilev's ballet. Larry Novikoff came there looking for me in what was for that gentle soul a fury of impatience.

"What's the matter with you? Madame has been waiting all this time for you in the rain!"

But Madame was not angry; she was in a high mood. She had three cavaliers that night—Larry, myself, and a Russian named Pitoeff who was married to a famous French actress of the day. Pitoeff, a Parisian by adoption, was to be our guide.

Dandre was not with us. He was not often with us on these excursions. I think he would have liked to come, but Madame did not encourage him. When she was out adventuring she wanted no sobersides along. And when she managed to go out without him she was like a young girl who has slipped from under the watchful eye of her duenna.

I had a very good notion of the places in Montmartre where

one went to see the sights—and where one might be seen—and I suggested to Madame that it might be wise for her to wear a veil.

"A veil, Hurokchik? What for? What if someone does see me? I am not going to hide behind any veil! And, besides, how can I drink champagne through a veil?"

So we saw the sights, and anyone who was a tourist in Paris in the Twenties knows well what the sights of Montmartre were. They were moderately naughty, and extremely expensive; the Parisian has always known how to relieve a foreigner of his money. Between midnight and five in the morning, Madame was amused and amazed by turns, but I can swear that she was never shocked.

She was always restless, hungry, seeking. She wanted to see and hear everything. When she was giving eight, sometimes nine performances a week at the Manhattan Opera House, and I would come back-stage after the curtain, there would be countless business details to discuss. And yet, after the business session was ended, "Now, Hurokchik, where shall we go tonight?"

Florence Mills, the Negro singer, was the rage that season, and Pavlova must hear her. So we went to the Plantation one night. Alas, it happened to be a night when there was a disagreement between the management and the waiters—or was it the dishwashers?—and the strikers had tossed stink bombs into the club. The stench was awful.

"Anna, let's leave," I urged her.

But she would not budge. She had come to hear Florence Mills, and she meant to hear her. "What's the matter, Hurokchik? Must you have only perfume around you?" she taunted me. In her determination not to let anything spoil her precious hour of gaiety, she was even able not to smell the offensive odor.

And there was another time, after the close of the New York season, when she danced a benefit for the Russian Church of New York at the Plaza Hotel. After the performance I found her entertaining the Metropolitan. Awed by the stately, bearded church-man, I kissed her hand and turned to leave.

"Oh, no, you stay!" she commanded. I stayed, and she charmed the Metropolitan right out of the door.

"Well, Hurokchik, what shall we do tonight?"

We rode in the park. It was an April night, brisk, but with a tantalizing scent of spring in the air. We rode about twenty-nine dollars' worth.

When I took her home, Dandre was sitting glumly alone.

"Where were you tramps all night?" he demanded.

She turned his anger aside by simply ignoring it. "It was a good performance," she said, innocently casual. "I think we made a nice sum of money for the Church."

Knowing her hunger, and not infrequently her despair, I found it all the more tragic that a heartless fate should have bound her for life to Dandre. Whatever the romantic attachment she might have felt for him when she was a young untried ballerina and he a gallant admirer in St. Petersburg, it had long vanished when I knew her. He was coldly correct, with a stubborn concern for minutiae. Even while she admitted the usefulness of this virtue, she found it a constant irritant. The rigid conservatism of his class possessed him to the point where nothing new, no change of any kind was desirable, or indeed possible to him. When she talked with yearning of going back to Russia, when she grew eager and animated over news of the progress of the Soviets, his fleshy face turned stonily pale. He wanted none of it.

At first the drama of his disgrace for her sake was enough to bind her to him. Later he became so necessary to her career that she could not imagine continuing without him. In his mind alone were recorded the thousand details of management; in his hands the solution of the thousand little problems of the company, the tours, the finances.

Once, indeed, he left her. It was during her second season with

Mikhail Mordkin, either 1912-13 or the next year. In the middle of the season Dandre walked out and took the boat back to London. When we were on tour there were weeks when she did not speak to him. But she could not cut herself off from him entirely. It would have been like cutting herself off from her work.

For his part, it seemed to me that he was afraid to let her stop working. It was always Dandre who egged me on, each season, to get the contract signed for the next.

She talked of taking a year off, of enjoying life. She talked of a villa on the Riviera, where she would do nothing but bask in the sun, tend her flowers, and cook delectable Russian dishes for the Novikoffs and me. She even talked of some day having a child. But the child remained a dream child, the villa a dream villa, and even the beautiful year of just living—all were dreams that never came true.

Dandre was always planning for the year to come, the tour, the repertoire. Even before the season was at its half-way mark, he was suggesting to me that it was time to discuss next year's business. And I, sorely tempted—as who would not be, by a contract with Pavlova's name on it?—would go to her.

"Coming back next year?" I would ask, as we sat over a supper in some American town.

She would shrug, and her answer was without enthusiasm. "What else is there to do?"

The "Royal Party"

Still, in New York or Paris, visiting with film folk in Los Angeles or getting off a train in Jackson, Mississippi, we were a gay troupe of gypsies. We were especially gay as the train drew near to Los Angeles. Twenty years ago, no less than today, the film capital was a shining oasis for touring artists: The picture folk embrace them not only with their own brand of imaginative and expensive hospitality, but with an appreciation and understanding which is more precious to performing artists than a thousand swimming-pool carnivals. The stops of a coast-to-coast tour are strung like beads, with New York—the start and the finish—as the clasp of the necklace, and Hollywood the glittering pendant. Indeed a number of artists, the urbane Artur Rubinstein for one, have made Hollywood their home.

Pavlova was adored by the picture people. We visited at Pickfair, and the irrepressible Doug Fairbanks, who was finishing *The Thief of Bagdad* at the time, showed us his bank book. It recorded a balance of just $13. He and Mary had put every cent into *The Thief*.

To Pavlova's company she and her immediate entourage were "the royal party." Though her concern for her girls was unremitting, Madame kept herself and her close associates rigidly apart from the dancers and musicians. This was perhaps a natural outgrowth of the caste system in which she had been trained in the Imperial Ballet, but it had its effectiveness in maintaining discipline. And anything that can maintain discipline in a ballet company is worth the effort.

On the other hand, she was generous with her girls. She paid them well. Ivy House was always full of her girls, visiting her.

Their Christmas gifts were of acute importance to her. She began shopping for them at the beginning of the tour, and each present was designed for the recipient. She could not resist an occasional copy-book morality; she might give a box of knitting or sewing materials to a girl who spent the long train journeys with idle hands. But for the most part the gift was what the girl wanted, not what she should have.

At phonographs, however, Madame balked, after she had given the first one and found that it was used principally to play jazz records. She was not convinced American jazz was the best kind of musical education for young ballerinas.

69

Her parties—for birthdays, name days, Christmas, Easter—were events for which she planned weeks ahead. On a trip to Capetown, South Africa, she carried not only the presents, but the Christmas tree in cold storage on the boat for three weeks. Her Christmas party that year took place on the Equator.

I was not at that party, but there was another Christmas we spent together. We had a week in Colorado Springs. The week before Christmas is not infrequently a lay-off week, since business is not at its best just before the holiday, and it is a good time for the company to rest and store up energy for the strenuous days ahead.

That was a beautiful week. Madame wore my feet out—her own were tireless—shopping for her Christmas party.

Wherever she was, she managed to have Russian food for her parties. She would have a suckling pig sent from New York to whatever little town the Russian Easter found her in. She had pirozhki—pies filled with meat or rice or fish or cabbage stuffing; she had smoked salmon, blini with caviar. And it was fresh caviar. She had to have sour cream, and Mrs. Novikoff was an expert sour-cream hunter.

We all ate together, frequently in Madame's hotel room. Dandre carried an electric plate, on which he prepared weak tea for Madame about half an hour before she went to the theatre. She watched his diet, and took a mischievous delight in shaming him before the rest of us so that he would not have the face to eat the rich foods which were making him fatter and fatter.

But frequently after we had gone on to the theatre, a waiter would stagger up to Dandre's door with an enormous tray of dinner. Madame never knew about those clandestine dinners which were putting pounds on him despite her diets.

Pavlova enjoyed Larry Novikoff's quiet seriousness. Once, it is true, she slapped him on the stage in London, just as she had slapped Mordkin years before, to the noisy delight of the English

70

press which made quite a thing of what it called, with characteristic English whimsy, "the quarrel in fairyland."

But the incident which involved Novikoff was nothing like the affaire Mordkin; she was at odds, not with Larry, but with herself. It was one of the rare occasions when her dissatisfaction with her life broke through her restraint in public.

Actually she adored Larry, leaned on him and trusted him, as she very well might. He is a rare person in the theatre, a fine and sensitive artist who is never guilty of advancing himself at another's expense, who perhaps has not had all the recognition he deserves because he is so much the reverse of aggressive. His stage manners are the most beautiful I have ever seen—and I have seen all kinds—for the obvious reason that they are an accurate expression of himself.

And she loved the stream of merry-hearted talk with which Mrs. Novikoff kept us all entertained. She even enjoyed my practical jokes.

I played one of them on Theodore Stier, our musical director. He was the most agreeable of conductors, from a manager's point of view. He got along with a minimum of rehearsals and never fought for an extra one. He considered himself rich with twenty-two musicians. When we came to New York he tremblingly asked for eight more men. "We're playing in the Metropolitan Opera House—please—you must!" he begged.

Stier was an Austrian, but during World War One he began to call himself a Czech. Considering the hysteria with which any national of the Central Powers was faced in America, you could scarcely blame him.

In Chattanooga we were entertained by a professor of music who was also a Czech. Incidentally he was the music critic of the Chattanooga paper. The afternoon of the performance he took Stier on a drive to see the Civil War battlefield. Stier came back in high spirits.

"He'll give us a good notice," he said.

The professor came to the performance with a young girl from his office, whose job it was to get the background facts of the story. She wanted to know the box-office figures, among other things, so naturally she was sent to me. I told her the orchestra was conducted by S. Hurok.

The next morning was bright and sunny. Early as it was, we were a happy company getting on the train. Stier came into the car, bouncy and cheerful, with a large bundle of the morning newspapers under his arm; he had bought dozens of extra copies to send to his friends. He kissed Madame's hand and sat down to read the notice.

Madame watched him, the corners of her mouth twitching. I had let her in on the joke. For herself, she never read any critics except H. T. Parker, the illustrious H.T.P. of the *Boston Transcript*, whose like for culture, charm and humanity I do not expect to see in my lifetime. There was a learned man who never paraded his learning, a man with taste and without affectation, whose zest for art in all its forms was matched only by his forthright eloquence in writing of it. Some of our best critics today are proud to confess that they sat at his feet.

Poor Stier! As he read the notice that morning, his happy face grew thinner and thinner. It was a fine notice, and it ended with a tribute to the music "conducted, as usual, by S. Hurok!"

He was a good sport. I suppose we were all good sports, making the most of our fun and ignoring the hardships of touring in this country twenty years ago. But Madame was the best sport of us all.

Ballet in Jackson, Mississippi

I found out how good a sport she was in Jackson, Mississippi. Jackson then had a population of about 15,000. You crossed the Mississippi River by ferry from New Orleans; I was sitting in

Madame's drawing room playing cards when without warning we found ourselves on a boat, train and all. The hotel in Jackson was too small to hold us, and the company was scattered in boarding houses and private homes all over the town.

I began to wonder why we had come to Jackson—I had never been in that part of the country before—but my question was answered when I met the local manager. She was a very happy woman that day. She had been a piano teacher for some years in New York, and now that she lived in Jackson her one ambition had been to bring Pavlova to her home town.

Jim, our carpenter, followed me out to the Country Club where I was lunching. He looked scared.

"Madame can't dance there, Mr. Hurok," he said. And he described the auditorium. It was an old garage which had been made over into a movie theatre. "The stage is nothing but a little platform. It will fall through if you put forty people on it."

I called the lady manager, but she had nothing more constructive to offer than acute distress. So Jim went to the lumber yard and bought what he needed, and with two carpenters to help him, he built a stage that afternoon. It was an odd-looking stage, with wallpaper tormentors, but at least it was safe.

The dressing rooms were nothing but a cellar full of rats. We cleaned and aired the musty basement and put up wallpaper partitions. It was pretty bad.

The program for the evening was "Les Sylphides," "The Fairy Doll" and the usual group of divertissements.

It was my habit to look in on Madame before the performance and during the intermissions. This time I did not dare to face her. I stood up in back of the house, and when the first intermission came I disappeared, so that Stier, who had to walk up the aisle from the pit, would not see me.

But there were moments in "The Fairy Doll" which always made me laugh, and Madame listened for my laugh. She also

73

kept an ear cocked for my applause, which is still, I must confess, good and loud.

Beside me stood the lady manager's husband. He was fascinated with "The Fairy Doll," in which the prima ballerina makes a number of exits and entrances. He slapped me vigorously on the back.

"That's good! She certainly knows her business. That's what the public wants—lots of encores!"

I can take ballet knowledge or leave it alone. The show should be able to stand on its own, and does, with people who have never seen ballet and cannot read a program. But in my despair that night, this exhibition of ignorance left me crushed. I was about to crawl away into the black night of Jackson when Stier came up the aisle, mopping his face with his handkerchief.

"Come along," he said, taking my arm. "You're not fooling Madame. She knows you've been here all evening."

I knocked on her dressing-room door, frightened to death. But she was smiling.

"Hurokchik, what's the matter with you? Does something hurt you?"

"No, no! I'm just ashamed to face you. The stage, the dressing rooms here . . ."

"Why, that's nothing! How can people in these little places see me if I don't come here to dance? No matter what kind of stage, I can dance better here than anywhere."

And when the roof leaked in Montgomery, Alabama, she read me another lecture on the obligation of the artist to the public in the provinces. It was hair-raising, that night. There was a thunderstorm during the performance of "Snowflakes," and the hole in the roof was so big that the lightning for the storm in the ballet was real. The scenery and costumes were wet, the stage was slippery with water and Pavlova did her pirouettes in a puddle.

"Never mind, Hurokchik," she told me afterward. "These are

the people who need us, and it gives me more joy to dance for them than at the Metropolitan Opera House."

Twenty years ago, outside of the largest cities, there were no good theatres. The floors were so bad that Madame always carried a canvas floor cloth, and one year she had a floor made of plywood which could roll up like a carpet.

Since those days I have been talking to the local newspaper men, making propaganda for better theatres. And if anyone still doubts the value of the New Deal's WPA, let him talk to me. Everywhere now in the small towns, thanks to the Federal Government which supplied at least sixty per cent of the funds, and to the Elks, Shriners, and other civic-minded organizations, there are fine municipal auditoria, with good spacious stages where scenery can be flown, with modern switchboards which make bad lighting inexcusable, with space for musicians in the pit. The people of America can now enjoy good symphonic music, theatre and ballet almost anywhere.

And so we traveled up and down the land, eating, drinking, laughing—and playing poker. I am an atrocious poker player, but Madame was even worse. Her poker face was about as subtle as a six-year-old's. When she held a poor hand she looked glum. When her hand was good, she put on a big act of indifference. She hummed, she looked around, she chattered about random trifles. I don't think she ever succeeded in making good a bluff, unless it was at my expense.

When she lost, as she often did, she would say, "Dandré, pay up for me." But when she won, she would gather up the pennies and nickels and dimes and tuck them away in a little purse. "This is my own money, for me," she said.

At last the tour was over. I put her on the boat and went back to my office in Aeolian Hall, feeling like a boy who has played hookey from school. It was like plunging into an icy bath to realize that there were other artists besides Pavlova, and that some of them were under my management. I dove into my work with an appetite sharpened by my guilty conscience.

Importer of Talent

That spring, the spring of 1922, I went abroad for the first time since my premature voyage, a decade before, in answer to Chaliapin's summons. My dream had come true: I was Chaliapin's American manager as I had vowed I would be, and I was Pavlova's manager too. I had managed a dozen other leading artists since those tentative Zimbalist concerts, had made a name for myself with music for the masses at the Hippodrome, and earned flattering interviews in the New York Times.

So at last I was an impresario, journeying to Europe in search of talent for the next season. And I went on the Majestic, first class.

The boat was crowded, as all the trans-Atlantic liners were in those careless years between one world war and the next. I shared a stateroom with three fellow-passengers. Al Jolson was on the boat, and J. J. Shubert and the late Edgar Woolf, who in those days was writing songs and sketches for vaudeville and afterward found his niche in Hollywood.

There was also a tall, good-looking brunette, a buyer making her annual trip to Paris for a Fifth Avenue store. She was a knowing traveler, but as for me—well, it was the dining-room steward who made this particular match. After all, it was my first trip in style.

I liked to dance and so did she, and there were long beautiful nights on deck. My principal trouble was that she was going to Paris and I was going to London.

Fast steamers have their disadvantages. It is scarcely until the third night that one can decently sit up on deck with a lady, and the fourth night before discussions of Einstein's theory are in order—and by next morning you are already in Cherbourg. There is never enough time. The proper romantic period is a minimum of seven or eight days. I never could figure out how the trans-Atlantic gallants made the conquests they boasted about on those five-day steamers.

On the last night my charmer turned coy and declined to tell me at what hotel she would be staying in Paris. I found a way around that. After I got to London I asked a friend who was going to Paris before me to do a little detective work. A day or so later I had a cryptic wire from him: "LADY AT CONTINENTAL."

I phoned her at the Continental from London, and she was so startled that she forgot to be coy. We met in Paris, and she traveled with me to Berlin and Frankfort and back to London, where I saw her off to America and the Fifth Avenue store again, her little fling on the store's expense account already over.

So began a friendship that endured some little time. I mention this small diversionary campaign only because my girl was representative of a curious element of the traveling population in those years.

Everyone who journeyed back and forth across the Atlantic in the Twenties knew the buyers. Chic, sharp, groomed with that machine-made Fifth Avenue smartness, our New York business girls are the handsomest en masse but less interesting individually than the European woman. Forgive me, my dears, my diminishing hair and expanding waistline give me the right to criticise—if I had married one of you I would have felt I had married quintuplets, you are all so much alike.

The buyers adorned the first-class decks of every liner. They wore a sleek armor of knowing everything about everything, and indeed they did know almost everything. They knew how to travel and how to drive a shrewd business bargain; they held their own at the bridge table and the bar. But the one thing they did not know was how to be happy.

Under their Daché hats and Schiaparelli frocks, inside the

shell of sophistication, they were scared little girls, easily flattered because so little secure in themselves, and to me, at least, their painful uncertainties, the scent of their inner fearfulness were perceptible even through their Chanel Number Five.

They came, for the most part, out of families with very modest incomes, and they were girls who either went to work directly from high school or skimmed through college with the single idea of getting into the business world with the least possible delay.

In those boom days they were pushed—those who had a native business sense—from salesgirl to assistant buyer to buyer in very short order. And they emerged at once from the narrow walls of the store, with its time-clock routine, its mountainous detail, its beat-last-month's-sales-or-get-out psychology, into the super-charged elegance of a first-class trip to Europe and luxury liners, luxury hotels and merchants in Paris, Lyons, Brussels, Prague ready to wine and dine them and turn their heads with costly gifts with the single purpose of selling them merchandise.

They gazed with longing at the glamour boys of the theatre, the concert, the literary world whom they met on these trips, but the glamour boys, with the inherent snobbery of the talented for the merely business-successful, passed them by. The successful businessmen flattered them, sold them and went home to their own leisure-class wives. And the less successful, the boys out of their own class who might have loved them for themselves— these they looked down on as inferiors, and quite naturally, because they made more money, and they had a luxurious free trip abroad every year. It would have to be a powerful romance which would make one of these girls give up her trip abroad.

This is not a portrait of my own young lady, who had managed somehow to rise above the disturbing circumstances of her career and to preserve her integrity and honesty. But she was rare. I was curious about these girls, and more than a little sorry for them.

And through them I had a glimpse of the business world of which I had never wanted any part, and I was happier than ever in the free-style career I had chosen for myself.

Groundwork for a Spy System

I spent a brief, happy holiday in London that first time, awed by the somber solidity of the city, charmed by the quicksilver artistic life that ran under its substantial surface. I visited Pavlova at Golders' Green and tasted the delight of Ivy House, the unpretentious serenity of it in its shady greenery, already filling up with Anna's treasures, her pets, the fabulously expensive and exotic gifts from her worshipers in all corners of the globe.

And I began, in London, in Paris, in Berlin, in the cafés and restaurants and hotels of the small as well as the great cities, to make friends among little people. The artists, the celebrities, the famous managers were my pride and my delight. My natural gregariousness with all kinds of folk has repaid me a thousand-fold in the years since.

What I was doing, more or less deliberately, was laying the wires for my private spy system in the entertainment world of Europe. Those were the days, remember, when America still scorned its home-grown talent. Except for Broadway, there was no audience for an American tenor, an American violinist, an American orchestra conductor. Our gifted boys and girls went abroad and acquired, along with their training, Italian names and Central European reputations before they could expect their fellow-countrymen to listen to them.

So the obvious market place for the talent buyer as well as the fashion buyer was Europe, and it was on the orginality, the quality, the variety of my importations from Europe that I was to make my name in the next fifteen years.

From the mystic Mary Wigman to the fiery Escudero, from

Shan-Kar to the astonishing Piccoli, the concertina-playing Raphael of tender memory, the delicate clowning of Trudi Schoop, even our glorious Marian Anderson was among the surprises from abroad which I offered to America. To many of them, I am not too proud to say, I was tipped off by my anonymous friends, the small-time promoters, the newspaper critics, the hotel managers, the headwaiters and café proprietors who came to know my pleasure in good wines and good food as well as good entertainment.

It took years to lay my wires, and many good dinners and many bottles of vintage wine in many cafés. A large capacity for eating and drinking is an essential item in the equipment of an impresario.

Trans-Sentimental Journey

The nearest Pavlova was coming to the United States the next season was Canada, and then only en route to the Orient. An entire season would pass before I could see her again. So, one chilly autumn evening, I took a train for Quebec.

The Canadian liner was waiting at Farther Point for the inspectors, and I went down with them in the cutter early in the morning and climbed aboard. The steward, not concealing his surprise at the early visitor, led me to Madame's table. None of the party had yet come in to breakfast. I sat down and waited.

They came in one by one, first the Polish ballet master Pianowsky, then Volinine, and finally, fussing with his pince-nez, Dandre. With each one came the roar of surprised recognition— "How did you get here?"—"Wait until Madame finds out!" But Madame kept us waiting interminably. At last Dandre, who was not a patient soul, jumped up and went to fetch her.

"Why are you hurrying me so? There's plenty of time!" she protested, but she left off packing her little bag and came to breakfast.

80

It was a lovely surprise. She threw her arms around my neck and kissed me. She had to know all about how I got there. But mostly she wanted to know whether this meant I would accompany her to Japan.

We had nearly five days to Vancouver. I suppose there are not many women for whose company a man would ride for five days on a train. But there was ever only one Pavlova.

I remember the stop in Calgary. There, for some reason known only to railroad men, the train paused for several hours. We sat together in the park, under the great trees flaming red and orange and yellow, and talked about everything. She told me all she knew about her father, about her mother—out of respect to Pavlova, her mother had been allowed to live on unmolested in Pavlova's house through the Revolution. We talked about religion. Anna did not share her mother's orthodox piety; she was in her own way anti-religious. She understood a good deal about the forces which brought the Revolution to Russia.

"I am a Jewess," she told me earnestly, and made me promise not to tell while she lived.

The train carried us on to Vancouver, and we had two days before the boat sailed. Being Pavlova, she had to spend some of the time looking at shoes. She had never fewer than thirty pairs of shoes—they occupied an entire trunk by themselves—and yet she could not spend an hour in any town without looking for new shoes. When the new shoes she had bought did not fit into the trunk she would make room for them by giving away some of the old ones. The old ones also looked new; she scarcely ever wore a pair of shoes more than a half dozen times.

We went into every shoe store in Vancouver, and she must have tried on a hundred pairs. I was getting very tired of shoes, but not Madame.

"Just wait, Hurokchik. Even when we've finished with the shoes, I won't let you go."

81

At last I dragged her away from shoes, and we took a cab and drove out of town to Stanley Park for a little fresh air.

On the last afternoon, Dandre went ahead to the pier with the baggage, warning me to be sure to get Madame to the boat on time. As usual, Madame put off leaving until the last minute. *The Empress of Canada* was waiting for us, and I directed the cab to the pier.

We climbed the gangplank with scarcely a minute to spare. Dandre stood watching for us on the deck, peering through his pince-nez, scowling with impatience.

"Why didn't you keep her another hour?" he scolded.

Anna dragged me to her stateroom, large and luxurious. "See how nice it is, Hurokchik! Now will you change your mind and come to Japan with us?"

But I had traveled as far and been gone from my office as long as I dared. I kissed her good-bye and hurried down the gangplank, and stood there waving until the big liner swung away from the pier and Pavlova's small lacy handkerchief was a vanishing speck in the distance.

New Ballets and an Injured Knee

Some demon statistician once estimated that in her lifetime Anna Pavlova traveled 350,000 miles on tour, enough mileage to take her fourteen times around the world at the Equator. There may be artists who have traveled farther to carry their gift to the peoples of the world, but certain it is that Madame danced for audiences of more varied skin colors than any other ballerina. She danced for the Chinese and the Japanese and the Zulus; she danced for all the kings and queens; and especially she danced for the common folk.

As she traveled, she studied. She engaged Japanese teachers in Tokyo, learned the exquisite Hindu-Javanese language of the hands in India, and when she came again to America she brought with her a group of new ballets, Oriental Impressions, and the young Hindu dancer Uday Shan-Kar, who later came under my management at the head of his own company.

Pavlova was always ready to embrace the new, the strange, the exotic. It is curious that for the American tour she did not live to make in 1932 she had engaged Vicente Escudero, the Spanish gypsy dancer who also became one of my remarkable artists—remarkable for more than merely his artistry.

It was Pavlova who urged me to bring Isadora Duncan back to America, and who was keenly excited about Isadora's Russian children, as I shall mention in another place. It was Pavlova, too, who first suggested Mary Wigman to me. It was in Pavlova, of all the artists I have met, that I saw in its fullest flower that eager curiosity, that interest which knew no boundary lines of nation or language or tradition, that open-minded, open-armed welcome to art of all kinds, only if it be good art. This readiness to examine and accept the new is one of the happy heritages Mother Russia bequeaths to her children.

Along with her Oriental ballets, Pavlova brought Novikoff's fine revival of *Don Quixote* with Karovin's decor and costumes, which sold out in advance virtually every performance for which it was announced.

And also, Madame brought with her an injured knee.

There are several versions of how she hurt her knee. Dandre wrote that in *Amarilla*, absorbed in the part, she fell to her knees. She herself mentioned that she hurt it in Japan while dancing the *Bacchanale* with Sascha Volinine.

Ballet dancers frequently have accidents, but they are usually minor ones and they usually happen to the less experienced dancers. Rarely have I known our great ballerinas to sustain accidents; the chances lessen with the perfection of technique, and an accident usually needs some outside agency, such as a bad stage or a partner's mistake, to help it along. Irina Baronova went so far as to break a bone in her ankle, but she was enjoying a snowball fight in a St. Louis park when she did it.

With Pavlova it was an iron rule never to miss a performance. I saw her dance once in St. Louis with bronchitis and a temperature of 103, resting between ballets on a sofa in the wings. She danced in Boston, but she stood sobbing in the wings and had to change the échappés from her left foot to her right in the Swan. After the Boston performance she sat in her room in the Copley-Plaza, drinking milk and crying openly like a child. It looked as though the 1923-24 American tour would have to end right where it began.

Mrs. Novikoff had done massage as a volunteer nurse in the Imperial Hospital during the war. She looked at the knee and saw that it was contracted and swollen.

"I'll look after your knee," she told Madame. "I'll treat it with massage and hot compresses, but don't let anyone else tamper with it."

"But I have a masseuse," Madame said.

"Never mind," Mrs. Novikoff told her in her forthright way. "I've seen that masseuse. She shakes you like a dog with a bone, but she doesn't do anything for your knee."

In New York Madame went to an expensive doctor who gave her some sort of medication. "Come back after your tour," he said, "and if the knee isn't better I'll cut out the cartilage."

A promise guaranteed to give a dancer perfect peace of mind!

Another expensive doctor in Chicago—this one was a Russian —insisted that it was all due to Madame's tonsils, which must come out.

Fortunately Madame was willing to continue with Mrs. Novikoff's treatment. And when she saw the swelling actually going down, felt the knee getting stronger, she forgot all her anti-religious leanings and fervently crossed herself, kissed an icon, and finally kissed Mrs. Novikoff's hand.

As the tour went on, the knee continued to improve, though she danced continuously, with only a week's vacation before Christmas. When the company came back to New York for the season's climax at the Metropolitan Opera House the knee was perfect except for a tiny lump which was barely noticeable.

The sequel to the story came in Paris that summer, when Madame went to see a celebrated doctor much favored by dancers. She told him what her friend had done all through the tour.

"Your friend did a good job," the doctor told her gravely.

Farewell Performance

After 1926 Pavlova did not return to America. She made her English and Continental tours, traveled to South Africa, to Australia, with a small company. I saw her in Europe every year.

In the summer of 1930 she telephoned me in Paris. I was taking the *Leviathan* back to the States in a few days. Wouldn't I come to Southampton, where they were playing, and spend some time with her before I left? I could board my boat at Southampton as well as at Cherbourg, couldn't I?

No invitation could have been more welcome. We spent four days together, wandering about the town, going to performance, playing poker. It was like old times.

She was thinking of bringing her small ensemble to America the next season. I was opposed to this and I said so.

"Well, since I'm not going to be your manager this time, I'm going to have a good time with you," I said. "I'll come backstage and be your cavalier."

"Yes," she said, and then she began to cry. "I'm coming to see you off at the boat," she declared suddenly.

Dandre protested. She was due to leave for another town on her provincial tour.

"I have to see that he has a nice stateroom," she insisted.

I tried to dissuade her. "It's so damp at the dock; you might catch a cold," I said.

Then she turned on both of us. "You can both go to the devil!" she stormed. "Don't you know I may never see him again?"

Her feeling was so strong that Dandre and I kept silent. She came to the boat.

She looked over my stateroom on the *Leviathan* minutely, made sure that the bed was soft, that I was in a part of the ship where I would not feel the vibration too much.

She spoke to the purser. "Take good care of my friend Hurokchik," she admonished him.

She gave me detailed advice on getting enough sleep, on eating the right foods, on taking exercise on deck.

Then we said good-bye.

She had been right, of course, in her intuition. I never saw her again.

The first news came in a cable to the New York newspapers datelined The Hague, January 20th, and was headed "PAVLOVA MUFFS FIRST DATE IN 30 YEARS." "Pavlova arrived here on Saturday, Jan. 17th, from Paris on her final world tour. On her arrival she was suffering from a cold contracted when she was in a train wreck coming up from the Riviera. . . ." The cold developed into pleurisy, and she died on the twenty-second. She would have been forty-six years old on January 31st.

Her death was tragically unnecessary. To the eye she was still beautiful, and her flesh fitted her slender bones with the perfection of a girl of twenty. But she was not a girl of twenty.

She should not have been making those killing tours, traveling in the bad winter months, sitting in cheap, ill-heated trains on long, jolting rides, suffering fatigue, courting illness.

When she was touring America with me she was at her peak. She had to keep her company occupied most of the year, she had to finance new ballets for the repertoire, provide herself with the best partners; her expenses were high, but her earnings were correspondingly high.

Nor had she squandered her money. She had lived modestly always. No lavish hotel suites, but only a nice room; no costly furs or jewels. She had beautiful jewels from her young ballerina days in St. Petersburg, but she kept them in a bank vault, and I never saw her wear them. She had no need of expensive clothes; she had elegance in anything she chose to wear. Her entrance in a room full of people was a dramatic moment. The way she placed her feet on the floor when she sat was an art. She needed no adornment, and desired none.

She had not even the excuse of financial need for her constant, grinding work. Otto H. Kahn managed her securities for her, and at her death there was close to a half million dollars in the estate, between Europe and America.

Why then did she work until she died of it? I have my own theory, of course, as everyone who knew her had. I believe she could not live without working, because she had emptied her life of everything but work, and it was by then too late to turn back and taste the kind of living she had missed. In another world, under another system, she would have been cherished like a jewel. She would have worked perhaps a few months of the year, would have danced perhaps once or twice a week. She would have had time and leisure both for working and for living, for love and children and the exquisite art of being happy.

Her estate in this country was quickly turned over to Dandre, but in London it was a different matter. He was not considered her legal husband, as indeed he was not except by common law, and the London courts had to be convinced that he had been useful enough to her to deserve to be her heir. Also the Soviet

Government, watchful in behalf of its citizens, laid claim in the name of her mother, still living in Leningrad.

I remember going to Dandre's lawyer in London with him, to make a statement on his usefulness to Pavlova on her American tours.

In the end the Soviet garnered about $150,000 for the obscure old lady in Leningrad, and Dandre was awarded the remainder.

East Wall 3711

I could not wait to get on a boat that spring after her death. Instead of going to Paris, as was my custom, I rushed directly to London.

I called Dandre, and we met for lunch at the Metropole. "You remember," Dandre said, "we met you here just ten years ago." Anna had always liked the Metropole because it faced the Thames, at the corner of the square, and she had reserved a room for me there in 1922. It was there we had had our first dinner together in London.

Dandre took her favorite table, placed a vaseful of her favorite flowers, lilies of the valley, on it. With Dandre opposite me, his familiar round face with the pince-nez, in that setting, I felt strongly that she was sitting there with us.

Afterward we went to the crematory at Golders' Green, where she had liked to go walking.

I remember the number: East Wall 3711. There in an urn was the handful of ashes that had been Anna Pavlova.

CHAPTER FOUR

The Turbulent Goddess

*I*SADORA DUNCAN moved through my life like a rocket ship, by means of a series of explosions. But the manner in which she first appeared on my horizon was of the most decorous, even the most routine.

On a night in 1922, while I was sitting in Anna Pavlova's dressing room at the Manhattan Opera House during a performance of the ballet, a member of my office staff brought me a cablegram. It was from Isadora in Moscow, asking if I would arrange an American tour for her and her Russian children.

I showed the cablegram to Madame.

"Ah, Hurokchik, that's a most interesting thing!" she said. "Of course you must bring Isadora back to America. With the children, too! Good. Very good."

Isadora! The name will forever chime with greatness to the ears of my generation. But I wonder if the young people now growing up know how much they owe to Isadora. Do they know it is because Isadora once lived that young girls walk with their free, long-legged strides on the streets of American towns? That their backs are straight and strong, their heads high, their bodies healthy and beautiful, their minds free of the conventions, superstitions, tabus that enslaved their grandmothers?

Isadora was born a revolutionary. There were four young Duncans, children of a rebellious mother who divorced a husband she

89

did not love and made an uncertain living by giving music lessons in San Francisco.

Elizabeth later took over Isadora's school in Berlin; Augustin became an actor; Raymond took to sandals and Greek robes, let his hair grow long and founded an ascetic cult of weaving and primitive crafts.

And then there was Isadora. The youngest, she was also the most creative, the most daring—and the most tragic.

At six she borrowed a half dozen neighborhood babies, not one of them old enough to walk, and sat them in a circle, teaching them to wave their arms. At ten she left grammar school, which could teach her nothing she cared to learn, and with Elizabeth organized her first school of the dance. At twelve she and the other Duncans were touring the coast around San Francisco with their own little theatre. She could have been no more than sixteen when she set forth with her mother, armed only with her little white tunic and her great courage, to conquer the world with an idea.

She was tall—five feet six inches—and slender, with reddish hair and a tip-tilted nose which might have made her a piquant Irish beauty, but which somehow blended into classic purity when she danced. Later, ten or fifteen years later, she was a lush Aphrodite, and still later, when I knew her well, she was Hera, the queen goddess, ripened to the full curves of maturity, with the shadows of twilight already dark on her face.

But in those early days at the turn of the century she was a slender nymph, chaste and a little sentimentalized, the nymph on Keats's Grecian Urn.

There was no place in the theatre for her simple, artless poetry of motion. Augustin Daly tried to make a pantomime actress of her and failed. In New York, in London, in Paris, poets and musicians, the sculptor Rodin and the painter Carrière, theatre people like Ellen Terry and Eleonora Duse, embraced her at once, and the great ladies of society patronized her and invited her to dance in their drawing rooms.

They clapped their gloved hands, murmured, "How delightful!" and told her how much money she had brought in for the Orphans' Home. And meanwhile she and her mother and her sister Elizabeth and brother Raymond slept on the bare floor of their studio and went hungry. She might have starved to death if a knowing manager, Alexander Gross, had not taken her firmly in hand.

He put her on the stage of the Urania Theatre in Budapest, and sold out for thirty performances.

From then on Europe was at her feet. In Berlin she became the "Heilige, göttliche Isadora." In Munich the students fairly tore the roof off the Künstlerhaus. In Bayreuth she danced for the greatest intellectuals, in her gauze tunic and bare feet, to the dismay of the matriarchal Frau Cosima Wagner and the greater glory of Wagner and herself.

As one manager to another, I bow to Gross, although I never knew him. She was the same Isadora, dancing in the same little tunic, now white, now red. Yet before Budapest the public ignored her; after Budapest it adored her.

Gross did not make Isadora; she made herself. But without him she starved for lack of a public. A manager does not make an artist. What he makes is an audience.

He led her over a well-planned path from Budapest through the little towns of Central Europe, to Vienna, Munich, Berlin, gathering an audience as an avalanche gathers snow. In the end all Europe was her audience.

She was feted in St. Petersburg, visited by the leading ballerinas. She spent a day with Pavlova—and merely watching the endless exercises, which years later I came to know so well, left her exhausted, though Pavlova was fresh and gay to the end.

Pavlova might have returned the compliment, for in her *Iphigenia in Aulis* Isadora danced continuously, impersonating the entire cast of the Greek tragedy, for forty-five minutes. Yet Isadora could never have submitted to the discipline of ballet. It was not in her to submit to any discipline. In her art as in her life she functioned not at all by rule or training, only by inspiration.

She abhorred ballet, which she called a distortion of the human form. But the ballet people embraced her, and her ideas. To them she was the Renaissance of the dance, and they eagerly enfolded her principles of natural, expressive movement within the framework of their never-dying, ever-changing art. Still her dream was the same: a school where she could teach little children, their young minds and bodies yet unspoiled, to express beauty in pure movement. She set up a school in Berlin, moved it to Paris, to London, back again to Paris. She came home to America in 1908 to earn money for her school and a tour which began as a disastrous failure ended under the guidance of Walter Damrosch as a financial success.

There were a few shining years; a child by the strangely gifted stage designer Gordon Craig, who was Ellen Terry's son; another child by the lover she called Lohengrin.

But the woman who gave herself so unstintingly to art and love could not be happy for long. Tragedy took her for its own when the car carrying her two beautiful children to Versailles backed into the Seine.

When the war came to Paris in 1914 Isadora was gravely ill; the third child, the child she had dreamed of to comfort her, had died at birth. She gave up her school at Bellevue to the wounded as a hospital, and began her wanderings anew.

She came to America again, school and all, in 1915. Her studio on Fourth Avenue and 23rd Street was a salon for artists and writers. Otto H. Kahn set her up at the Century Theatre, where for four weeks she and the children danced and Augustin, the actor-brother, declaimed Greek tragedy and Biblical poetry—to a painfully empty house. In the end she had to appeal through the newspapers for funds to pay a $12,000 debt and passage for herself and the children to Naples. Frank A. Vanderlip, banker and art patron, came forward with $3,000, and a number of responsible citizens to endorse her notes for the rest, and she sailed away on the *Dante Alighieri* with her children, declaiming her disgust at Americans growing fat on the war while Europe bled.

Still another time, in 1917, she was in New York. She danced at the Metropolitan, was feted magnificently at Sherry's by Lohengrin, who talked of leasing Madison Square Garden for her school. But the party at Sherry's ended with Lohengrin in a fit of jealousy dragging the cloth from the banquet table and dumping a thousand dollars' worth of crockery, viands and vintage wines on the floor. Instead of being installed at Madison Square Garden, Isadora sold an emerald to one opera soprano, an ermine coat to another opera soprano, and pawned a fabulous diamond necklace —all were gifts of Lohengrin—to establish her pupils at Long Beach. When those funds were gone, Gordon Selfridge, the London merchant, paid her passage to London. But she went alone. Her little girls, the "Isadorables," had grown up and wanted to make their careers in America. Thus ended Isadora's first school, the one she had clung to with all her strength for so many years.

In 1921 Isadora was invited to Russia by the Soviet Government. The story of Isadora's Russian days has been eloquently told by Irma, the one pupil who remained faithful to her and her ideas to the end. To found a school for little children in the chaos of those days, without money, without food, without heat for the big house the Government placed at her disposal—only Isadora would have dared.

The good will and the interest of People's Commissar of Education Lunacharski were hers without stint. But where could a government, struggling for a foothold in an exhausted country, coping with famine and disease and counter-revolution, striving to get the wheels of a broken-down industrial system turning—where could that government find the means to support a school of the dance?

It was Isadora's young Russian husband, Essenine, who explained the situation laconically. Asked by a reporter in New York whether Lunacharski gave financial support to Isadora's school, he said, "He gives advice, yes. But money? How can a man give what he has not?"

Isadora finally went on tour through the provinces to make money, and nearly died of starvation herself. And always there was the mad poet Essenine, tormenting her with alternate moods of love and contempt.

This was the Isadora who cabled me that she wanted to return to America with twenty-five of her Russian children. I imagined the tender pride with which she would show them to her countrymen who had never accorded her the honor she deserved.

After she left in 1917 I had managed the "Isadorables." Anna, Lysel, Gretel, Theresa, Erica and Irma, six lovely young creatures, had become the pets of chic New York. Vanity Fair gave them pages of beautiful Arnold Genthe photography. The artist Winold Reiss "immortalized" them—the word belongs to the enthusiastic magazine writer, not to me—in his decorations for the Café Crillon, the Stork Club of the day.

With the pianist George Copeland, the six, calling themselves the Isadora Duncan Dancers, sold out six performances in Carnegie Hall in June—an unheard-of achievement—and made a successful tour. In October I presented them at the Metropolitan Opera House with an orchestra, another unqualified success.

Woman from Mars

With Pavlova spurring me on, to say nothing of my own enthusiasm, I moved quickly to bring Isadora and the Russian children here.

I concluded negotiations with Isadora. Then came a real setback. The Soviet Government declined to give permission for the children to leave the country. Some of them were only eleven and twelve years old—too young, said Moscow with finality.

But Isadora cabled in a paraphrase of the inscription over the New York City Post Office, "Storms, winds, or snow will never stop me from reaching America."

She flew from Moscow to Berlin, but not alone. With her was another kind of child, a problem child, who would prove to be more trouble than a whole schoolful of children, Serge Essenine.

He was twenty-seven; in New York the reporters relentlessly ferreted out Isadora's age on her passport as thirty-eight. He was even then considered the leading poet of Russia, with prophecies that he would grow into another Pushkin. In Moscow he was the leader of a gang of self-styled "hooligans," given to drinking and carousing in a time when good Russians were working twenty-four hours a day to build up a new country. But the Soviet Government, with its weakness for pampering artists, never disciplined him.

Nor did Isadora, though his exuberant drinking bouts were a constant disruption in her school.

Isadora confessed to me long afterward that she had arranged the trip expressly for his sake, to show him the big beautiful world beyond the impenetrable wall of the Soviet borders. She would have given him the moon if she could. Though she had fought her life long against marriage as an enslavement of women, she married Essenine before they left Russia. She remembered how

95

poor Gorki and his sweetheart had been hounded from American hotels.

Essenine responded to the capitalist world like a child—a spirited, unstable child of poverty—who has been pushed into a monstrous toy shop and told he could do what he liked. He could not get enough at first of beautiful clothes, beautiful luggage, shaving lotions, hair tonics, luxurious masculine accessories. Or of liquor. Or women. And then, surfeited, guilty, his inner hungers still unsatisfied by this superficial banquet, he became unruly and downright destructive. That was what Isadora was bringing with her, but I did not know it at the time.

At the Adlon in Berlin Isadora gave an interview to the press. "I love the Russian people," she said, "but it is very comforting to return to a place where one can have warm water, napkins, heat. Not that the Russians believe in giving up luxuries! On the contrary, but they believe in luxuries for all, and if there is not enough to go around, then everyone must have a little less."

She went to Paris, crossing the border as a Soviet citizen with a promise to the French Government that she and her husband would not engage in any propaganda. "I only want to earn money for my school!" she protested.

She took her grown-up child for a little trip to Italy, to see the great art of the Renaissance. She arranged for the translation and publication of his poems in French.

Meanwhile I had announced her first appearance at Carnegie Hall. The announcement fell curiously dead. The box-office men at Carnegie had little to do.

At last the day came, a Sunday in October, when the S.S. *Paris* was due to land, bringing Isadora back to her own country. I went down to the pier and climbed aboard, more than a little excited.

In the lounge I found Isadora in her long cape and white felt hat, holding court for a vast gathering of reporters and photographers. Under her cape she wore no Grecian draperies, but a handsome Paris suit, blue with wide yellow and orange stripes, and an orange blouse. She was handsome and smart, and it pleased me to see that she was offering herself, not as a freak, but as an artist who could be a woman like other women off the concert platform.

She was happy, and she was beautiful. Her face looked older than the thirty-eight years to which she confessed, but it was lovely in its happiness, radiating warmth and friendliness for her countrymen who stood around her. Her rounded, womanly arms moved gracefully; her voice, not throaty, not shrill, was sheer music.

She had come to her native land in the happy mood of the interview she had given in Berlin; out of the chaos and suffering of Soviet Russia in its birth pangs, she had emerged into the familiar and pleasant world where good things to eat and drink, nice things to wear, soft beds and hot baths were hers for the taking. And she had with her her beloved poet.

Her eloquent hands gestured toward him as she presented him to the press as the leading imagist poet of our time.

From Isadora, the woman from Mars, the free-lover, the scandalous beauty whom they had come to interview, the reporters turned to Essenine. The tall Russian youth in the peasant smock, with glittering blue eyes and a thatch of straw-colored hair, was picturesque.

"What kind of poet?" one reporter asked, and wrote down "imaginative poet." That bit of illiteracy, too, was in the stories about Isadora and her husband from then on. It was already clear, if I could have read the signs, that Isadora and the American newspaper men did not talk the same language, that out of her years in Paris with the writers and artists she spoke as foreign a tongue as the Russian Essenine.

Isadora passed out a prepared statement.

"Here we are," it said, "on American territory. Gratitude, that is our first thought. We are the representatives of young Russia. We are not mixing in politics. It is only in the field of art that we are working. We believe that the soul of Russia and the soul of America are about to understand each other.

"The work of the American Relief Administration is unforgettable. Above everything else I wish to emphasize the fact that today there are only two countries in the world—Russia and America."

It had been prepared by Serge, Isadora told me, with Vladimir Vetlugin, the brilliant young Russian, now one of the story wizards of Metro-Goldwyn-Mayer, whom she brought as her secretary. The last sentence, with its pedantic little air of the teacher addressing her pupils, was Isadora's own touch. The statement in its friendly naïveté showed how pitifully unaware Isadora was of the America to which she had returned.

This, remember, was 1922. The wave of reaction to the war, to Wilson, to liberalism, was rolling up in a fearful tide. It was a year when red was the color of all evil, and to call a man a Bolshevik was to damn his eternal soul as well as to send his earthly body to jail. Suspicion and mistrust of the Soviet Union are still a force to be reckoned with in this country in 1946. In 1922 it was not suspicion but sheer, unreasoning terror; it was not mistrust but the bitterest hatred.

Into the arms of this America came Isadora, fresh from Moscow with her Bolshevik husband, smiling, friendly, confiding.

As the first slap was dealt her, a lesser soul would have quailed and fled; a wise one would have sealed her lips and danced.

But Isadora was neither weak nor wise. She was a warrior. She had fought for her convictions all her life, and always against odds. She fought this time too. And as the press handled her more and more roughly, so she grew more and more violent and extreme. It was a battle in which she was inevitably the loser, but she went down fighting.

But on this Sunday morning in the gracious lounge of the *Paris* all was still serene. The reporters stuffed the statement, unread, into their pockets. They had more interesting questions they wanted answered, human-interest questions.

Their sharp eyes went from the startlingly handsome young man back to Isadora, the beauty still beautiful in decline. If her husband spoke only Russian, and she spoke no Russian at all, how did they converse?

"There is one language that everyone understands," she told them, with her radiant, disarming smile.

While all this was going on, the immigration inspectors beckoned me aside. They were very sorry. The law by which an American woman who married an alien automatically forfeited her citizenship had gone into effect some two months before. With a Russian passport and a Bolshevik husband—the whole proposition was too hot for them to handle on the spot. Isadora and her husband would have to go to Ellis Island.

The reporters, who quickly surmised that something was brewing, clustered around me panting for the news. I told them the fact without embellishment: it was a trip to Ellis Island for Isadora and her poet.

The captain offered them the hospitality of his ship so that they would not have to sleep on Ellis Island that night. I hurried away to call my lawyer.

I went back to the boat that evening to reassure her that the lawyer, Nathan S. Goldberger, was ready to make an appeal to the Department of Labor if it became necessary. And then it was my turn for an adventure. As I stepped off the gangplank an immigration inspector stood in my path.

"You'll have to come with me," he said. "If you don't come quietly we'll have to use force."

I went, meek as a lamb, to the inspectors' office on the pier. And there I was obliged to remove every stitch of clothing on me, while

99

sharp eyes peered into every pocket, and hands felt of the linings of my suit and topcoat. When I was permitted to put my clothes on again I felt that every shred of my Constitutional rights as a citizen had been trampled. I was ready to fight the whole Department of Labor.

Riding uptown, seething, I stopped to buy the morning papers, which were already on the stands. Immediately I felt much better. There were the nice big headlines, "ISADORA ON ELLIS ISLAND!"

The next morning the papers had denials from the Bureau of Immigration that any orders had been issued to detain her. Heywood Broun wrote caustically of the "blundering boorishness" of America's welcome to Isadora. Arthur Brisbane wrote a protesting column which appeared on the front page of the *New York American* and was syndicated throughout the country. Celebrities wrote to the newspapers in protest: Anna Fitziu, the singer, sent a blazing letter to the *Times*. The papers were full of Isadora for a week.

Meanwhile on Monday morning I hurried to Ellis Island. There was a long wait while a special Board of Review questioned Isadora behind closed doors. At last the doors opened and Isadora strode out. She was free to enter her native land.

"They held me," she told me in a quick aside, "because I came from Soviet Russia." And in fact a statement was issued later, explaining that she had been held by the Department of Justice because of her long residence in Moscow, and because there was some suspicion that she and her husband might be acting as "friendly couriers" for the Soviet Government, carrying secret documents. This explained, too, my strip-tease on the pier the night before. But what those documents or their purpose might be, no one ever attempted to explain.

"Well, they found me innocent, not guilty," Isadora said gaily as we boarded the ferry. She seemed to share none of the indignation of her friends who had written to the newspapers. To her the

Chaliapin and S. Hurok

Chaliapin as Boris Godunov

Chaliapin
as Mefistofele

Chaliapin
visits the Bowery

Anna Pavlova

Anna Pavlova and S. Hurok
in a park in Calgary

Anna Pavlova
and Laurent Novikof
in *Autumn Leaves*

Isadora Duncan and her husband, Serge Essenine

(Wide

Isadora Dun
with children
of her school

Marian Anderson and her mother

Marian Anderson singing at the Lincoln Memorial, Washington, D. C., Easter, 1939

Mrs. Franklin D. Roosevelt presents the Spingarn Medal to Marian Anderson

Marian Anderson rehearses at home with her accompanist, Franz Rupp

Alexandre Glazounov and S. Hurok

The Saengerknaben

(Cosmo-Sileo

Mary Wigman

Vicente Escudero

Argentinita and S. Hurok

(Maurice Seymour)

Alexandra Danilova and Leonid Massine in *Boutique Fantasque*

Trudi Schoop

(Alfredo Valente)

experience was an amusing adventure. She had never expected, she said, that the human brain could be capable of devising so many questions.

They had asked her if she was a classical dancer. "I do not know," she answered, "because my dancing is personal."

"What do you look like when you dance?"

"I have never seen myself dance!"

I readily believe that the session was as baffling to the investigators as to Isadora.

One of the reporters broke in on her account of the inquiry with a point-blank question. "Are you a Communist?" he demanded.

"Rot!" she exploded. "Rot, rot, rot!"

One-Woman Parade

When the ferry docked, a crowd was waiting. Isadora stepped off and, grandly gesturing the taxicabs aside, she set forth on foot to the Waldorf-Astoria. In her red-leather Russian boots and Russian caracul hat, with her startling red hair and her long cape flying, she marched from the Battery up Broadway, up Fifth Avenue, a triumphal parade of one, with me, Modeste Altschuler the Russian Symphony Orchestra conductor, and even young Essenine panting behind her free-striding, heroic figure.

At the Carnegie Hall box office, meanwhile, the treasurers suddenly found themselves very busy indeed. Thanks to the United States Government and the New York newspapers, three performances were sold out within the next twenty-four hours.

At the first performance in Carnegie Hall the following Saturday Isadora made her first speech.

"Why must I go to Moscow after illusions that don't exist when you in America also need the dance for your children? Why does not America give me a school? America has all that Russia has not!

Russia has things that America has not. Why will America not reach out a hand to Russia, as I have given my hand?"

Thus began the Duncan progress through America. From that day never a phone rang but I trembled to answer it. If I laid my head on my pillow at night, I never knew what alarm would rout me out of my bed before morning.

It was my duty to protect Isadora from her own unwisdom, for her sake as well as mine. I saw in her first speech the ruin of her entire tour. I talked to her.

"Dance," I pleaded. "Leave speeches to the politicians. You can teach the public more with one gesture of your arm in the 'Marseillaise' than with thousands of words of oratory."

I described to her the state of mind of the public to whom her words were addressed. The fear of revolution was too strong. They would not listen to her; they would only turn against her.

Gracious, sweet-tempered, agreeable, her handsome head bent at an attentive angle, she listened to me. She always listened to me. And the next time she did it again. It was as though she could not see an audience without telling them what was on her mind, as though she felt it a form of deception to keep her thoughts to herself. Impetuous, undisciplined, Isadora would speak, and the blows rained on her uncompromising head.

As company manager with Isadora on tour I chose Sergei Kournakoff, who had been Pavlova's secretary. Sergei has since achieved well-deserved recognition as a military expert and author on the subject of the Red Army. He qualified perfectly for the Duncan tour, first, because, a gifted linguist, he spoke Russian, English and six more languages, and could talk to both Essenine and Isadora; second, because as a son of the old Russian aristocracy he had the soothing charm to reassure the managers, ladies' committees, and not infrequently the mayors and police officers of whom Isadora ran afoul.

But third, and most important, as a former captain of artillery he had the firmness, if anyone had, to cope with the turbulent pair. No one, not even a four-star general, could really exert authority over Isadora, and Isadora herself could not control her husband. Kournakoff did his noble best.

A complication in the management of Isadora's tour was the fact that we had Prohibition in those days, and Isadora needed a bottle of champagne, or at least of whisky or bourbon before she went on the stage. I, when I was with them, and Kournakoff when I was not, had the additional duty of finding a source of supply in each city.

Lecture to the Boston Brahmins

The first explosion occurred in Boston. Essenine opened a dressing-room window in Symphony Hall, tossed a red flag out on the chilly air and shouted the Russian equivalent of "Long live Bolshevism!"

The manager of Symphony Hall called me in New York. Mayor Curley was furious. The performance must be canceled.

I got Isadora on the phone at the Copley-Plaza.

"He's a darling, but what can I do? He had a drink or two. Mr. Hurok, don't be disturbed. He won't do it again."

Somehow we placated the Mayor and the outraged Bostonians. And the next day Essenine did it again.

This time a crowd gathered on the street and Essenine made a speech. Fortunately, Russian was not spoken in Boston in those days any more than it is today. The performance went on.

Essenine appeared in a box in full Caucasian costume, the boots, the fur hat, the belted black coat with cartridge clips. There was no doubt of it; he was a beautiful young man.

The next morning in New York I opened my newspaper and choked on my coffee.

"RED DANCER SHOCKS BOSTON . . . Isadora's Speech Drives

103

Many from Symphony Hall." The more flamboyant newspapers had her tearing off her red tunic and waving it above her head while, completely nude, she delivered an oration.

I telephoned Boston. It was true, or most of it. Isadora had waved her red scarf, not her tunic, above her head and shouted: "This is red! So am I! Red is the color of life and vigor! You once were wild here! Don't let them tame you!"

At that point a number of dignified Bostonians rose and stalked out of Symphony Hall. But the young men from Harvard burst into cheers. Encouraged, Isadora embarked in full sail.

She talked about Gorki's division of the world into the black, the red and the gray people. The black people were the tyrants, the ex-Kaiser and the late Czar. The red were, obviously, the lovers of freedom like the Russians, like herself.

The gray were the Bostonians. "I could hardly dance here," she protested. "Life is not real here. Mr. Franko [the conductor] was doing his best, but he could hardly play here. We are red people, Mr. Franko and I."

This was bad enough, but as Kournakoff went on I felt my very spine curling up my back.

All her life Isadora had carried on open warfare against what she considered the curse of Puritanism which blighted the free spirit of America. She had rebelled against marriage, had deliberately had three children out of wedlock—not furtively, but proudly, as one who stood before the world and said, "I am a free creature and this is my right and the right of all women." And she had been a good and loyal wife to the men who loved her, had never disparaged them, had always cherished them in honor and respect, though they had not in every case behaved as well to her. In later years she was offered thousands of dollars by publishers for the love letters she had stored in a special little trunk, but she would never consent to the betrayal of her lovers, though she was penniless and actually starving.

104

Yes, odd as it may sound, according to her own principles, Isadora was a moral woman. She was also a woman with a mission: it was her sacred obligation, she felt, to cure America of the Puritan disease. She preached the health and beauty of the human body, as of the human spirit; she called upon America to tear aside the veils of prudery.

And here she stood, in Boston's Symphony Hall, in the core and center of that New England which had laid the curse upon America. Here she stood, moreover, incensed and outraged already by the criticisms cast at her, by the hostility of the city officials.

So I should not have been shocked, I suppose, when Kournakoff unfolded the climax of his tale.

She stood on the stage of Symphony Hall and pointed to the replicas of Greek statues which adorn that somber sanctum of music.

"Those are not Greek gods—they are false! And you are as false as those plaster statues. You don't know what beauty is!"

And then she tore her tunic down to bare one of her breasts and cried out, "This—this is beauty!"

This act of defiance the newspapers never revealed in so many words, nor, in all the accounts by Isadora's friends and adorers, have I seen it reported. But it was true to Isadora, to her self-dedication and to her violence. I record it in justice both to her and to the newspapers, for it was the cue which led the press thereafter to treat her with the contempt, the disrespect, the sly innuendo which they would accord to a fan dancer. They give a professional strip-teaser today more gracious consideration than Isadora received from them twenty years ago. It is the tragic fate of all rebels to be born too soon.

For myself, I did not sit in judgment on Isadora, then or later. Even if I had enjoyed that comfortable feeling of superiority which gives some of us the right to pass judgment on others, I would not have had the time. I had work to do, immediately, if the tour was to be saved.

"Hold everything," I muttered into the phone, "I'm taking the next train."

When I reached Boston Mayor Curley had made the next move. He announced that Isadora would not appear again in Boston as long as he sat in the Mayor's seat.

I talked to the reporters and tried to explain Isadora's point of view. "Let her tell us herself," they insisted. And so, half because I thought her eloquence and sincerity might win them over, but mostly because I had no choice, I consented to a press interview at the Copley-Plaza.

Isadora was primed to talk, and talk she did. She attacked New England Puritanism as a disease that infected Bostonians with a peculiar virulence. She poured acid on their "concealed lust." She said she would rather dance completely nude than "strut in half-clothed suggestiveness" as chorus girls did in commercial entertainments. She described Bostonians as chained, enslaved by their Brahminism, crying out to be freed—and she had come to free them. She called them vulgar, diseased, smirking, base.

That was the Boston incident. It followed her like a flaming trail across the country. The story that she had torn her tunic off and stood nude on the platform of Boston's Symphony Hall pursued her relentlessly, although she denied it later in Chicago, saying only that the audience in Boston had seen what she was feeling, not what she said and did.

In Washington Billy Sunday demanded that that "Bolshevik hussy" be deported.

The tour proceeded to Indianapolis. Again an excited long-distance call. Mrs. Ona B. Talbot, the local manager, described to me how Isadora and her husband had barely set foot on the soil of Indianapolis before Essenine began making a speech, right on the railroad platform.

"The Mayor won't let her appear here!" Mrs. Talbot protested. Again we soothed the ruffled feelings of outraged citizenry. Again Isadora promised not to talk.

Nor did she. But there were four policemen in the hall when she danced, and one on the stage. The Mayor of Indianapolis was not letting any "nude dancers" get away with anything in his town. But it was common knowledge in Indianapolis that a business men's banquet had enjoyed an anatomical exhibition by two show-girls not many evenings before, and Mayor Lew Shank had made no outcry. Of course Isadora was foolish, but unlike many of her detractors, she was no hypocrite.

So the tour proceeded, punctuated by the indignations of may-ors and leading citizens, the anxieties of local managers, our heroic efforts to keep the wheels turning and the show going on.

In Louisville Kournakoff got wind of a plot by the local post of the American Legion to cut the electric-light wires of the concert hall and plunge the performance in darkness. That day Isadora was to be the guest of honor at a Rotary Club luncheon. Kournakoff told Isadora the invitation had been withdrawn, and went to the luncheon himself, explaining to the Rotarians that Isadora was indisposed. The commander of the Legion post was there, courte-ous but watchful, and Kournakoff outdid himself, in a speech thick with charm and decorum. Isadora discovered the trick that evening, of course, and denounced him as a "Russian Cossack." But the electric wires remained intact and one more performance was saved from disaster.

In Milwaukee, by the desperate device of telling the hotel clerk Miss Duncan was ill, we kept the reporters away for twenty-four hours. But they followed her to teas and supper parties in her honor, and she said what she had to say to them there. Never was a woman more generous in supplying to her enemies the ammu-nition with which to destroy her.

The pity of it was that she had her friends as well as her enemies. Who can say how many of the thousands in every city who crowded her performances to the doors came out of curiosity, with the hope of being entertained by another scandal? Nor does it matter. She might have won them to her, if she had been content to let her dancing carry her message to them. If she had put a curb on her too-eager tongue, and planted the seeds of her ideas in quiet and patience, she might still have seen her dream come true in her own country. She might have had her school in America.

But neither can you put a curb on the west wind, nor counsel patience to a cyclone.

Turkey and Gold Stars

Yet she was a good trouper, and the tour, like every tour, had its lighter side. In Memphis, for some reason I no longer recall, her accompanist failed to make connections. Frantic for a pianist, my manager went to the Catholic music school, the Conservatory of Saint Cecilia. The professor of piano, a tall, soft-spoken Irish gentleman, assured him he could play the Liszt "Funeraille" and would be glad to help out in the crisis. He was brought to Isadora for a rehearsal.

It was the day after Thanksgiving. Isadora reclined on a sofa, waving her arms in an approximation of the dance while the angular professor stooped over the keyboard. Suddenly the music stopped.

"Pardon me, Madame," the professor said. "I must rest. I am exhausted."

Isadora was at once all sympathy. "Of course, my poor man, I understand. The music is so powerful—you feel it too deeply . . ."

"No, Madame," the professor carefully corrected her. "It isn't the music; it's the turkey I ate yesterday that I feel."

In Cleveland it was the blue velvet backdrop and the blue floor-cloth which failed to arrive. My manager was desperate, but the theatre manager reassured him.

"You're lucky your set is lost. We've got something here . . . Madame Duncan has never danced in such a set," he said.

My manager asked to see it. "It's in the storehouse—you'll see it tonight at the performance."

"But listen, she insists on something simple."

"Just leave it to me."

My manager hurried to the theatre two hours before the performance to make sure. What he saw frightened him out of a year's growth. The theatre owner had had somebody make him an en tout cas set, something that would do for any occasion. It was brand new, just completed, spick and span—and a horror. With twisted columns, palm trees, draped curtains painted in, and whole galaxies of gold stars, it looked like a cross between a Christmas tree and a Victorian bawdy house.

Isadora listened to his report. "Has it many gold stars?" she asked.

"Many."

"Ah, I'm sorry, I really can't dance in front of a thing like that." And you couldn't blame her. But the situation was saved here too. From somewhere a set of shabby curtains were dug up, dusted off, and draped over the set—chipping a piece off the theatre owner's heart for every column and palm tree that was hidden—and Isadora danced.

Isadora and Essenine were installed once more at the Waldorf when, at about three one bitter morning, the telephone shrilled in my ear.

I lifted my head and reached for the instrument. It was Isadora herself.

"Come quickly! He's killing me!" There was stark terror in her voice panting over the wire.

I dressed in frantic hurry and rushed out of my hotel—the Great

Northern—onto an eerily deserted 57th Street. The taxi could not drive fast enough down Fifth Avenue.

At the Waldorf I found the room clerk, a wildly harassed young man. We raced over the cushioned carpets, past the clusters of fat-armed chairs, now strangely empty, that crowded the sumptuous old lobby, and rode upstairs.

We knocked at the door. Silence within. Were they both dead in there?

Finally the young man turned the knob. The door opened and we stepped in.

The room was a shambles. Chairs overturned, draperies askew, clothes lying tangled in corners where they had been flung.

There was every sign that two cyclones of temperament had met and battled here. But there were no bodies lying lifeless on the rug, no trails of blood.

The clerk touched my arm and pointed to the bed. I peered, and distinguished at last the shape of a human form—no, two human forms, so closely intertwined that they seemed to be one.

The cyclones had met, battled, blended and subsided. Isadora and her husband were fast asleep in each other's arms.

Silently the clerk and I stepped back out of the room and closed the door.

It was shortly afterward, as I recall, that the Duncan-Essenine menage departed the Waldorf, at the Waldorf's request, and found refuge at the Brevoort on lower Fifth Avenue.

Evening with the Poets

Essenine received an invitation: the Russian-Jewish poets of New York City had arranged a party in his honor at the home of one of them, Mani Leib, in the Bronx.

Mani Leib and his wife had befriended Essenine some time before, and had gone as his guests to some of Isadora's recitals. The

Yiddish poet had, in fact, been standing in the wings with Essenine at the Brooklyn Academy of Music when an incident which began as merely embarrassing and awkward turned into one of peculiar pathos.

Isadora had stepped forward to announce an encore. She was in the habit of speaking to the audience, not only in the form of orations, but in small intimate asides, footnotes to the dance. The size of an auditorium never intimidated her. She could make four thousand people in the Metropolitan Opera House feel that they were chosen guests at a small private recital in her studio.

So it was no surprise when, from the announcement that she was going to dance Scriabin's "Etude," her musical voice went on to describe the composer as her favorite, and to heap praise upon his genius, the beauty of his work, the emotions it stirred in her.

Her accompanist, Max Rabinowitsch, meanwhile sat quietly waiting at the piano. Perhaps, concentrating on what he was next to play, he had missed the beginning of her remarks, or perhaps he could not hear it all, sitting behind her and to the side. It came over him as a sudden, if inaccurate, discovery that she was heaping all this praise on him as her collaborator in the concert. With perfect stage manners he rose and bowed his gratitude.

The audience responded with a hearty round of applause. Isadora, startled, looked around. And then, with her characteristic insistence on hewing to the line of truth no matter where the chips flew—or whom they bruised—she cried out, "No, no, it was about Scriabin I was talking!"

A dreadful moment. Rabinowitsch, mortified before a packed house, got up and left the stage.

In the wings, Essenine whispered, "What happened?" It was explained to him. Essenine cursed and said, "I'll beat her for this." He had already beaten her once that evening, in the dressing room during intermission. And when his friend asked him how he could do this to a great woman, a great artist, he had retorted, "She an artist?" and made a derogatory and uncouth noise with his mouth.

Meanwhile Isadora had followed her accompanist off stage. She begged him to come back and play, without success. He was too painfully humiliated.

Isadora stood a moment, confused. Then she turned and went back on the stage. She danced the Scriabin "Etude" as she had said she would, singing the accompaniment as she danced.

"Crazy woman!" was the popular reaction. But there were many in that audience who said, "Poor Isadora!" and who were not far from tears.

But to get back to the poets' evening. Mani Leib had a fine large apartment near the Grand Concourse, in the Bronx, and it was there that the party was to be held.

Essenine arrived, very handsome in a new suit and a white silk shirt. And with him, to everyone's astonishment, came Isadora.

She had not been expected, nor even invited. But she came, resplendent in a purple velvet wrap and a white evening gown with amber-beaded shoulder straps and a skirt that swept the floor. The wives of the Yiddish poets in their inexpensive little black dresses —poets, especially Yiddish poets, don't make much money—were dazzled, were panting as though they had run the four flights up to the apartment.

Word spread through the neighborhood like magic that Isadora was there. In a few minutes the living room was swarming with faces the host had never seen before.

Like every story about Isadora, the story of what happened at that party has been distorted out of all semblance to the truth. The tale that persists is that Essenine responded to his host's kindness with a disgraceful anti-Semitic speech, that the Yiddish poets gave him a good drubbing for it and that the occasion ended with the guest of honor in the hands of the police.

To which the yellower journals gratuitously added the titbit that Isadora had stripped off her clothes and danced in the nude.

A student of journalism might enjoy discovering the seeds of fact out of which grew this orchid of fantasy. Not that the truth was less lurid; it is only different.

Isadora, naturally, was at once surrounded by admirers. The poets, the young intellectuals sat at her feet, around the trailing folds of her beautiful white gown, and vied with one another in composing dithyrambs to her beauty, her grace, her art.

Across the room, Essenine watched. Again she was stealing the stage from him. It had been like this ever since they had crossed the border of the Soviet Union. In Moscow, everywhere in Russia, he was the great Essenine, the young genius, the new Pushkin. Even Isadora herself had bowed to his immortal gift. But in Berlin, in Paris, all over America, who had ever heard of Essenine? It was Isadora, Isadora, only Isadora. And here, at his own friends' home, at the party which was to have been in his honor—again it was Isadora.

And so he watched from across the room, and glowered. And drank and drank. His host knew he must not get drunk, and had warned the other poets that the guest of honor must not get drunk. But the house was full of strangers, high with the stimulation of Isadora's presence, and those who could not get close enough to Isadora gathered around Essenine as the secondary celebrity of the evening. They plied him with liquor, and he got drunk, very drunk.

There came the inevitable moment when someone asked Isadora to dance, and Isadora graciously arose to comply. Whereupon Essenine sprang across the room and tore her beautiful dress from her shoulder.

The amber beads scattered over the floor. The next day Mrs. Mani Leib's little daughter gathered them up and has cherished them since. By a curious chance this little girl grew up to be Julia

Levien, who has been recognized as an interpreter of Duncan dancing, although she never saw Isadora then or later.

Isadora was at once led away into another room. Essenine flung himself toward a window and was barely restrained from going through it. Instead he leaped for the door and, coatless, hatless, in his white silk shirt drenched with perspiration, ran down and out into the snowy street.

The poets ran after him, terrified lest he be hurt, certain he would catch pneumonia at least. They followed him down the Grand Concourse, where he ran in and out among the speeding cars, shouting in Russian, "Hey, Amerikanski!" At last the traffic officer caught him and handed him back to his distraught hosts. This was the only part the police played in the performance, a walk-on role.

Back in the apartment the tussle continued, with the poets no match for a Russian peasant lad with the strength of an enraged bull. From the bedroom Isadora sent word that cold water be poured on his head, but the only effect was that he got wet—and madder. A doctor among the guests advised tying him up. Reluctantly, the exhausted poets consented.

They cut down a length of rope from the clothes dryer in the kitchen and bound his hands and feet, first tenderly wrapping his wrists and ankles with towels pulled from the bathroom rack, and bringing little sofa cushions to place under the rope lest he be hurt. And while they worked tearfully over him, he lay on the floor and wept and swore at them, and once he called Mani Leib "Jid!" which is the contemptuous Russian word for Jew and which is used generally among the peasants as a swear word for anyone who angers them, Jew or good Greek Orthodox. This was Essenine's entire anti-Semitic speech.

In the end Essenine, subdued, begged to be unbound, and they released him. He put on his coat and hat and went home alone, consenting only that one of his hosts go down with him to find a taxi in the snowy dawn. Isadora, afraid to go home, stayed the night, talking, and in the morning her hosts and another friend took her home.

Disarrayed, her lovely gown torn, her lined face haggard in the morning light, Isadora in her purple wrap still looked a queen. "We took her arm down the wide steps of our apartment house," Mani Leib says, "and beside her, I felt myself so dusty!"

When they went into the suite in the Brevoort, Essenine was in bed. Isadora bent over him. He looked up, smiling, and when he saw her face he pushed her away.

Her friend asked her why she endured all this from him.

"You're too young—you wouldn't understand," Isadora answered.

When the weird story of the evening with the poets appeared in the papers the next day, Isadora telephoned me. Her voice was full of laughter.

"What do you think of my darling?" she caroled.

For every one of Essenine's scandalous outbursts, Isadora had only one excuse: he was a poet, a genius; how could you expect him to behave like ordinary men?

Her friend Mary Desti offered the explanation that he was an epileptic. Epileptic he certainly was, and in that affliction he was a member of a noble company of geniuses, Dostoevski for one.

But neither answer is complete. Essenine, outside the Soviet land which adored him, suffered intensely from neglect. An egomaniac, spoiled by the adoring Russians, he missed the nectar of public adoration abroad, and was the more bitter because Isadora had become increasingly the more important of the two the farther they went from Moscow.

He was violently jealous of Isadora, so jealous that he denied she was an artist at all. This together with his ailment, together with the emotional instability which very often goes hand in hand with artistic gifts, together with the adolescent "hooligan" behavior he

115

was accustomed to indulge in at home with impunity—it all added up to considerably more than a handful.

Only once, that I know of, did Isadora attempt to discipline him. One night on tour, she and Essenine and Vladimir Vetlugin drove out of Memphis to a roadhouse, where they had supper and a good deal of bad Prohibition liquor. Essenine, as usual, became unruly, there was a lively row, and in the end Isadora and Vetlugin took the only taxi and drove back to town, leaving the poet sitting in a tree in his dinner jacket, in a pouring rain. He walked back to Memphis, through mud up to his ankles, and crawled into their hotel in the morning, a very bedraggled young man.

The Orator

Dr. William Norman Guthrie, the distinguished liberal minister of St. Marks-in-the-Bouwerie, invited Isadora to dance in his church on Christmas Eve and to give a talk on "The moralizing effect of dancing on the human soul." The invitation was suddenly withdrawn, and an explanatory statement credited to Bishop Manning appeared in the newspapers which refrained from mentioning Isadora's name, but made it perfectly clear that she would not dance at St. Marks or any other church within the diocese.

She danced at the Brooklyn Academy of Music on Christmas night. As she was dancing a curious hum of excitement spread through the audience. Her costume had slipped from one shoulder, and half her bosom was bare. Isadora danced on, unmindful or uncaring.

It was a painful thing to stand at the back of the house and watch her dance on, without making a move to readjust her costume. It was one of the nightmare experiences of a manager.

And yet, remembering it now, I remember another, more recent nightmare moment. The same grotesque accident befell one of our loveliest ballerinas; I shall spare her the mention of her name.

116

She struggled throughout an entire *pas de deux* to salvage her modesty. And I am not sure but that her embarrassing tussle with a shoulderstrap was more painful to watch than Isadora's indifference. Isadora merely ignored the costume, or lack of it. By giving her uninterrupted concentration to the dance, and thus making the simple assumption that the dance was of supreme importance at the moment, she invited the audience to follow her example. Perhaps she was right. To repair the damage in full view of the audience had the unfortunate effect of calling vulgar attention to it.

As the program ended the audience exploded into wild clamor. Isadora stepped out before the curtain and made the most impassioned speech of the entire tour.

Again I asked her, for perhaps the fiftieth time, to forego speeches and restrict herself to dancing. Again she was, for the fiftieth time, willing and eager to comply. She promised to be good. I confess that, in her own way, she kept her promise this time. But with what embarrassing results for me!

I went to Isadora's farewell recital with, for the first time since the S. S. *Paris* had slid into her dock that Sunday in October, a mind free of anxiety. It would soon be over. This was the last concert. A feeling of relief, of well-being, buoyed me and I walked with a light step through the crowd of standees to my favorite vantage point at the back of the house.

My happiness was premature.

While Isadora danced, in my cheerful frame of mind I was able to savor, for the first time since she arrived, the heroic beauty of her person and her movement. Her face was lined with years and suffering, but her body, with the fullness of ripe womanhood, was a caryatid come to life.

She is a great woman, I was thinking as the final curtain fell, already forgetting the months of long-distance alarms and excursions she had put me through.

She stepped out before the curtain to take, as I thought, a bow. My heart stopped. She was going to make another speech!

"I'm sorry I can't talk to you today," she said in her clear musical voice. "My manager, Mr. Hurok, forbids me to talk. He is standing back there, at the back of the hall . . ."

As one, the audience turned. I could feel, like a burning spotlight, the baleful glare of a thousand pairs of eyes, the eyes of Isadora's worshipers hot with indignation at the man who had gagged their goddess.

The standees near me began to edge away. I edged away myself, out of that concentrated stare of hatred, toward the door. As the door closed behind me I could hear Isadora again, talking now about Beethoven and Wagner.

And yet we parted friends. Isadora told me she still planned to bring her Russian children to America, to show her countrymen what she had achieved in a school nurtured by the whole Russian people.

Isadora made money on that tour, as I should know. The lurid headlines which trumpeted her march across the country caused mayoral apoplexy and occasional cancellations, but they also assured long lines at the box offices where she did appear.

Yet she had to borrow money, I have been told, to get back to Europe. If that is true, the answer lay hidden in the beautiful trunks that Essenine took to Moscow.

In those trunks, which he would permit not even Isadora to touch, were stuffed hundreds, thousands of dollars' worth of expensive clothes and luxurious trifles—the child gone wild, or the peasant greedy, in the great wide world.

There were even Isadora's own beautiful gowns and lingerie. She returned to Moscow with scarcely more than the clothes she wore on her back. The rest, she said, had strangely disappeared or been lost in their travels. She found all her lost wardrobe in those handsome, heavy trunks of Essenine's.

Twilight of a Goddess

I saw Isadora again in Paris in 1927, the year of her death. A letter came to me at the Hotel Continental.

She hoped I had forgiven her, she wrote, for all the trouble she had caused me in America. Would I see her, if only for a few minutes?

I picked her up at her studio hotel on the Left Bank and we went to dinner together. She told me of the unhappiness of her last months with Essenine.

They had gone back to Moscow, after a succession of scandalous incidents in Paris and Berlin which closed to them, one after another, all the best hotels. The faithful Irma in Moscow had kept Isadora's school going in the ballerina Bachalova's house at 20 Prestchistenka.

But her "darling," the beautiful and unbalanced youth around whom her life revolved, would not stay with her there. He would not, it soon appeared, stay with her at all. He presently began to be seen with another woman, and she received messages warning her not to communicate with him any more.

He had threatened to leave her many times. In New York, once, she had actually counted out $400 to pay for his trip back to Moscow and handed it to him. And when she reproached him with marrying her for her money, he pulled the wad of bills out of his pocket and tore them into little bits before her eyes.

Yet in Berlin, whither she had sent him with her faithful maid, Jeanne, after the French Government had insisted he leave Paris—this after he had wrecked their suite in the Crillon—he told newspaper men, "Of course I married Isadora for her money!"

And in the very next breath he vowed, "I love Isadora madly, but her drinking makes it impossible for me to live with her."

119

Isadora, be it said to her credit, never disparaged either him or her love for him. Her excuse for him was always, "He is a poet!"

It was inevitable that he should die a suicide. But not without originality. He had talked of suicide in New York, where the Woolworth Building had tempted him; he would jump from the tower, he said, with the manuscript of his last poem in his hand. On second thought, he might fall on an innocent passer-by, even on a baby carriage. He would not like that.

Back in Moscow, he appeared on the Red Square one night with an armful of firewood and the intention of lighting his own funeral pyre and throwing himself on it. This time the indulgent Soviet police arrested him and he spent the next six months in jail with this rebuke of the judge to meditate on: "Your life is not yours to throw away; it is a property of value to the community."

In the end he went to the Hotel Angleterre in Leningrad, to the very room in which he and Isadora had stayed on their first journey together. On that visit he had pointed out to her a hook in the wall and said, "Good for a man to hang himself from."

He cut his left wrist and, while it dripped into an Etruscan vase Isadora had once given him, he wrote in his own blood a poem addressed "To a Friend":

> "Good-bye, my friend, good-bye!
> You are still in my breast, beloved.
> This fated parting
> Holds for us a meeting in the future.
> Good-bye, my friend, without hand or word.
> Be not sad nor lower your brow.
> In this life, to die is not new,
> And to live, surely, is not any newer."

And from that fateful hook in the wall he hanged himself. Thus fantastically ended the fantastic life of the second Pushkin.

Isadora told me about the little locked suitcase. He had kept this suitcase close by him always when they traveled across the ocean and all of Europe, back to Moscow. He roared at her if she so much as put out her hand toward it. When she opened it she found between seven and eight thousand dollars in American money —money she had given him whenever he had asked for it, money he had collected from us at the office as advances for Isadora.

He left behind three widows and five volumes of poetry. To his first wife, the actress Zinaida Meyerhold, whom he divorced for Isadora, he bequeathed his heart. To Isadora he left his blood in the little Etruscan vase. To Sofia Tolstoy, granddaughter of the great writer, he left his brain. He made no disposition of such worldly properties as the royalties from his books.

This was left to a Soviet court to untangle, and it was found that while he had divorced Zinaida to marry Isadora, he had never divorced Isadora, and therefore had never legally been married to Sofia.

Later, when Isadora was in Paris, Soviet officials came to her with some 300,000 rubles, royalties from Essenine's books which legally belonged to her as his widow. She was penniless, virtually starving, but she would not touch the money. She instructed the bearers to give it to Essenine's mother and sisters. This I learned, not from Isadora, but from her good friend, Mary Desti.

The Isadora who sat in her littered studio telling me these things was, I think now, already marked for death. Empty bottles, unwashed glasses were scattered about the room. The famous blue curtains were tightly drawn to shut out the light of day.

Isadora herself was sadly changed. Her beautiful body was shapeless with flabby muscles and fat; her hair was dyed a dreadful shade of reddish-purple.

But behind the still-beautiful eyes in her parchment-yellow face, as she talked, lay the irreparable loss of her love, the great love of

121

her later years. Cruel, contemptuous, taunting, openly unfaithful, Serge Essenine had embodied her dream of immortal beauty immortally young, and she had forgiven him everything with an Olympian generosity.

I saw in the declining Isadora that evening a creature who had never really been a part of this world, a goddess out of the Greek myths, magnificent, queenly, whose love, like her art, like her life itself, was on the grand scale, out of all proportion to the small desires and frailties of ordinary human beings.

Her own frailties were on the grand scale, as I learned a few nights later. That night we sat at the Café Royale until three in the morning, talking. We had long since finished our boeuf à la mode, the best in Paris, and a change, for once, from Isadora's invariable diet of rare roast beef, salad and champagne.

We talked about her book, which she was writing. She had already spent the publisher's advance of $500 and must wait until she delivered the manuscript for the remaining $2,000. We talked about the children in Russia, whom she still wanted America to see. She would arrange luncheon for us, she said, at the Soviet Embassy with Ambassador Rakovsky. This luncheon we did, in fact, have within the next few days, and Rakovsky said he would do what he could to persuade the Soviet Government to grant permission for the children to make the trip. Isadora told me she had written to Arthur Brisbane in America, asking his help for the project. Brisbane had always been her friend.

We parted at last at the door of her hotel with a promise that we would dine together again soon. A day or two afterward I called her again.

I had a guest with me, my charming buyer from New York whom I had the good intention of marrying one day, and I asked her if she would mind Isadora's company at dinner. She was enchanted at the prospect of meeting the celebrated Isadora. We called for Isadora and went to a restaurant of her choice.

122

The dinner was good, the wine plentiful. Isadora was in an expansive mood; the melancholy vapors that had hovered about our previous meeting were apparently dispelled.

She wanted lots and lots of gay company. Her lovely eyes, glittering, searched the café for faces she knew. Her shapely bare arm was perpetually upraised in a beckoning gesture.

First one, then another, and at last a stream of young men began to pour down upon our table. More chairs were brought, then another table and still more chairs. More wine, too. The chatter swirled about the heads of my young lady and myself, a chorus of male magpies paced by the resonant bells of Isadora's voice commanding a train of waiters.

The dinner for three was swelling into a royal feast at my expense, and I was not enjoying my guests. The sight of Isadora surrounding herself with these parasites was acutely distasteful to me. And also, it seemed, to my young lady.

She leaned toward me and whispered, "Perhaps I should develop a headache?"

I reassured her, but she was determined to put an end to the charade. She put her hand to her forehead and looked at me piteously. I touched Isadora's elbow.

"I'm sorry," I said. "Miss—— has a bad headache. I'll have to take her home."

"Why must you? Let her go by herself. You stay."

I demurred at that, and Isadora was piqued.

"You Americans! All you do is drink ice water. You have ice water in your veins! You know nothing of the art of living!"

My young lady had pushed back her chair and a young man in beret and open-throated shirt was already snatching it from under her to sit closer to Isadora. I paid the check as it stood then, mumbled good night as we left her, a lavish queen ·surrounded by a horde of young courtiers with empty stomachs and emptier pockets.

A few days later I was having tea in the garden of the Continental Hotel when an attaché of the hotel brought over a Frenchman in a headwaiter's shiny dinner jacket.

"M. Hurok? You owe 26,000 francs to the Café. . . ."

"Impossible!" said I, whereupon he produced a restaurant check. Scrawled across the back of it in Isadora's handwriting was:

"American impresario S. Hurok, Continental Hotel."

Charged on the bill was a 2,000 franc tip!

The headwaiter was reasonable. We settled for half the amount. But when Isadora called, I was at first too angry to see her.

Then I thought, how absurd to be angry! Isadora was a great woman, a great human being. If I had lost 25,000 francs in business I would not have given it a second thought. More than once I had spent that sum on a party at the Claridge for people who meant nothing to me, who came and went in my life, leaving nothing of value. I wished I had more, much more than 25,000 francs to give Isadora, enough to subsidize her school so that she could teach American children to make a better world.

I went to see her. We rode out to the Bois de Boulogne, to Armenonville, and sat on the terrace.

"Forgive me," she begged. "You were always so kind in America. If I had had the money, you know I would not have asked you for it."

We talked of the children again. "There is one thing you must promise me. I want nothing for myself. I don't know how long I shall live, and I don't care. Once I finish my book I don't care what becomes of me.

"I want America to see my work. Promise me only one thing: you will take the children to America."

The children. Always the children. Was she thinking of her own two children, tragically and needlessly killed twelve years before? It was as though she had a premonition of her own death,

and wanted the one image of herself, the only one she had left—
her Russian children—to carry her spirit to her own country which
scorned her.

She kissed me good-bye.

The next time I had heard of Isadora, she had killed herself with
her own scarf in an automobile in Nice.

Killed herself?

Yes, I firmly believe that Isadora killed herself.

Perhaps not deliberately—to die by the twisting of her scarf in
the wheel of a moving car was perhaps too fortuitous a method for
one to choose who planned to die.

But I am certain that she wanted to die, that she longed to die,
and that if she had not died by this curious accident she would have
died by another.

I know that Isadora loved life as perhaps no human being had
ever loved it; that she was the embodiment of life, rich, generous,
zestful life, to those who knew and loved her. I know also that she
lived life to the fullest, gave herself unstintingly to art and to love,
and that the petty concerns in which the rest of us bog down, the
struggle for bread or for power, never caught her feet in their
quicksand.

But when I think of her at the end, I see her sitting again in her
empty room, the curtains drawn tight to keep out the light of the
sun which she had loved. I think of her mourning for her lost children, for her lost love. I think of her mourning, too, for her lost
country, the country she loved and which never did her honor,
which instead heaped her with calumny and scandal-mouthing
headlines.

She was a great revolutionary. Because of her, women were freed
at one stroke from corsets and from convention. The bodies of
little children were freed. She brought sunlight and fresh air into
the lives and the thinking of all of us; she cut the bonds of spirit as
well as flesh.

Yet this great woman sat alone at last in a darkened room, clutching the solace of alcohol and perhaps of stronger medicines, poor, unattended except by a horde of hungry young men and a few devoted friends. She sat there, withdrawing further and further from the life she had loved and which had dealt so tragically with her.

She was without honor only in her own country. In the Soviet Union she was adored, she was idolized. With her on her last journey went a huge wreath of red flowers inscribed, "The heart of Russia weeps for Isadora." If she had stayed in Russia, she would have lived to enjoy a noble old age crowned with honors and usefulness. I am certain of this. She never stopped growing; in Russia she developed singing and dancing together. Who knows what she might still have done?

But what she longed for was the recognition of America.

With every word she spoke to me, those last days, she uttered the unconscious wish for death.

"Until my book is finished . . . I don't care what happens after my book is finished . . . I want nothing for myself . . . Promise me only one thing, that you will take the children to America."

The promise was asked of me as by one on her deathbed, and I gave it in that solemn spirit. I went to Moscow to see the children. They were lovely. Irma chose some fifteen of them, and I brought them in Irma's charge to America for a successful tour in 1928.

Mary Desti wrote, after seeing their performance at the Manhattan Opera House, that Isadora "had to go to Europe to gain recognition as an artist, to Russia to create her school, and to heaven to see it dance in America. I wonder if America will now support this tremendous task her one pupil, Irma, has carried so far and is now offering them—to gather to their hearts this legacy Isadora Duncan has left them. . . . If not, Isadora will have been born in vain and American children will lose a great heritage from a great American."

America did not, but neither did Isadora live in vain. The touch of her free spirit is on the bodies and minds of young Americans today.

Whenever I am in San Francisco and the reporters gather around, asking questions about this or that dancer, I remind them of San Francisco's greatest daughter.

I ask them why they are so interested in these other dancers, when one of the great dancers and one of the great women of history was scorned and all but laughed out of her own country—and San Francisco did nothing to help her.

And I ask them why, in all the beautiful parks of the beautiful city where she first learned to love the sunlight and the good clean air of life, there is still no monument to Isadora.

CHAPTER FIVE

Up and Down in the Twenties

*I*F SOMEONE were to draw a graph of my progress in the Twenties, it would look like a cross-section of some part of the Himalayas hitherto unexplored by man. Right at the start it would climb to a towering peak, beginning in 1921 with two great names —Pavlova, Chaliapin—and others as well under my own management, and dozens of concerts by the finest artists of the day by arrangement with other managers.

Isadora Duncan came the following season. Tetrazzini and Titta Ruffo went on tour for me, singing the most beautiful arias and duets in all opera. Pavlova and Chaliapin continued to head the roster for the next several years; the Russian Opera Company appeared under my name; Chaliapin toured as the head of his own opera company. An old handbill in my files advertising Pavlova at the Manhattan Opera House December 22-27, 1924, with Laurent Novikoff and Alexander Volinine, lists as well: Chaliapin, Zimbalist, Gluck, the French tenor Lucien Muratore, the baritone Joseph Schwarz, the coloratura Elvira de Hidalgo, Madame Schumann-Heink, Artur Schnabel, the Metropolitan mezzo-soprano Ina Bourskaya, the violinist Rudolph Polk, the Russian pianist Alfred Mirovitch, the Cherniavsky Trio, the Folies Bergères, and the composer Richard Strauss.

I had spent most of the preceding decade preparing myself for just such goodly company as this. My Hippodrome concerts had caught the friendly eye of Adolph S. Ochs, publisher of the *New York Times*, in whose large-minded view the metropolis was not so huge that any worthy effort was lost in it. Several times in several years my private formula for creating an audience was spread across the pages of the Sunday magazine section. I remember once telling the reporter what I saw of humanity while from my vantage point in the lobby of the Hippodrome I watched six thousand people file in to take their seats for a Sunday concert.

A man and his wife would come in. Perhaps his Sunday dinner had not been good, or she had found the children naughtier than usual, or they had had a disagreement about money. That they had quarreled was obvious; they were not talking, not even looking at each other. He stalked ahead of her, and she followed nervously. Well, by the first intermission he was relaxing in his seat and she was gazing around to see what the audience looked like, by the second intermission they were holding hands, and at the end, after they had heard their favorite air as an encore, they walked out arm in arm, smiling. That, I told the reporter, was an example of the power of music.

No More Quartets

But I had learned other things during those years of preparation, and mostly the hard way. I learned, for example, never to present a quartet.

The Metropolitan Opera Quartet was to sing a Sunday concert for me. The Metropolitan Musical Bureau had the tenor Martinelli and the baritone De Luca, and Charles Wagner managed Frances Alda and Emma Lazarus. I engaged the four, named them the Metropolitan Opera Quartet, and advertised the "greatest operatic ensemble" in quartets from *Rigoletto* and other operas, in duets and solo arias.

129

Five days before the concert the Metropolitan Musical Bureau telephoned. Giovanni Martinelli could not arrive in time from Italy. We had a lengthy pow-wow, and at last I agreed to accept Charles Hackett in Martinelli's place. Hurriedly I began to advertise the American tenor from the Chicago Opera.

Two days later they called again. Giuseppe De Luca's wife had fallen suddenly ill, causing him to miss the boat. I knew that De Luca would not willingly forfeit his $1,250 fee, so it must be true. I settled for the American, Marshall, who has since very sensibly left the crazy music business and is now selling either wine or shoes, I forget which.

On Saturday afternoon I serenely left New York for the weekend. Sunday afternoon I was back in town, and dropped in at the Hippodrome to see what business was like. There was Charlie Wagner running around the lobby, a very troubled man.

"Hackett has a bad cold—can't sing," he said.

I was speechless.

"Don't worry, Sol . . . Take Kingston . . . You can get him for $500 . . . Save you a little money . . ."

I found enough voice to protest that I couldn't do this to the people who came from all over the city to the Hippodrome; the Hurok audience—they trusted me—how could I ever run another concert?

But the concert took place; the announcement was made from the stage, where incidentally there were 1,150 seats, all filled, and not one person in the audience asked for his money back. Thanks to Frances Alda, whose gracious manner on the stage gave the whole performance a gala grand-opera tone, whose singing was moreover truly beautiful, the public went away smiling and satisfied, and even I was willing to admit it was not a bad concert after all. But I vowed I would never present another quartet—and I never have.

All my resources of program-making were called into action by the Hippodrome concerts. Great music by great artists at a two-dollar top, drawing from every category of the musical world: that was my objective.

When I announced a symphonic concert with two fine artists, the pianist Josef Lhevinne and the soprano Helen Stanley, I was not prepared for the indifference of the hitherto-eager ticket-buyers. It was not until Saturday morning, thirty-six hours before the concert, that the appalling truth struck me. I was going to have my first empty house.

It was during that period shortly after the Armistice when European royalty—those whose heads still wore crowns—were making visits to this country, and America was in a fever of prince-worship. The King and Queen of Belgium happened to be the adored guests of the moment.

Inspiration burst upon me. It was too late for the Sunday papers, but my advertising man, Larry Weiner, was able to get a quarter page in the Sunday edition of the old *Evening Telegram*.

"Their Majesties THE KING AND QUEEN OF BELGIUM," it said in very, very large type. Then underneath, in the smallest type the newspaper would give me: "have been invited to." And then, in large type again, "the HIPPODROME for the most EXTRAORDINARY CONCERT" and so on. When my secretary came in I had her send a special-delivery letter, enclosing tickets enough for their entourage, to the royal party who were occupying an entire floor at the Biltmore.

We draped a box in the Belgian colors, and the people who jammed the Hippodrome were privileged to hear the finest of music. Which was what they had paid for, after all.

And, speaking of the power of music, not one protest came to me on the fact that their Majesties did not appear.

131

Music in Ocean Grove

There was another huge auditorium, within easy striking distance of New York, which tempted me as the Hippodrome had tempted me. It was in Ocean Grove, New Jersey, that curious seaside community which had been founded by a rather strict religious sect whose precepts, however, did not forbid entertainment of an artistic sort being given in their tabernacle. It was managed by the Ocean Grove Camp Meeting Association. Billy Sunday held his famous revivals there.

July 4th, 1917, fell on a Saturday night, a good date in every way for a concert in a seaside resort. I hit upon the glamorous Anna Case, who had the additional virtue of being a New Jersey girl, and could thus be advertised as Jersey's own songbird.

We announced the sale of tickets. The announcement fell completely and utterly dead.

Maybe, I thought, a concert was not enough. Maybe we need a lecturer. I wired Senator Bob La Follette, father of the present Senator Bob, the intransigeant statesman who had filibustered single-handed against our entrance into the war.

We made that announcement, and it too fell dead. Not a ticket moved.

I sent a man out to Ocean Grove to snipe posters and window-cards. My man discovered that there was some feeling against our display material, that, in fact, the Asbury Park press refused to carry my announcement.

"They want to see you, Mr. Hurok," he phoned. So I went down to Asbury Park.

I was ushered into the managing editor's office, and found four or five men sitting around a conference table. They eyed me in a way that made me feel a bayonet was not an inch from my ribs.

The man at the head of the table began to ask me questions. Who was I? Where did I come from? What kind of affairs had I been managing in New York? What was my connection with La Follette? And, finally, was I in sympathy with Germany?

He showed me a clipping from the New York Sun, in which a typographical error had made my innocent invention into a sinister sounding organization, the "Von Hugo Musical Society." That, coupled with La Follette as speaker, had set the patriotic Asbury Park press on a manhunt for pro-German propagandists.

I convinced the press of my 100 per cent Americanism, but they still wanted no part of La Follette. The Ocean Grove elder, Mr. Smith, declined to allow the Senator in the tabernacle.

I long ago learned that in nine cases out of ten it is better to give the newspapers the whole story, and I did. It became a cause célèbre. La Follette wired me, asking if I wanted to cancel the lecture. I wired back, saying no, I still wanted him to speak. It went on for days. And the tickets began to go at the box office.

In the end La Follette bowed his grizzled head before the storm of protest and cancelled the lecture. On the recommendation of the Camp Meeting Association I engaged a Dr. Newman who spoke on a religious subject. Anna Case sang beautifully before a sold-out house.

I went on to present a whole summer season of concerts that year. Galli-Curci sang for me at Ocean Grove, and Elman, McCormack, and Schumann-Heink. I made $10,000 out of that season.

But it was a strange place. Jimmy Vinson, whom I brought from the Hippodrome to handle the box office for me, came back with a load of stories of the curious questions people asked him across the ticket counter. So many old ladies demanded to know when the next train left for Red Bank that in self-defense he memorized the time table and gave away railroad information free while he sold tickets.

I did a second season in Ocean Grove the next summer, and

then no more. It's a wise man who knows when to stop, as Chaliapin used to say about aging tenors.

Loves of a Coloratura

During these happy years of earning my wings as an impresario I came to know virtually all the great of music, and in one way or another to manage most of them. Many were the jeweled prima donnas' hands I kissed, and among them was the hand of Luisa Tetrazzini, she of the breath-taking coloratura voice. She returned after the Armistice, having spent most of the war in Italy singing for charity. I sent her and the fine baritone Titta Ruffo on tour together in 1922-23, and learned something more about prima donnas than I had known before.

This charming little woman had an amazing romantic career. I could scarcely keep up with its rapid-fire changes of heart. A frantic call from Detroit or some such city would warn me that there was going to be serious trouble over the pianist unless I came at once. By the time I got there, the trouble spot was no longer the pianist, but the 'cellist.

In her latter years her romantic involvements cost her the fortune her art had made for her. She married late in life a man younger than herself. Many men misled her and took advantage of her generous heart.

I visited her in Milan during her retirement, and she cooked with her own hands the *spaghetti alla Milanese* for our dinner. Afterward she insisted, with a purposefulness I did not understand, that we go driving in her American Packard, almost the last memento remaining to her of the great years. We went through a forest outside the city, to one of the beautiful cemeteries, and she led me into a small, beautifully proportioned mausoleum. There inside, confronting me from all the walls, were photographs of Luisa Tetrazzini in every one of her great operatic roles.

134

"See, my darling Hurok," she said, a serene satisfaction shining in her face. "It is my future home. I wanted you to see it."

Bankruptcy à la Russe

Where there are mountains there must be valleys and the higher the one, the deeper the other. So the mythical graph-maker who is charting the course of my career in the Twenties must now prepare to take a nose-dive to the bottom of his page.

In the spring of 1922 I walked about in a roseate haze. Chaliapin had come and gone, leaving me breathless and somewhat in the red. Pavlova, after a season that filled me with joy and more than repaired the dent Chaliapin had made in my bank account, had bid me a tender *au revoir*. I had brought the two greatest figures of music and the dance to America, was bringing them again the next season—and they were both Russian. I was successful, proud and so happy that I must have glowed like a neon sign.

Then I heard about the Russian Opera Company.

They had been stranded in Tokyo during the Russian Revolution, and had made their way with difficulty to the West Coast of the United States. They had a fine big repertory of Russian Opera. There were ninety-three members of the company.

That last item should have given me pause. But I was then and I suppose I am now a sucker for anything Russian.

It seemed to me that their coming was especially designed by a kindly Providence to make my dearest dream come true. Could I have discovered or invented a more perfect setting for my treasured jewel, Feodor Ivanovitch, than an authentic Russian Opera Company? Now I could present to America my own *Boris Godunov*, in Russian, with Chaliapin surrounded by Russians; it would be a *Boris* the Moscow Opera itself might well envy. (After all, Moscow did not have Chaliapin, and I did!)

I met the company in Chicago. I was appalled at the shabby sets and costumes, and set to work at once dressing up the productions, reorganizing, getting together a good orchestra.

We were opening hamper after battered hamper, each one shabbier as to contents than the last, until we came to one with a prima donna of the company standing guard over it. She blushed, stammered and finally allowed us to untie it. Wrapped in a tinselly tarnished costume were the remains of a Russian Easter cake she had brought all the way from Shanghai.

I cheerfully advanced the Russians money to live on during the summer. In the fall I took them to Boston, where Olin Downes wrote his praises of them in the *Boston Globe* and I lost from $3,000 to $5,000 a week. Springfield, Providence, Syracuse, Buffalo, Montreal, Detroit—the last two welcomed the Russians with good folding money and I was cheered, until we reached Chicago.

Chaliapin came on to do three performances a week of *Boris* in the four-week season. I paid him $3,500 a performance.

And so for four weeks I went to see Russian opera every night. For four weeks I gave parties at the Congress Hotel, and the late Eddy Moore of the *Chicago Tribune*, Claudia Cassidy who was then writing her trenchant criticism for the *Journal of Commerce*, Maurice Rosenfeld of the *News*, Herman De Vries of the *American*, Carl Hackett of the *Post* and dozens of others came and drank and ate with me and shared my happiness. Chaliapin, my noble ornament, was happy too; he was among his own people, who treated him like a god. For four delirious weeks I walked on air while my pockets were quietly emptying to the tune of $60,000.

Back to New York and the Jolson Theatre, where in a last-ditch fight against disaster the Russians changed their pace and did an operetta. Called *A Night of Love*, it bore no resemblance except in name, alas, to Grace Moore's wonderful film, especially not at the box office. Every Saturday my company manager came into the office to get $5,000 or $6,000, to cover the deficit for the week.

I sent them to Mexico. The reports from Mexico were hair-raising; Russians have a genius not only for getting into scrapes, but for getting into scrapes of the most complicated nature. I never understood half of what was going on with my Russians in Mexico.

Descriptions of their arrival in Mexico reached me in Paris. Rivalries fizzed up and ran over. On the train platform in Mexico City a prima donna slapped another prima donna's face.

One of the ladies managed to win the favor of my Mexican impresario, with the result that the other lady and her loyal cohorts simply up and left Mexico City in the middle of the engagement. Back in New York, the dissident contingent sued me for the salary they should have earned had they stayed to finish their Mexican contract. Believe it or not, I paid them off.

Some members of that lamented company are still in New York; some of them have studios and teach singing. I hear from them when someone is in difficulties, or when there is a funeral. We are still the best of friends.

Chaliapin and THE BARBER

Meanwhile, Chaliapin, who had been costing me money quite on his own since the Chicago production of *Boris*, wanted his own opera company. He wanted to tour America in Rossini's *Barber of Seville*.

This was a curious choice of opera. Chaliapin's role, Don Basilio, is a minor one. Aside from stage business, which he performed in an exaggerated Commedia dell'Arte style which was the sheerest clowning, he sang one aria four minutes long during the whole opera.

But when anyone asked him why he wanted to sing *The Barber* Chaliapin drew himself up to his six feet four and roared, "Do you buy artists by the yard?"

137

By this time it was 1926. Chaliapin and the Russians, between them, had cost me all I had made on Pavlova and the one season of Isadora Duncan, plus all my other artists. I was bankrupt.

There was money, however, for Chaliapin's company. Since I had lain awake, years before, after losing other people's money in my attempts to bring music to the masses in the Brooklyn armory, I had foresworn outside financing. But with Chaliapin wanting an opera company, and money ready to hand, I succumbed to the temptation.

The company was organized with Elvira de Hidalgo to sing Rosina, the baritone George Dubrovsky, a Lithuanian tenor named Bobrovitch, and a chorus. We took it on tour.

It was an extraordinary tour in more ways than one. America, I had comforted myself, had not been ready for Russian opera. Now it appeared America was not ready for Italian opera either.

In Columbus, Ohio, we found the auditorium had a stage with a ceiling. No loft, no lines to fly the scenery—the ceiling was no higher than the height of an ordinary room. It was impossible to fit the set. Frank Kaiser, who later became chief electrician at the Radio City Music Hall (and a happy man he must have been in that dream world for a stage electrician) was traveling with the company. He could rig up a show on a plowed field within two hours, provided only there was a telegraph pole on it.

Kaiser went to a storehouse and hired a set of white walls, which he cut down to fit. He had no borders, just spotlights in the wings. The company's shadows danced on the white walls while they performed.

One critic said, "The most extraordinary thing about the performance was the scenery—so European!"

Chaliapin caught a cold, which, complicated by his slight diabetes, incapacitated him for four or five weeks. He returned to New York, and the company and orchestra sat in St. Louis, drawing salary and not playing.

At the end of the tour the company's backer had dropped $120,000.

The Opening Night That Sold Thirty-nine Seats

While this fantastic tour was going on, I was busy in New York. I was presenting the Habimah Players.

This was the Hebrew Theatre of the Moscow Art Theatre. A more beautiful, more exquisitely perfect acting company I had not seen outside of the Moscow Art Theatre itself. They performed in Hebrew, and their finest production was that immortal play of Hebraic legend, *The Dybbuk*. This haunting story of the scholarly youth who becomes a victim of the fascination of black magic, and whose ghost enters into the body of his fiancée, was done afterward in Yiddish by Maurice Schwartz in his Yiddish Art Theatre, and even had a production in English at the Neighborhood Playhouse on Grand Street with Mary Ellis as the bewitched girl. Some day I hope to see it done as a ballet, with Nora Kaye in the role.

I saw the Habimah Players first in Paris at the Madeleine Theatre, and the production was *The Dybbuk*. While casting *The Barber* and discussing the scene designs with Constantin Korovin, I was as always on the hunt for new things.

The house was full of American producers. Morris Gest was there, Lee Shubert, Al Woods. After the *Beggars' Dance* Woods walked up to Gest in the lobby.

"Who in America would want to see those shabby clothes, those dirty whiskers?" he asked. They went out of the theatre together.

But I disagreed with them. I disagreed so heartily that I went backstage and began discussions which led to the signing of a contract to bring them to America the following season. In my enthusiasm I was able to find money for this great company.

139

I have not yet known the importation of a Russian company of any kind to go forward without running afoul of the immigration authorities. This case was no exception. Someone in Paris must have whispered to our Consular staff that he had it on good authority the Habimah Players were all Communists. My opening night in New York was postponed five or six times, but at last, with a monstrous cable bill, I got them here.

The opening was to be on a December night at the Mansfield Theatre. At six o'clock that evening half the scenery had not arrived. With one of my secretaries I rushed down to the dock, picked the scenery out of a pile of what looked like hopelessly jumbled junk, and got it onto the transfer truck. The curtain went up at 9:15, and I caught my breath again and ambled out to see how we had done at the box office.

I had planned this opening carefully. Not alone my own humble opinion, but the admiration of great men like Chaliapin, Gorki, Stanislavsky, all the serious theatre men of Europe had raised this company to the rarefied atmosphere of great art. I had prepared the newspapers, the magazines; I had circularized the organizations which would normally be interested.

To give the opening the prestige I thought it deserved, I set the opening night scale at $10 a ticket.

I was a little surprised, therefore, when I arrived at the box office and discovered that we had sold exactly thirty-nine tickets. Besides the critics, the feature writers, and the numerous celebrated persons I had invited as my guests, there was just $390 in the house.

During the intermission I was hurriedly called backstage. The company had had time to glance over the baggage which had come up from the dock, and there was one trunk missing. So valuable was that trunk, that the actors declared they could not go on with the performance until it was found.

Again I was confronted with a mysterious trunk. There had been Chaliapin's trunk with the filched hotel towels, the Russian prima-donna's trunk with the Easter cake. Now the Habimah Players' trunk. What could be in this one, I mused, as I taxied for the second time that night down to the dock with my secretary and my transfer man? And what, I wondered, was the fatal fascination of trunks for Russians?

By the time we reached the dock, I had discarded various theories, including a dismembered body, in favor of a very simple explanation. These players had suffered unbelievable hardships in the Russian Revolution. They had starved, had eaten potatoes fried in castor oil. Perhaps they had succumbed to the lure of security, of never again having too little to eat, too few warm clothes to wear. Perhaps they had taken to saving gold—*valuta*, the only reliable money in those days of diving national currencies. That was it; the precious trunk was filled with gold!

We found the trunk—it was not as heavy as it should have been to bear out my theory—and carted it up to the Mansfield. Meanwhile the actors had consented to go on with the performance on condition that I would have the trunk at the theatre by the time the curtain came down. Down it came, to a burst of applause. The curtain calls were many.

Then, without stopping to take off makeup, the company gathered around the trunk. The stage manager unlocked it and flung back the lid.

It was full of newspaper clippings.

"What is this?" I blurted. "Are these torn bits of newsprint so important to you that you were willing to stop the show until they were found?"

"We have no property, few possessions," they told me. "These torn bits of newsprint are our wealth."

I have thought about that trunk a great deal in my life among the artists. Even among the artists, there have not been many to whom the recognition of their art is so much more important than the cash.

141

From the Mansfield we took the company to the East Side, and then on a short tour. Some are back in Russia, with the Moscow Art Theatre. Some of them are living and acting today in Palestine. Some remained here: Benno and Batami Schneider are in Hollywood; Benjamin Zemach is in New York. They teach their incomparable theory of acting to some of our more serious artists of the theatre, and they work in the theatre and the films when opportunity for their unique talents presents itself.

I think part of the failure of the Habimah to take hold in this country was the language barrier, part the strangeness of the experimental form. They were ahead of their time. The more sophisticated theatre public of today would welcome the sensitive, beautifully integrated form with its speech, music and dancing, and the language would not prove a difficult hurdle for the art of great acting.

Philosopher on a Park Bench

This was when I really scraped bottom. Chaliapin was gone, Pavlova was gone, although I did not guess then that neither would return. My backer was disgruntled $120,000 worth, which is a large order of disgruntlement in any currency. I had even, in the confusion, got myself divorced, and parted with my girl, so that I had no family, not even a pillow to hide my head under.

I went to my room at the Ansonia Hotel one night. I had spent thousands of dollars at the Ansonia, had housed most of my artists there, including Chaliapin. On this night I put my key in my door and found it would not open.

I went down to the desk. "My key won't open my door," I said.

"I know," the clerk answered, shamefaced. "The door is plugged." This was the first time I had heard the hotel man's phrase for what to do to shut out a paying guest who hasn't paid. I owed some $500 on my bill.

142

"But can't you give me a room for tonight? I haven't anywhere to go at this hour."

"You'll have to see the manager," the embarrassed clerk told me.

The manager, a Russian, was very sorry. The decision to put me out of my room had been made by the Board of Directors.

I was broke, and I was alone. But oddly enough I was not sad. The nights I spent on benches in Central Park I did not spend debating the comparative advantages of jumping out of a window. I spent them enjoying the fresh air and the peace of the city after midnight.

Nor did I think of going to my friends. I remembered what Tolstoy had said when he was very ill. "Don't publish any more bulletins about my illness," he told the doctors. "What good do they do? My friends will be saddened, my enemies cheered."

I kept my troubles to myself, kept my clothes in order as best I could, kept my office and my secretary at 55 West 42nd Street, and kept my ear to the ground for a chance to get started again.

The chance came sooner than I had had any reason to hope. And it was one of the gentler ironies of fate that two opera companies put me into the hole and a third one pulled me out of it.

For a long time I had played with the idea of operas in concert form. The cumbersome baggage of scenery and costumes, the trappings of lights and properties, the chorus, the stage hands and technicians, the large orchestras—it had all become nightmare to me during the days of my decline and fall.

All that paraphernalia, it seemed to me, weighed down the wings on which the music should soar. Maybe the only thing it weighed down was the manager's spirits when he saw all the red ink on the books.

I took my idea for tabloid opera to Lee Shubert, and he liked it. He rented me the Century Theatre for a series of Sunday afternoons.

143

The first opera was *Eugene Onegin*—my Russian weakness again. But the cast was well chosen; the music lovers were eager to hear the infrequently performed music in capsule form. My first Sunday afternoon left me with a profit of $2,500.

The second was *Samson and Delilah* with Margaret Matzenauer as Delilah. It too was a nice success.

Then I went into a series of Wagnerian performances with Ernest Knoch as conductor. Johanna Gadski, who had never quite recovered her position in the public esteem after the anti-German war hysteria, was available. Her good friend, Geraldine Hall, still smarting over the injustice done to an innocent artist, was eager to guarantee the financial success of the series to give Gadski her opportunity.

Meanwhile, a beating of drums was rocking the New York theatre public: the great Max Reinhardt was coming over from Germany. His sponsors were Otto H. Kahn and Adolph Zukor, his manager Gilbert Miller, and the Century Theatre was to be turned inside out to house his productions in style. For one thing, an entirely new stage had to be built.

Before a project of such splendor I was willing to bow out of the Century for the remainder of my Sunday afternoons, especially as there was a financial consideration and an offer of the Jolson Theatre on Sunday evenings rent-free.

Through these several fortuitous circumstances I was already all but back on my feet. I was even able to bring the Isadora Duncan dancers from Moscow. Irma Duncan and some fifteen of Isadora's Russian children appeared at the Manhattan Opera House and not only made me happy by keeping my promise to Isadora, but incidentally improved by another notch the health of my reviving fortunes.

The Wagnerian concerts continued merrily at the Jolson Theatre. Meanwhile George Blumenthal, Oscar Hammerstein's secretary, had brought a group of German artists here. They were practically stranded, and he asked me to do something about them. Here was another opera company, this time German, practically to hand. Miss Hall was interested, and Gadski was enthusiastic.

So I reorganized the company, provided a better orchestra, arranged a short tour and the German Opera Company took off with a repertoire of Wagner's *Ring*. That first season the company went to Philadelphia, Baltimore, Washington, Cleveland, Pittsburgh, Milwaukee, Chicago, Indianapolis, St. Paul, Cincinnati.

We carried two of practically everything, even trumpet players. In Chicago we gave two performances of *Götterdämmerung*, and immediately after the second performance the trumpet player went to the hospital. I think the poor man died. Whatever the scientific truth may be about the German *Übermensch*, Wagner certainly assumed it was a fact and that his operas would be performed exclusively by supermen.

Before we ever left New York, one of our two Mimes, who was also our stage manager, fell ill and died.

The other, Hanker, had a leave of absence from the Staatsoper in Berlin for precisely two months, November and December. The first of January he was due back in Berlin.

With my first Mime lost to me through natural causes, I camped on the doorstep of the German Embassy in Washington to save my second Mime from vanishing Cinderella-like in the middle of my tour.

I wrote cables by the yard, pulled wires for weeks until my hands were calloused. Nothing moved the German official mind. Unless Hanker returned—and on time—he would lose his pension and his hope of ever again singing in his native land.

Now this may seem like a small problem, but it is no small thing to find a singer with a Wagnerian repertoire in America at a moment's notice. I hurried to Chicago and found a Mime there—he could sing the role, that is, in *Das Rheingold*, but he could not sing it in *Siegfried*. Nor was there time for him to learn it, for the role

145

of the dwarf in *Siegfried* is a considerable one, even for Wagner, and even though he is disposed of in the second act. There is still the first act, in the cave, and quite a bit of Mime.

We were scheduled to give *Siegfried* in Milwaukee. I sat with my three conductors in the hotel and told them why we would have to cut Mime out of *Siegfried*. Two of the conductors refused pointblank to have any part of the job; they would not conduct *Siegfried* without Mime. I couldn't blame them. To give *Siegfried* without Mime is like giving *Boris* without Godunov.

I turned to Ernest Knoch.

"Knoch, you have to help me," I pleaded. He had no faith in the project, but out of the goodness of his heart he took the score and a pencil and got to work on the job. He would, he said, restore portions of Siegfried's forging songs, which are usually cut.

The theatre was just outside of Milwaukee. I remembered all the times we had cut and shaved and sawed up our productions to fit them onto impossible stages, just to keep the show going on. The bad theatres we had to cope with all over America had given us plenty of headaches. Why, I thought, should the primitive theatrical housing situation always work against us? Why not make it work for us, for once?

With this thought to ease my conscience I sent Frank Kaiser, the demon electrician, to the local manager. He was to say the stage was too narrow to set the cave scene. Either we cancelled *Siegfried*, which would be a pity, or we would cut the cave scene. Cutting Wagner is, after all, no crime—no performance of Wagner is ever given as he wrote it, except possibly in Bayreuth.

The manager agreed that the cave scene could be cut, agreed to explain the situation to the public. And so we gave *Siegfried* without Mime. Nobody stoned us. As a matter of fact at the last performance, which was *Götterdämmerung*, Mme. Gadski drew me out to take a curtain call. We moved out of Milwaukee with our honor unblemished in the public mind.

The season was a great success. Encouraged, I grew more ambitious in my plans for the second season. When I went abroad in the summer of 1928 I spent a good part of my trip in Germany, engaging an entire new cast, ordering scenery and costumes. I added *Tristan und Isolde*, *The Flying Dutchman*, and Mozart's *Don Giovanni* to the repertoire.

We had a tremendous season in 1928-29. I felt we had conquered the United States for German opera that winter. We had done a good job, my bank balance was as robust as it had ever been, and for the second time in my life I knew when to stop.

There have been attempts to duplicate my German opera tours, but for some reason they have never been successful. For myself, I had become interested in other projects.

I remember Johanna Gadski with a kind of homely warmth. Her death after an automobile accident, in which her husband Captain Tauscher and her friend Geraldine Hall were injured, was a painful shock to me. She was a fine Wagnerian artist who was equally at home in French and Italian opera.

Despite her heroic voice, she was not heroic in stature. Offstage she was an old-fashioned German *hausfrau*. There were dinners I remember at her big stone house in the woods in Zelindorf, outside Berlin—knackwürst and sauerbraten and good Moselle wine, and her two grandchildren in stiffly starched clothes and starched company manners. There was a birthday party one night, and when I left at 4:30 the guests were still toasting Johanna with another glass, and yet another. One Wagnerian lady carried me off Walküre-fashion to the Adlon, but she was less the Brünnehilde type than the Isolde.

Patriarch of Russian Music

In 1929, back on my feet, I turned again to the music that is closest to my own heart, the Russian. I brought to America the patriarchal composer, Alexandre Constantinovitch Glazounov.

To me it was a moving moment when the old man, stooped with years of bending over scores, a world of kindness in his wrinkled face under the shaggy white hair, stepped off the boat onto American soil. But I had already learned, to my chagrin, not to count on America sharing my feeling for him. When I offered him for a conducting date to the New York Philharmonic, the Philharmonic, which had been playing his music for years without paying him royalties simply because it was not protected by copyright, turned me down.

Once he had arrived, however, I found there were many Americans who venerated him as I did. Stung by the Philharmonic's rebuff, I organized an orchestra in New York for him, composed mostly of his own pupils from the Leningrad Conservatory; Glazounov may not have written the greatest Russian music, but he was one of Russia's greatest teachers. My own wife, Emma, was one of his pupils.

For that New York performance I took the Metropolitan Opera House, and Walter Damrosch made a speech before the concert, introducing Glazounov, in which he spoke of me as "the king of managers, a credit to New York." When Glazounov stepped on the podium the audience stood up, and many of them were in tears.

The Detroit Symphony offered only $500 for Glazounov's performance as guest conductor, but Ossip Gabrilowitsch added another $500 out of his own pocket to the fee.

Serge Koussevitzky gave him a glowing welcome in Boston. When he left Chicago, Frederick Stock and a group of his friends got up a fund of between $7,000 and $8,000. This they presented to him as royalties—so they said—for the many performances of his works in this country.

The old man was not well. He was ill for a while in Chicago. When he recovered, I brought him back to New York by way

148

of Niagara Falls. He saw the ice caves, the breathtaking spectacles which have become to Americans a honeymoon joke, and he said, "If I don't live a day more, it was worth the trip to see Niagara Falls."

He was ill in New York too. Every afternoon I went to see him in his room at the Alamac Hotel. And every afternoon while I was there calls would come up from the lobby: "Mr. Suchandsuch is here to see Mr. Glazounov." The lobby was full of musicians with scores under their arms, all wanting to see Mr. Glazounov.

"This is ridiculous!" I said. "Alexandre Constantinovitch, you must rest. What do all these people want?"

"Oh, they want me to look at their music," he answered.

"It's impossible," I insisted.

"Well, all right. Just let me see the young man with the quartet."

The next week the same sad-faced young man was in the lobby when I came.

"What is he doing here?" I asked Glazounov. "I thought you would look at his quartet and send him away."

"Yes, but, Salomon Isaievitch, it's a very bad quartet and I haven't the heart to tell him."

"Please," I begged, "give him back his bad quartet and send him away. I don't want you bothered by tenth-rate composers!"

Five days later the same long dreary face was in the lobby again. I was really angry. When I got to Glazounov's room I was ready to explode.

"Please, Salomon Isaievitch," he said. "Sit down, be nice, listen a moment. I rewrote his quartet—now it's all right, it's good—let him have it now and he will go away."

Walter Damrosch, who was musical director of the National Broadcasting Company at the time, gave a reception in Glazounov's honor at his home. He had played Glazounov's Third Symphony over the air that night, a special broadcast. Kadroff's Quartet of Russian singers sang at the party, to Glazounov's delight. Damrosch, who himself has done so much to spread the gospel of good music to America, could not do enough for Glazounov.

Before the composer left these shores his former pupils in New York gave a banquet in his honor at the Hotel Commodore. There were six hundred guests, and one by one his pupils among them rose and told what this gentle old man had done for them.

He had been not only a fine teacher and a top musician, but a man of great heart as well. He had a special concern for the talented boys and girls of poor families, and, though he was not a Jew, he made a very special place in his heart for the Jewish children only because their way was made peculiarly difficult. Jewish applicants were not admitted to the conservatory on the same basis as others; they were obliged to pass an additional, and additionally hard, examination.

Mischa Elman's father had told me years before a story about Glazounov. The pupils stood outside his studio waiting for their auditions. Glazounov would say to his assistant, "Well, who is the next?"

"A boy named Elman is waiting, from Odessa. Soandso recommended him . . ."

"What nationality?" Glazounov would ask.

"He is a Jew."

Glazounov would nod his shaggy head. "I don't think we need to examine him. Let him come in."

There were many tender and affectionate anecdotes told of Glazounov at that banquet. But the story I liked best was the one Glazounov told himself.

In 1910, he told us, Baron Guinzburg in Leningrad had come to him with a worried face.

"Alexandre Constantinovitch," he said, "what will become of you? You cannot teach forever, your music is played throughout the world but you get no royalties, and yet you are forever giving away your money to poor young musicians."

"I have enough—there is only my mother to support—I have no children to provide for," Glazounov told him. Guinzburg was not satisfied.

"No, you must save. I will put 100,000 rubles in the bank for you today provided you will add to it from your own income regularly every month. Only in this way will you have enough to keep you in your old age."

Glazounov agreed. But a year later when the Baron looked at Glazounov's bank book, there was a balance of only 50,000 rubles. He had not only failed to put in his share of savings, but had even given away half of the Baron's stake. Guinzburg scolded him severely, and put back the 50,000. Glazounov promised to do better.

By the time of the Revolution, the account was virtually bare. Guinzburg, like most of Russia's wealthy men, fled to Paris. Glazounov, who had not asked for his help in the first place, continued blithely on his way, giving his money where it pleased him to give it.

In 1923-24 the composer made a short trip to Berlin and Paris. In Paris Guinzburg came to see him.

"Well, Alexandre Constantinovitch? Are you still a poor man?"

"So I answered him," Glazounov told the guests gathered to honor him, "as I will tell you now. Guinzburg, a very wealthy man, left Russia, left everything behind. I have nothing to leave—but you. This is my wealth, this is my savings, these pupils and friends in this room, and I think I am far richer than Baron Guinzburg."

Glazounov had his gentle humor. When I first asked him, in Paris, to let me arrange a conducting tour for him in America, he said, "Hurok, I am heavy artillery. What will you do with me?" I told him then that I did not expect to make money out of his tour, but that I was proud and grateful to bring him to my adopted country.

It was from Glazounov that I first heard the name of Shostakovitch. When the press came to interview him on his arrival at the Hotel Astor—this was December, 1929—he told them that a composer called Dmitri Shostakovitch would be one of the greatest to come out of Russia.

The patriarch went back to Paris where, still on leave from Leningrad, he died a year later. I had been in the Soviet Union in the interim, and had seen Steinberg, Rimsky-Korsakoff's son-in-law, director of the Leningrad Conservatory. Steinberg told me they were planning a great celebration of Glazounov's fiftieth anniversary at the Conservatory, the next year when he was due to return.

Back in Paris, I went to visit him. I told him about the celebration that was being planned for his return to Leningrad on his anniversary. He was very ill, and I knew he would not live to see the celebration, but his dim eyes brightened as I talked of it. Three hours later I received a call at my hotel that he was dead.

CHAPTER SIX

"S. Hurok Presents"

*M*ANY THINGS HAPPENED to me in the Thirties, most of them wonderful. I heard Marian Anderson sing for the first time in a Paris concert hall; Artur Rubinstein became my friend; my lovely Emma became my wife.

Another thing that happened to me was the Ballet. And then there was a thing that was important because it did not happen to me, though it happened to nearly everyone else in the business. I was not swallowed.

My unwillingness to lose the identity of S. Hurok acted like a giant vitamin pill. Since I refused to be a little part of a big business, I had to become big business myself.

The steps by which the National Broadcasting Company and the Columbia Broadcasting System developed enormous concert booking organizations were as logical and as inevitable as similar growth in other industries. The United States Steel Company, needing coal to make steel, went into the coal business, acquiring control of mines to supply its blast furnaces. The networks, needing artists to make music, went into the artist business.

It began when Marks Levine, then head of the Daniel Mayer office, proposed to George Engels, NBC's program head who also managed the modest NBC Artists Bureau, that they get together and build up this bureau. In 1930 those two energetic fellows joined forces in the NBC Artists Service. By the next year they had grown so big that CBS got busy building up a concert organization of its own.

The names of my competitors of so many years—Coppicus, Judson, Evans and Salter—vanished and then reappeared on the letterheads of the CBS concert department. To me it seemed as though all the concert managers of New York were becoming merged—I would have said, submerged—in the networks.

S. Hurok stood alone. I did not want to be merged.

So, feeling my way, I did three things. I made a deal with NBC, whereby I relieved myself of the expensive burden of booking tours, taking advantage of their enormous organization for that purpose, and making sure to keep my label, "S. Hurok Presents" on all my artists.

But—this was the second step—I kept for myself the plum of New York. Whenever my artists appeared in New York, I decided, I myself would present them without anybody's help.

And third, I kept my own publicity staff. I have clung to this staff through hell and high expense accounts, and the advertising and publicity which have come out of the Hurok office have proved to be one of my hardiest bulwarks against being swept down with the tide.

When the FCC advised the networks that it would be better to release their artist bureaus, we suffered nothing more than a change of offices. With the newly emergent National Concert and Artists Corporation we moved out of 30 Rockefeller Plaza into the old NBC Building on Fifth Avenue. And here, at number 711, we sit today, with my good friend Marks Levine, one of the most brilliant minds in the concert business, a near neighbor on the same floor. In fifteen years Marks and I have not had a cross word.

Dance Decade

In my determination to prove that I had a right to live alone
and like it while most of my colleagues were moving in together,
I redoubled my efforts to snare the interesting, the exotic, the
novel from abroad. I began with Mary Wigman.

The Nineteen Thirties might with reason be called the Dance
Decade. Out of my efforts alone came Wigman, Escudero, Shan-
Kar, Trudi Schoop, and not one but three separate Ballet com-
panies.

Others brought over the Jooss Ballet, the Chinese dancer-actor,
Mei-Lan-Fang, while a long list of American dancers, beginning
with Martha Graham, Tamiris, Doris Humphrey and Charles
Weidman, brought an earnest mood into Broadway theatres on
Sunday evenings.

All this dance activity did not impress me, remembering as I
did another and even busier dance decade. From 1912 to 1919
New York was entertained simultaneously and successively by
the Diaghilev Ballet Russe at the Century and the Metropolitan
Opera House, Pavlova at the Hippodrome, Mordkin at the Man-
hattan Opera House, Isadora Duncan at the Century in her ill-
fated Greek tragedy and in and out of the Metropolitan Opera
House as her stormy life permitted. There was also a season of
Gertrude Hoffman in a production of *Schéhérazade* at the Winter
Garden, while Ruth St. Denis, Loie Fuller, Maude Allen and
Albertina Rasch and their companies flitted in and out of New
York. And perhaps there were others; this is as much as one man's
memory yields up.

But despite all this dance activity, not Diaghilev with his sensational, stunning company, nor Isadora the iconoclast, had the
effect on the entertainment world in those days that the Ballet
had in the Thirties and is having today. Pavlova took the Ballet

to the remotest towns, and Diaghilev, both without and with Nijinsky, made well-publicized tours to the biggest cities, but never until 1940 did a ballet company rake a cool million in United States currency across its box-office counters in one season.

Furthermore, you cannot go to a Broadway musical today and not see a ballet, and both Broadway and Hollywood are constantly raiding our company for dancers and choreographers. This is a handsome tribute to a ballet impresario. It is also a handsome headache. I sometimes wonder if they will end by killing the goose that laid the golden egg.

Priestess of the Dance

The decade which was to end with the Ballet in gorgeous and glamorous flower, expensively dressed and lavishly orchestrated, began at exactly the opposite end of the dance scale.

Where we were to see an endless variety of costumes designed by our liveliest modern artists, we had in 1930 a single tunic, now long, now short, now one color, now another, but always with the same circular skirt and bathing-suit decolletage. Where we were one day to enjoy full orchestras led by distinguished conductors through the mazes of Wagner and Shostakovitch, Tchaikowsky and Leonard Bernstein, we listened in 1930 to a piano played by a thin, long-necked German youth and a collection of curious drums and gongs under the hands of a plump German maiden.

And where we were to feast our eyes on a luscious Toumanova and a beauteous Baronova, on lovely young faces and exquisite pink silk legs, we gazed in 1930 on Mary Wigman.

Pavlova had mentioned her to me long before. By 1930 she had become a religion in Germany, and American girls had already begun to make pilgrimages to Dresden, to sit at her bare feet in the Mary Wigman Schule and drink in her strange new art.

156

Besides the shrine in Dresden she had a branch school in Berlin, managed by a disciple. All over Germany there were Mary Wigman groups, led by other disciples. The entire populations of schools, factories, gymnasia would turn out for their weekly *Massengrüppe*, their session of mass dancing in the Mary Wigman manner.

To her schools came a collection of queer young people, mostly girls, a few boys. They ate, drank and slept Mary Wigman, and worked with the devotion of fanatics in her classes. Germany in those years had a peculiar approach to sex. The relationship was intellectualized. In her school there were constant tense affairs between boys and girls, and girls and girls, and boys and boys, practiced on a high intellectual plane, rationalized on the basis of a mutual absorption in Mary Wigman. Wigman in Germany had become a cult.

I signed a contract with her for the season 1930-31, but I could not guess how the American public would react to this strange woman.

She was not beautiful nor too young, but she was fascinating. She had a superb muscular body, built on Amazonian rather than Hollywood lines.

She had three points of beauty: a warm smile, beautiful wide-apart gray eyes, and a head of chestnut hair, waving almost to her shoulders, so thick, so vibrant that it seemed to live a life of its own. Her voice too was pleasant and low, and she spoke beautiful English without an accent but with a definite British inflection. This, however, could not help her on the stage.

My first announcement brought a mailbag full of letters, most of which startled rather than encouraged me. They were from ardent worshipers who had seen her in Germany, or had actually studied with her in Dresden. They sounded quite mad; I could not believe, nor even wish to believe, that there were enough of them to make even one full house. One letter, however, was from a young man who said he had recently returned from a trip to Germany, was familiar with Wigman's work and had an idea he could publicize her in America. I hired him on the spot, and he was the head of my press department for fifteen years after.

Wigman arrived in November. She looked stuffily German in a black cloth coat trimmed with some sad fur of uncertain ancestry and a tired, aging hat (for her second season she arrived in a mink coat and mink-trimmed turban) out of which flowered her extraordinary hair. With her she brought her accompanist and composer, Hanns Hasting, a weedy young man with protruding eyes in a pale face, and the sturdy girl percussionist, Meta Mens. Her baggage consisted of a trunk of costumes and a series of oddly shaped cases in which were her precious Hindu drums and Balinese gongs, together with a few primitive flutes and reeds.

I had penciled in a scratch tour, depending pretty much on how she would be received in her opening performance at the Chanin, now the 46th Street Theatre. Meanwhile, my new press agent had deluged the newspapers with background stories. He wrote of the three great dancers, Pavlova, Duncan and Wigman. He also made obscure references to the history of the human race, the inner meaning of the Wigman dance, the *zeitgeist*, the sub-conscious. Occasionally I wondered whether I was offering the public a form of entertainment or a course in the philosophy of Nietzsche and Schopenhauer with a glance at Sigmund Freud.

That first night at the Chanin Theatre proved without a doubt that whatever it was, dance or discourse, the public wanted it. The house was wild, the notices next day fantastic. Here and there a veiled, almost shamefaced reference to her personal unattractiveness crept in. But on the whole the critics, like the public, felt a power, a personal dynamism here that could not be ignored.

The meaning of her dances was a constant embarrassment to me. She danced "cycles," groups of related dances whose relationship existed only in the mind of the performer, as far as I could see. There was one in particular, called "Monotonie," in which, to a thin little melody composed of two phrases of four notes each endlessly repeated, she stood in one spot and whirled. The effect of that whirling figure, now slow, now fast, now crouching, now erect, was pure hypnosis. Every dance ended with the dancer falling to the floor in the abandoned posture of a dead faint.

Before a performance she went into a mystic silence. For three or four hours she lay alone in a darkened room, her ears plugged against sounds. On no account could she be disturbed.

And she emerged from each performance with a real jag on. Every artist leaves the theatre or concert hall stimulated, wound up, eager for company and live talk. But when we went to supper with Wigman we panted to keep up with her accelerated stride. Her gray eyes glittered and a constant stream of highly literate, highly articulate chatter poured from her lips. She sped along, both mind and body, as though full of champagne, or as though she had been in a trance all evening and had emerged from it to discover all over again, with a kind of hysterical delight, the land of the living.

There was no question about the trance-like possession of her dancing, or the mysticism of its content. But she danced it with a sternly disciplined technique.

Still I wanted to know what it all meant. When we sat together on trains, in restaurants, I would say, "Miss Wigman, the newspaper boys are always asking me, what do your dances mean? I'd like to be able to tell them."

"Oh, the meaning is too deep; I really can't explain it."

So I began making up my own meaning. One day I told a reporter that Mary Wigman was carrying on the work that Isadora Duncan had left unfinished.

The story duly appeared. Miss Wigman read it. She read it through from beginning to end, put it down, and said nothing at all.

The next town on our route was Toronto. I got her settled comfortably in her hotel room and then I tried an experiment.

"The newspaper boys are coming up to see you," I said. "I have some errands to do. You won't mind being alone for your interview this time, will you?"

"Not at all," she said. I left.

When I came back there were two or three reporters sitting in the room, busily writing on their wadded copy paper, and she was talking. I stole in and sat down inconspicuously.

"And so, where Isadora Duncan left off, there I began," she was saying.

The formula was right, after all. Our slogan, "Priestess of the Dance," the bracketing of Wigman with Pavlova and Duncan as the third of the great dance trinity, the polysyllabled references to anthropology and philosophy—it all took. The scratch tour was a march of triumph.

The next season was even more triumphant, a full-length coast-to-coast tour, and she played to capacity everywhere. In Cincinnati, where the local manager, J. H. Thurman, offered her as one event in a subscription season, people took to watching the death notices in the newspapers to see if any ticket-holder might have been considerate enough to die and leave vacant a seat for the Wigman performance.

We established a school for her in New York that year, an enormous studio in Steinway Hall with a black linoleum floor. I gave a New Year's Eve party there, with the guests sitting on cushions on the floor. An entire delicatessen store was set up in the studio for the occasion, shelves laden with canned delicacies, enormous roasts of beef, turkeys, salamis ready for slicing laid out on the counter. The waiter stood behind the counter like a storekeeper, with a huge carving knife in his hand, making up sandwiches to order, complete with mustard, cole slaw, Russian dressing and pickle. I added my own impromptu version of Mary Wigman dancing to the entertainment.

The third season she returned with her group. It was a dismal flop. One stocky Amazon, providing it was the miraculous Wigman herself, was all right, but a whole group of thick-waisted, thick-legged German girls in wide-skirted bathing suits was too much.

Lincoln Kirstein put the case of Mary Wigman very well. What she did was to create the illusion that anyone could be a dancer, with the result that she encouraged all kinds of awkward, unhappy souls to dance. Kirstein called her a dangerous woman, dangerous, that is, for the dance, because she was professionalizing amateurs. Because of Wigman, people who should have been in the audience were on the stage.

Yet she expressed a spirit of the time, or she never would have ridden on such a tide of adulation. Hers was the sick intellectuality of a dying era, an escape, a merging of the self with infinity. Wigman never dealt in her dances with life or people, only with the cosmic, the infinite, the remote, the barely conscious stirrings of an unhappy, neurotic mind.

She created an audience for our modern American dancers; even Broadway choruses displayed some diagonal arm movements for a season or so, and the Roxyettes (the Radio City of that year) went briefly angular.

But the Wigman frenzy passed as swiftly as it had come. Martha Graham is today using the material of our lives and our history in her dances, giving us the drama and poetry of real life. She has grown into the great modern dance interpreter of America, and so closely does she approach the theatre that if she chose she could today become one of our greatest dramatic actresses.

Mary Wigman strode down Broadway one evening in 1933 with Hasting, the stocky Meta, and some of the office staff. It was late, after a performance, and the morning papers were out.

That was the day of the last legal election in Germany. Wigman begged for the newspapers, and the lot of them hurried down the steps into Childs Restaurant in the Paramount Building basement to read the election returns.

She was happy that night. The Hitler gang had been beaten.

But despite the fact that her money—more money than she had ever had in her life in Germany—was deposited in a New York bank, that she had a thriving New York school, that she had an adoring American audience—despite all this, Mary Wigman went back to Germany.

The last we heard of her, she was organizing pageants of 10,000 people at a time for National Socialist party gatherings. Whether she became a Nazi or not, we don't know. In any event, she stopped writing to us.

Gypsy in a Hotel Room

Anna Pavlova was to have returned to America in the season of 1932, after the long absence since 1925. Death intervened with its own flat finality. But Madame had planned to bring with her on that tour the Spanish gypsy dancer, Vicente Escudero. Again as with Duncan, Wigman, and Shan-Kar whose turn had not yet come, it was Pavlova pointing the way for me.

Escudero arrived in January with his pianist, his guitarist and his two gypsy girl partners. Carmela was a slender girl, very young, soft-voiced and shy. Carmita was small, muscular, full of fire, with a voice that rattled Andalusian dialect in shrill machine-gun staccato; she indulged a tendency toward the shrewish when she talked to Escudero, whose favorite of the moment she was.

We were prepared to handle the gypsy as one would handle a bomb with a very short fuse. Though I had had quite normal contractual dealings with him myself, his reputation was picturesque.

162

But the wiry little dark-skinned man with the aquiline nose greeted me with a childlike trust, his thin lips parted in a happy smile which showed a row of small, even, white teeth. In his tight-fitting Paris suit, his long, black, very kinky and thickly greased hair brushed forward to hide his unglamorous bald spot, he looked more like an Arab peddler of linen napkins who used to wheedle Emma outside our hotel in Paris than like the world's greatest male dancer.

We established him and his entourage at the decorous Hotel Barbizon-Plaza. Within an hour the trim suite with its sleek modern furniture was a shambles.

Escudero was hungry and called for food. When it came he sat down at the table, but he disdained knife, fork or napkin, using his fingers quickly and efficiently. At the same time Carmita scurried around, unpacking. Her method was to pull everything out of a suitcase and toss it on the bed, the chair, often enough the floor. Petticoats and stockings somehow got on the table, where they mingled cosily with Escudero's dinner. He did not mind.

Throughout, he chattered in a steady stream of Spanish. The Mexican painter, Miguel Covarrubias and his wife, Rose, had come to meet Escudero, whom they had known in Paris, and Miguel translated what was translatable. His talk was an imaginative series of anatomical and bathroom references combined with allusions to a variety of incestuous relationships.

Once I thoughtlessly dropped my hat on his bed. He leaped across the room, one hand clutching half a broiled chicken, and with the other unceremoniously swept my Homburg onto the floor, while he muttered the direst predictions of doom to come as a result of my ignorance.

In preparation for his arrival, we had stirred up the Vogue, Vanity Fair and Harper's Bazaar set, who knew of him in Paris and had taken him up as a chic enthusiasm. Now we arranged to introduce him with a cocktail party. Our list of guests was very smart indeed. Many of the artists and photographers had sketched and photographed him in Paris. He had been lionized by the painters, writers, *salonnières* who commuted between Paris and New York.

This facet of New York was comparatively new to me. I had lived in musical society for years; I had, with Wigman, become familiar with the radical-intellectual set, the low-heeled, long-haired girls and the thin, serious young men. Now with Escudero I came to know the expatriates-at-home.

I had been meeting them on shipboard and in Paris, but I had not seen them in such concentrated form in New York since Isadora, ten years before.

Ten years had made a change. The painters and writers who had worshiped Isadora had sat around her in a soft golden haze. These, in 1932, were people with a sharp edge to them. They glittered in their handsome and very expensive clothes. They bristled with wit. They talked in shrill, nervous voices, continuously. They competed for each other's attention, and the competition was murderous. Ten years had made a change in the world, and the symptoms of the change were apparent in the faces of these clever, gifted people who moved like migratory birds in flocks each year from New York to Paris to the South of France to New York.

The guest of honor, the wiry little Spanish gypsy with his white teeth and his kinky black hair plastered down with grease to make it stay, was embraced by them like a long-lost brother. He knew them all, and jabbered to them in a kind of French through which his Andalusian Spanish coiled and wriggled like a basketful of restless snakes.

No doubt those multi-lingual men and women understood him. For my part, Russian, some German and a hesitant acquaintance with French gave me little help. But they punctuated his conversation with little bursts of explosive laughter, and he laughed with them, happy as could be. Lucius Beebe, on his first assignment for the drama editor of the *Herald Tribune*, wove among the guests with glass in one hand and pencil in the other, very happy. It was a most successful party.

Escudero made a sensational debut at the Chanin 46th Street on January 17th. He gave several performances in New York and made a short tour. He came again the next year for a long tour which took him to the West Coast and back and kept him on this side of the Atlantic from October through January.

Curiously, he was one of the steadiest, most reliable performers I have managed. He and his people were disciplined troupers; everywhere the curtain went up on time and the performance ran on schedule. In all his business dealings this Spanish gypsy from the cave-dwellings of Granada was absolutely correct.

The contrast was startling. Before the footlights, he was electric. With his tight Spanish trousers fitted over his taut muscles like his own skin, nowhere a shadow of a wrinkle; with his flat-brimmed hat at an angle of scornful arrogance; with the little gesture of adjusting the elegant set of his short jacket, a gesture that called attention to the utter and unquestionable assurance, the superiority of this maleness—moving across a dark stage in the spotlight's eye, to the clean rhythm of his own heels and snapping fingers, he was fury leashed with a silk thread.

The excitement of an Escudero audience came to be a matter of course. If I had been led blindfolded and with cotton in my ears into a theatre where he was dancing, I think I could have told whether he was on the stage.

The climax of his performance was his Farrucca. Those who never saw Escudero may have seen Massine's Farrucca in the *Three-Cornered Hat*; it, too, stopped the show. But Escudero's Farrucca was not a concert or ballet piece. He danced it to the nasal, off-beat chords of a single guitar, and it was a fiercely feline thing, a thing of uncivilized animal ferocity held in check by the exact perfection of its style. When Escudero danced his Farrucca, there was not an eye in the audience that was not fastened to his taut figure in its skin-smooth trousers, following him as he stepped with cat-like delicacy, as he crouched, as he sprang and flung himself to the floor and sprang erect again with a suddenness that caught your breath in your throat, or even as he stood unwaveringly still for a timeless second.

And then he would come offstage after his bows, with the shrieks of the audience muffled by the dropping curtain. There would be sweat beading his brown leathery skin; his sunken eyes above the sharp cheekbones would be bright with excitement; his thin lips would be parted in a wide grin of happiness.

He would go on to the next number, and after the performance he would go on to the next town, and the reports came with comforting regularity from the company manager: no troubles, no hysterics, no fits of temperament. If there were clashes within the little troupe—and with two girls competing for his favors there must have been—he disciplined his females himself. We never heard any echo of them. If the trains, the hotels, the strange food of America troubled him, he made the best of it. A gypsy, after all, could find a way to feel at home anywhere, even if only by turning his hotel room into an instant and unbelievable chaos the moment he stepped into it. He ran through his tours with the precision of clockwork.

So I was caught unaware the one time his harnessed violence exploded, and it was the nearest I have been to witnessing manslaughter.

The trigger that exploded this human bombshell was his superstition. It was backstage at the Chanin, on his return engagement in New York. The stage was set with the simple black backdrop, and Escudero was walking about before the performance, not warming up—he never did—merely walking off the pre-curtain nervousness which every performer suffers, no matter how many thousand times he has waited for the curtain to rise.

The stage electrician was only trying to change a bulb in a border. But he put his ladder right over the path Escudero had taken for his pacing. And, unaware, Escudero walked right under the ladder. He might not have seen the ladder even then, if the unlucky electrician had not come climbing ponderously down at the moment Escudero was passing beneath it.

He uttered a howl which made even my few hairs stand on end. The stagehand's head jerked around, and when he saw what menaced him he turned and went away from there very fast. But Escudero was faster.

I ducked behind the backdrop and met the stagehand—his flight past me created quite a breeze. Escudero was right on his heels. I stepped in his path and stood there. And the gypsy bent on murder stopped, looked with sudden fascination and began to laugh. Because dangling from my hand, ascending and descending with a leisurely dignity, was a yo-yo top, of which I had only that afternoon mastered the art.

Escudero returned to Paris after his second season. He was in Paris during the Civil War, and has since gone back to Madrid.

Hindu God on Broadway

My enthusiasm for the dance, always keen, was now a guiding policy on my trips abroad in search of talent. My schedule of concert artists continued with additions and deletions each season, but the dance companies I imported became my trade mark for those years. In Wigman's third season and Escudero's second, I brought over my most exotic contribution to the American dance theatre.

I had seen Uday Shan-Kar first in Pavlova's ballet, *Oriental Impressions*, which she brought back from her round-the-world tour in 1924. I saw him again in the Paris Colonial Exposition, where he and his company performed for hours on end, without rest, the long and leisurely dramas of Hindu mythology. The costumes were sumptuous with all the richness of storied India, and the tawny bodies which moved in them through the elegant traditional symbolism were beautiful to watch. The music, too, difficult at first, grew poignant and haunting as the initial resistance of the Western ear was overcome by its strange sonorities.

But those endlessly long, involved dramas of the gods and their adventures were in no form for the American theatre.

Behind his thin studious face with the melting eyes, Shan-Kar was astonishingly canny. Together with his Hindu scholarship, with his ability to reproduce the ancient legends, their involved forms and hypnotic other-world atmosphere, together with his own great talent as dancer, musician and choreographer, he miraculously possessed an understanding of the Western theatre public and the specific limitations in time and space of a Western audience's attention. Perhaps the showmanship on which we in America pride ourselves is more universal than we think. At any rate Shan-Kar had it.

He had absorbed a great deal in his apprenticeship to Pavlova, brief as it was. When I began to describe to him the kind of concert program I needed, its precise timing as to beginning, middle and end, the need for intermissions and high points preceding intermissions, all the technical details of program-making for an American tour, he nodded understandingly and told me in his gentle, hesitant voice that he knew what I meant and was prepared to give me what I asked.

Physically it was as simple a show to transport as any. There were no settings. In the Oriental theatre illusion is a convention established by pantomime and needing only a few physical properties like the swords in a Chinese duel. Shan-Kar needed not even swords. His battle as Shiva against the Elephant God was mimed, with the sharp clang of a gong to signify the striking of blows. In one exquisite dance the two girls of his company took off their clothes, bathed, dried themselves, snatched their skirts and fled before an imaginary intruder, all without disturbing the clasp of a girdle, a jeweled hair ornament or even a bangle on their arms. Yet the illusion of the stream, the disrobing, the bath, the flight was perfect.

The costumes naturally went in trunks. The most complicated part of the baggage was the collection of oddly shaped drums, gongs and string instruments, and these had their oddly shaped cases. The packing of the drums was, however, a considerable chore. And it was just that chore which was the cause of the shocking disaster which nearly wrecked my tour, in fact came close to wrecking Shan-Kar's entire career as a dancer.

They came in December, 1932, fifteen slight, soft-voiced, shy, inconspicuous people. None of the men was very tall, and the two girls were tiny. One of them, Simkie, was a French girl who had embraced the Hindu faith for love of Shan-Kar. In her graceful draperies, her parted black hair hugging her small head like a smooth cap, the red disc painted on her forehead, she looked a more perfect Hindu than the Hindu girl in the company.

The company was full of Shan-Kar's male relatives. An uncle played among the musicians. One of his brothers made a specialty of a fierce tribal warrior's dance. The youngest, a thin lad who looked ten and was about fourteen, cavorted engagingly in the role of the Monkey King in the Shiva drama.

I had been optimistic about his chances of success in New York; I knew the critics would give his precise and beautiful performance a good send-off. But I never anticipated his being a smash hit.

That's what he was. He played twenty-five performances in New York alone that first season, and every one of them was a sell-out. Shan-Kar was good—but not that good. His art was, after all, very special. The complex symbolism, the fine hand move-

169

ments, the strange music, which many people found difficult to listen to through an entire performance, are not normally the ingredients of a popular success. Above all, there was no apparent virtuosity, no sensational technical feat which would make people gasp. It was all very beautiful, but it was even-toned, serene, soothing rather than exciting.

I scanned the audiences, curious to know what drew them in such numbers. And then I enjoyed a good laugh at my own expense. His audience was at least seventy-five per cent women.

To me he was a slight young man of less than average height, gentle, soft-spoken, not in himself an exciting personality. Seeing him through the eyes of a feminine audience, I realized that on the stage he looked six feet tall—all his company, especially his girls, being so small, he was actually the tallest of the lot!

He was beautifully proportioned, moreover, muscles smooth under a sleek golden skin. In those traditional costumes, which subtly enhanced his height, the breadth of his shoulders, the slimness of his hips, he looked impressively virile. Sex appeal was one item with which I had not credited him, but it showed in the box-office statements.

When he went on tour the same concentrated feminine audience flocked to him; he did very satisfactory business.

All of us had come to identify him, unconsciously, with the noble godly figures he portrayed. At the very least he was, in our eyes, a thoughtful and scholarly young man. He was that—but he was human too. On tour he revealed some very human and very disillusioning addictions.

Once a train had to be held while someone rushed back by taxi to the hotel, where he had inadvertently left his entire collection of well-thumbed movie-fan magazines. This was his favorite reading matter—not the lofty musings of Hindu philosophers, but the outpourings of the Hollywood gush girls.

It was midway in his second tour, which ran from October to

January of the following season, that the blow fell. A telephone call came from our company manager, Howard Potter, in Chicago. Shan-Kar had broken two of his fingers.

The catastrophe was a combination of drums and relatives. His brothers, whose task it was to pack the drums after each performance, had grown rebellious and demanded extra pay for this extra chore. When he refused, they fell on him and beat the living daylights out of the Hindu god.

The bruises were nothing, but in a Hindu dancer a finger is at least of equal importance to a leg. Several engagements had to be cancelled, and for several more his dances were modified in favor of the injured fingers. He got through the tour, but I found it difficult to get over the shock of this bad behavior, and its expensive consequences. I did not bring Shan-Kar back again until two seasons later, for a six-week engagement in 1936-37.

Again he was a sensational success, and I had more or less got over my mistrust of him and his brothers. I brought him back the following season for a coast-to-coast tour.

Shortly afterward I heard from London that he had been awarded by the Elmhurst Foundation a fund for the establishment of a school of dance study and research into Hindu lore in Benares.

In the latter part of the season 1932-33 I celebrated my new eminence as the dance impresario of America with a Dance Festival at the New Yorker Theatre, a week of performance by Wigman, Escudero and Shan-Kar. New York made quite a thing of it, and I was well pleased.

By the next December I had begun my life with the Ballet.

Funniest Girl in the World

But before we take off into the fluorescent upper ether of the ballet world, there are other vanished figures of the not too distant past knocking to be admitted here.

171

From Zurich there came a slender girl with short straight blonde hair cut in the style we used to call Buster Brown, with the agile body of a small boy and a small boy's face which alternated between blandest innocence and impish mischief.

We billed Trudi Schoop as "the female Charlie Chaplin." She was a clown in the great tradition of clowns, an exquisite mime whose range included every note from the flick of an eyelid to the most frightening, apparently self-destroying acrobatics. Surrounded by a company of gifted dancers, she performed theatre pieces without words, without scenery and with a minimum of costume. Like Chaplin's, her satire was gentle, without sting, winning you to laughter tinged with tears.

Her greatest creation was a character named Fridolin, a boy in a little black suit and a flat black hat like a country preacher's, whose innocent blundering in a naughty world led to catastrophe after laughable catastrophe. Another was *Die Blonde Maria*, the epic of a servant girl who, by a series of zany encounters, rises to opera stardom. *Want Ads* was a group of short sketches, the stories behind the brief items in the agony column: "For Sale, Wedding Gown, never worn" and "Honorable lady (middle fifties) seeks acquaintance, object matrimony."

Trudi enchanted the critics, who called her "the funniest girl in the world." Edna Ferber wired me ecstatically: "IN THAT SUNDAY NIGHT MOOD OF BOREDOM OR CURIOSITY I WENT TO SEE TRUDI SCHOOP AND HER DANCERS LAST NIGHT STOP I HAD NEVER BEFORE HEARD OF HER STOP ALL TODAY I HAVE BEEN TELEPHONING MY FRIENDS AS THOUGH I HAD MADE AN EXCITING AND BRILLIANT DISCOVERY STOP THIS TRUDI SCHOOP BALLET IS I THINK THE MOST AMUSING AND THE MOST AMAZINGLY FRESH ENTERTAINMENT IN NEWYORK STOP CERTAINLY EVERY ACTOR IN NEWYORK SHOULD BE COMPELLED TO SEE THIS PERFORMANCE IF ONLY TO LEARN SOMETHING ABOUT THE ART OF PANTOMIME STOP WITH NO SCENERY NO PROPS AND A LITTLE COLLECTION OF COSTUMES THIS TURNS OUT

TO BE FOR ME AT LEAST A DAZZLING EVENING IN THE THEATRE AND
A TRIUMPH OF SHEER TALENT AND SPIRIT STOP HAVE A SPECIAL
MATINEE FOR ACTORS WONT YOU PLEASE. . . . EDNA FERBER"

Miss Ferber spoke not only for theatre people but for audiences too. Three times I brought Trudi and her dancers and her composer brother, Paul, who made and played her music, across the Atlantic, and three times I sent them on tour. Disciplined troupers, the company fulfilled their obligations without a hitch.

By the fall of 1938 things looked really black in Europe. The war clouds hung lower and lower. Schoop elected to remain at home in Switzerland. I had no news of her through the war years, but recently she has written that she would like to return.

Eight Hundred Actors

In December of 1932 I brought over from Europe a new company. It had no fewer than eight hundred actors, opera stars, ballet dancers, piano virtuosi, acrobats, matadors, toreadors, picadors, trained animals and animal trainers, an assortment guaranteed to turn an impresario's hair gray overnight. But they never gave me a bit of trouble. They were all made of wood.

I had seen the Teatro dei Piccoli in 1930. The Theatre of the Little Ones went into the Grand Theatre des Champs Elysées for a two weeks' engagement and stayed there three months. Plump, smiling Vittorio Podrecca was the darling of the Paris artists, as he had been the darling of the chic Roman world before that, and every one of his miniature performers, made of wood but far from wooden, was adored.

This was precisely the kind of novelty I loved. It was unique, it had style, and it came of a great tradition. The art of the puppet theatre has an ancient and honorable history, dating back to medieval times when marionettes were at every fair in Europe.

173

Italy, particularly, was the cradle of puppeteering. There are families who have been puppeteers, father and son, for three centuries.

But a tradition is no guarantee that the art is alive. In Podrecca's hands a new kind of puppet theatre had been born, and it was so lively as to be almost alarming. Audiences who jammed the Champs-Elysées' two thousand seats every night for three months roared with uncontrollable laughter at the antics of his wooden actors, more lifelike than life itself, and inhumanly human.

Podrecca was a Venetian who had come to Rome in 1916, a sickly youth hidden behind large spectacles, a beard, and a mop of dank black hair. Too ill to serve in the army of Italy in that other war, he had rented a cellar in the Palazzo Odescalchi and set up a little stage at one end. On the thick stone walls he had frescoes painted, characters from the Commedia dell'Arte, loving, cheating, laughing, weeping, beating each other, and celebrating in their own violent way the immortal theatre.

For his technicians Podrecca went to the source and engaged descendants of those famous puppeteer families of Italy. For his material, however, he roamed the whole field of drama, opera, concert and vaudeville. He took acrobats, jugglers, dancers and trained animal acts from the music hall. But never were there such acrobats as his, performing impossible feats of balance, or such dancers whose arms and legs serenely parted from their bodies and as serenely returned. He reproduced with an uncanny wit the wonderful long legs and delightfully tinny voice of Josephine Baker, the American Negro girl who stood Paris on its head for twenty years. His concert pianist tore the pretensions of the concert platform to shreds.

Even hallowed opera was defenseless against his irreverent invasion. He condensed Verdi and Rossini to thirty-five unforgettable minutes, revived the fairy plays of eighteenth-century Carlo Gozzi with such skill that Prokofieff was inspired to compose his *Love of Three Oranges* on Gozzi's play, and Puccini wrote as his last opera Gozzi's *Turandot*. *Puss in Boots*, *Cinderella*, *The Sleeping Beauty*, composed especially for him by Respighi, became dream fantasies with exquisite settings and music.

The first performance of the Piccoli, that winter in Rome, was attended exclusively by children with their mothers and governesses. But the Piccoli never had a child audience again. This was grown-up theatre, sophisticated, coruscating, gorgeously funny.

The artists and musicians, the playwrights and the players, flocked to the cellar in the Odescalchi. Chirico and Picasso, Debussy and Respighi, Mascagni, Casella and Puccini, Pirandello and Eleonora Duse and Jean Cocteau all came. Diaghilev and Stravinsky were there, Stravinsky spending all his afternoons at the Piccoli matinees and Diaghilev pursuing him there to get the score of "Pulcinella." The new ballet was waiting to go into rehearsal, but Stravinsky protested the puppets were more interesting than any troupe of dancers, even the great Diaghilev collection.

None of these workers in the arts could resist the Piccoli, and no more could I. I signed Signor Podrecca and his eight hundred actors, to say nothing of 300 stage settings, 1000 costumes, ten puppeteers, eight technicians and ten full-sized opera and music-hall singers, including Mme. Lia Podrecca.

By the time they stepped off the boat in December of 1932, the Little Ones had been all over Europe, the Near East and South America, had given 12,000 performances in thirty countries, had played in the big Salle Pleyel in Paris, had been fantastically successful everywhere. They came with the blessing of Maestro Toscanini who called them "the finest entertainment on the contemporary stage."

I had taken the Lyric Theatre on 42nd Street, a house with the capacity for a bang-up musical. On the social and artistic side I had prepared a list of sponsors from the A of Mrs. Vincent Astor

175

to the Z of Mr. Bruno Zirati. The Theatre of the Little Ones had a publicity campaign to equal a million-dollar Ziegfeld production.

We opened the night of December 22nd, and when the morning papers came I was sure I had a hit. The raves were unbelievable. Wrote Brooks Atkinson in the *Times*, "The human race had best look to its laurels," and he went home and composed a two-column Sunday piece about us. John Mason Brown in the *Post* called it "as delightful as anything our contemporary stage has to offer." Bob Garland said in the *World-Telegram*, "Not for many a theatre-going moon have I heard more genuine enthusiasm in a local showshop. I caught a dramatic critic clapping his hands for joy."

So we were in. Or were we?

Three months later, when we had moved to the smaller Cohan Theatre, and finally out of New York to Washington, Philadelphia and Boston, I counted my losses and asked myself what had happened. What had happened was merely the greatest depression this country had ever suffered.

We pulled out of the hole with a motion-picture contract (*I Am Suzanne* was the name of the film, and very charming it was) and a tour of the presentation houses.

Speak to Me of Love

Artists came and went in the Thirties. They came with high hopes, both theirs and mine, and for the most part those hopes were fulfilled. But times were hard, the country was fighting its way up from the sticky slough and somè, like a very fat Italian coloratura with a beautiful but mechanical voice, like a sixteen-year-old French girl with a virtuoso violin, stayed but briefly in the spotlight and vanished again into the wings.

Others brought me prestige but no profit. The Moscow Cathedral Choir was one of these. The Salzburg Opera Guild was

176

another, a really marvelous company which made gay theatre out of opera; in better times there would have been capacity houses for them, but in the Thirties they were a luxury in the arts.

A Parisienne in a blue velvet gown who sang of love was a season's sensation. Lucienne Boyer was not beautiful, not even really pretty except for her eyes, which were two large dark plums. Her voice was next to nothing as an instrument. But she was the streets of Paris; she was a girl looking for love over the rim of a brandy glass at a café table, a girl tremulously in love under a corner street lamp, a girl in black despair on a bridge over the Seine. Her voice could be low in confidences, soft and soothing as the velvet of her blue gown. It could take on a jagged roughness as she tied a little shawl around her throat and sang of a woman of the Paris streets. It could soar with the happiness of a woman newly in love. In Paris she was the queen of her own intimate supper club, "Chez Elle."

She came with her personal manager, a shrewd Egyptian named Henry Carson, who was smooth as silk and, surprisingly, honest as well; her youthful composer-accompanist Jean Delettre who was euphemistically called her husband; and her French maid, very French, very nervous, who divided her time between pressing exquisite French lingerie and suffering bilious attacks.

Mlle. Boyer spoke no English, so we got her a secretary-press agent who spoke very proper school French.

This young lady came away from the job sporting a dazzling new French vocabulary never taught in any school. One of her principal tasks was to keep the blue velvet gowns rolling out of the sewing rooms of Bergdorf-Goodman like automobiles off an assembly line.

That blue velvet gown was a symbol of Lucienne Boyer and a clue to her exceptional style as an artist. Softly clinging and feminine, it called no attention to itself. It was a supple blue shadow out of which her hands, her fine shoulders and her mobile eloquent face emerged whitely. All the blue gowns were made exactly alike, except for one of a lighter material than velvet for an engagement at a Florida night club, and yet every one had to be fitted with maddening exactness. Only Lyons velvet would do, and only a very certain special shade of blue. Bergdorf's elegant titled sales-ladies, none lower than a countess and some bearing names out of the *Almanach de Gotha*, danced attendance on this blunt-spoken little brunette off the streets of Paris, who knew exactly what she wanted and would not be cajoled into anything less.

Boyer went into the Rainbow Room atop the RCA Building in Rockefeller Center, then dazzlingly new and glamorous with its view of the city from the sixty-eighth floor. She sang, in her blue velvet gown, with the long-stemmed red roses she loved, "Speak to me of love," "I—spit in the water," "Buy my roses"—and she was a tremendous hit.

Ben Franklin and Edgar Selwyn put together a show around her, a Broadway production, but containing mostly Hurok talent. Escudero with his gypsy troupe danced in it; Raphael, the bland, moon-faced Russian who played the classics unbelievably on the concertina, played in it. My Emma, for the fun of it, returned to her singing career in a group with Lydia Chaliapin and some others, and gave us the Russian songs I love. A magician mixed drinks on the stage as the audience called them, pouring Martinis and Scotch and champagne apparently out of the same bottle.

Nikita Balieff ambled on and off the stage as master of cere-monies, making his good-natured polylingual jokes. They called the show *Continental Varieties*, and had Henry Dreyfuss redecorate the Little Theatre in very chic style.

The show was good, not quite good enough to be a hit, but nothing to bring the blush of shame to a producer's cheek. I myself enjoyed it, as did others who knew the nice little places in Paris which I knew, where the art of intimate entertainment reached its peak of perfection.

Boyer acquired a flock of admirers, most of them gentlemen of a certain age whose hair was considerably thinner than their wallets. Mademoiselle's press secretary found her days filled with the task of writing thank-you notes for fabulous flower offerings, and returning with the most gracious firmness little boxes from Tiffany's and Cartier's.

As she offered a polite and smiling—but adamant—negative to all invitations which included private little suppers with champagne, this American girl lived in a state of constant astonishment at the Parisienne's strait-laced morality. Mademoiselle told her solemnly that love unhampered by marriage is far finer, far nobler, that it truly demands the best of each partner's character. These altogether French sentiments, straight out of de Maupassant—although I am certain Mademoiselle had not read them, but construed them for herself—impressed our very American young lady deeply. She has been a happily married woman ever since.

After *Continental Varieties* had run for several months I took over the show and sent it approximately *in toto* on concert tour, where it had a nice success.

Twenty-six Little Boys

Through most of the Thirties there could be seen, traveling the roads of America, a bus with a strange cargo. Twenty-six little boys, ranging from eight to twelve, wearing identical little sailor suits, carrying identical little bags, rode up and down the country each season. They were the Wiener Saengerknaben, the Vienna Choir Boys, one of the most charming as well as solvent attractions I managed in those years.

The boys came from the Castle Wilhelminenberg, outside Vienna, each year. They traveled with their teacher, Rector Schnitt, a good gentle priest who hovered hen-like over his boys, and was not averse to relaxing, once the lads were abed, over a little glass of Scotch with our company manager. There was also the choirmaster, Herr Gruber, a taciturn fellow whom we never got to know, and a patient, hard-working Sister who washed the boys' laundry and probably their necks and ears as well. Certainly they were the cleanest little necks and ears I have seen, before or since, on any little boys.

The Saengerknaben of Vienna were an ancient organization, only six years younger than the continent of North America, with a grant from the Hapsburg Emperor, Maximilian I, dating back to 1498. The Imperial decree founding the institution specified, among other items, a pair of new shoes for each boy every month, as well as roasts three times a week and no less than a pint and a half of wine at each meal, "such wine that the boys do not become ill from it." Even then the boys went on public concert tours, but certainly the music-minded Maximilian never dreamed that one day his name would be carried over the concrete roads of the New World of whose discovery he may not even then have heard, and even to a newer world on the other side of the globe, Australia.

The Saengerknaben had a virtually unbroken history through the long reign of the Hapsburgs until the end of the First World War. With the Emperor gone, the Church gathered a new group of little boys, many of them foundlings and orphans, some few dedicated by their parents to the organization. They had their board and keep, their education and their musical training, and when their voices changed and they could no longer sing they were supported through their further schooling until they were old enough to go out into the world and earn a livelihood at the trade or profession of their choice. In a deeply disturbed Europe, this was no small measure of security for a little boy fortunate enough to have a voice.

In return for this, the boys traveled for part of each year, bringing their enchanting music to the concert halls of the world, and earning a goodly sum for the maintenance of the institution. They worked hard, keeping up their studies while they traveled, cramming knowledge to make up for lost time during the rest of the year when they were at home in Wilhelminenberg. They were happy little men, astonishingly free from mischievous impulses, and in their approach to music they were as serious and knowledgeable as many a grown musician should be and sometimes is not.

They sang, a capella and with piano accompaniment, a long repertoire of sacred and folk music, including an impressive list of masses by Haydn, Mozart, Schubert, Bruckner and Beethoven. Their angelic voices soared in the waltzes of Johann Strauss with a childish version of the Viennese romantic atmosphere. They dressed in white wigs and knee breeches, some of them in little hoop skirts and demure maidenly curls, and quaintly acted out *Hansel and Gretel*, Mozart's *Bastien and Bastienne* which he wrote when he was only as old as the eldest of these lads, Haydn's *The Apothecary* and several other little operas. One of them was *Der Hausliche Krieg*, by Franz Schubert, who was himself a Saengerknabe.

As they traveled across the country our company manager wired ahead to the town which they would reach on Sunday, arranging for them to attend mass. The news that the boys were arriving spread through the town, and invariably a spontaneous welcoming committee of motherly women would line the streets, dripping with tenderness for the charming little boys.

And they were charming. Their scrubbed cherub faces shone, their close-clipped hair showed the vigorous ministrations of comb and brush despite an occasional rebellious cowlick. When a lady approached, there was the inevitable click of heels of the well-polished shoes, the quaint bow from the waist, guaranteed to melt any feminine heart. Our company manager thought it wise to post bodyguards around backstage at all performances, lest anyone be tempted to kidnap one of his precious charges.

Traveling by bus for thousands of miles may sound like undue hardship for the children, but their tour was arranged with frequent stop-overs, and there were regular pauses en route to give them time to run and play in a pleasant roadside field. The overhead baggage racks in the bus were turned into reasonably comfortable little berths with a soft blanket and a pillow for each. After lunch sixteen of the smallest lads were boosted up to their perches, eight on a side, and the others stretched out on the seats for a siesta. Rector Schnitt, the good Sister, and our company manager were watchful of nodding heads at other times, too, and catnaps were a frequent order of the day.

They must have thrived on the regime, however strenuous it may sound to anxious mothers reading these pages, for they bloomed like the fat cherubs in a Renaissance painting. No measles, mumps or other scourges of childhood assailed them while they were in our care, nothing worse than an occasional sniffle. Their tempers were as happy as their health, and the music that came out of those twenty-six rosy little faces was, quite literally, heavenly. The only tragedy was the sudden dropping out in the middle of the season of this or that lad whose voice had begun to change.

Nineteen thirty-seven saw the end of the Saengerknaben's tours; the Austrian Government prohibited foreign travel. The lights were going out in Europe one by one, the shadows closing in. I sadly said good-bye to the Vienna Choir Boys, knowing that those angelic voices would all too soon be raised in shouts of "Heil Hitler," whether they willed or not.

I have before me an article translated from the German, a history of the Wiener Saengerknaben written for our publicity staff by two earnest Austrian ladies dedicated to the choir boys.

"The Saengerknaben are only in their infants' shoes, at the beginning of a new era," they wrote with eager conviction. "Our work prospers and grows and is a cultural certainty of our country."

"A cultural certainty." I wince as I read these words today, when

Vienna is a smoldering ruin, when the culture of the German-speaking peoples lies a suicide, and all those little boys with their cherub faces rot among the nameless millions of unmourned youths who died for Hitler.

Tom Thumb and His Giants

The next season the same bus was on the roads of America again, with the same company manager, Boris Charsky. But when it stopped by the roadside for its passengers to stretch their legs in an inviting field, the farmer accustomed to halting his team and watching twenty-six little boys jump out would have suffered a violent shock.

Because instead of twenty-six little boys, he would have seen thirty-two black-haired men, some with beards, all fierce-looking and all six feet tall or over—and a thirty-third, a bantam of a man not quite five feet tall.

These were—and are—the Don Cossacks, a singing aggregation different in every way from the Saengerknaben except in the quality of their art. Diminutive Serge Jaroff, the most talented choral conductor in the world, and his giant singers from the steppes have been one of our most solid attractions in the years since 1937. Covering thousands of miles across America in their bus—since the war, they have been traveling on trains—they have been singing the songs of Old Russia and New Russia to a highly appreciative American public in more than a hundred cities each year.

They have given American audiences the thrill of the most masculine, most virile singing in the world, the singing of a Russian male chorus. I am hard put to it to discern America's favorites in their long repertoire. The church chorals are organ-like and exalting, but I think the stirring Red Army songs vie with that well worn and still beloved "Song of the Volga Boatmen" for first place.

183

When they traveled by bus the countryside was regularly amazed and amused to see these muscular, black-bearded giants stripped to the waist, going through a routine of strenuous calisthenics under strict army discipline. On the trains they have had their adventures too.

The most touching of these happened last season, when a late train and a missed connection left them stranded, thirty-two miles from another town where they could catch a train which would get them to their next concert on time. The company manager learned of a bus in the town and went to talk to its owner.

The garage man, a patriarch of at least three score and ten, was eating his lunch.

"Can you drive thirty-three Russian Cossacks to ——?" the company manager asked.

"Russians?" The ancient leaped to his feet, abandoning his lunch, and rushed into the garage. A moment later a motor began to cough and sputter, and out came a bus of the same vintage as its owner.

"Jump in," he cried. "Where are they? Sure I'll drive the Russians. Most wonderful soldiers in the world, the Russians!"

He drove the thirty-two miles, talking the whole way about the exploits of the wonderful Red Army, stealing a glance every now and then at the tall, foreign-looking men who sat with military erectness in the rickety seats of his bus. His wrinkled hands on the wheel trembled with excitement. When the bus rattled into its destination and groaned to a stop, he watched the men leave with real regret.

The company manager asked him for his bill, and he shook his head vigorously. He wasn't going to take money for driving Russian soldiers where they had to go, no sir! The manager pressed a wad of bills into his hand and ran for the train, unwilling to disappoint him with the news that his glamorous passengers had not been soldiers of Russia for twenty-five years.

Through the years these Russians, exiled from their land by accidents of war and civil war, upheavals in which little people have no voice in their own fate, have conscientiously adapted themselves to the land of their choice. One by one the beards disappeared, the last one vanishing only during the past season. When the time came for them to take their oath as American citizens, they were probably the best-instructed Americans in history: they had translated the Constitution into Russian, the better to understand it, and back again into English, and then memorized it in both languages.

CHAPTER SEVEN

So This Is Ballet!

$\mathcal{I}$N THE SPRING of 1933 I received a cable from my press agent who had been vacationing in Switzerland and had flown to Paris at my request. The cable was long, and the sum and substance of it was: "So this is ballet! Wheee!!"

The cable made me happy. If this young man, representative of a generation of Americans who had not been exposed to ballet in the grand style since Diaghilev made his two brief visits in 1916 and 1917, who may have seen Pavlova briefly in the Twenties, and whose familiarity with *tutus* and *maillots*, with *arabesques*, *entrechats* and *fouettés* stemmed from the Roxy and the Music Hall—if this young man could be stimulated to such roller-coaster excitement by an evening at the ballet, then perhaps the mournful predictions of Nikita Balieff would not come true.

Not only my moon-faced friend of the Chauve-Souris but everywhere in the concert business people were shaking their heads, and being sorry or glad according to whether they wished or did not wish to see me break my neck.

The Ballet Is Dead—Long Live the Ballet

When Diaghilev died in 1929 the company which he had held together by the sheer power of his personal magnetism split apart at once into a dozen atomic units. It was inconceivable that

186

there should be no more ballet, and so these units attempted at various times to organize repertoires and present seasons in Paris and London. One of these was the short-lived Balanchine Ballets 1933, with Tilly Losch as its luminary. A second, and far more enduring one was headed by Alicia Markova and Anton Dolin in England. A third was the Ballet Russe de Monte Carlo.

The original Monte Carlo company came by its name because it had the support of the Prince and Princess of Monaco, in return for which the company contracted to spend a season each year at Monte Carlo.

The directors were a curiously matched pair. There was the gentle French intellectual René Blum, whose brother Léon was leader in the Socialist bloc but not yet Premier of France. And there was Colonel Wasily de Basil, the Russian officer, tall, gaunt, cadaverous, whose right forearm was bigger around than a two-by-four and at least as hard from swinging the heavy saber on horseback.

Blum came by his interest in art, music and ballet by right of being a Parisian, an intellectual, a man of taste. Basil, finding himself an émigré in Paris after a life of soldiering, had managed a Russian Opera Company, a concert agency. The Frenchman and the Russian had their devotion to ballet in common.

Blum had taken the first step toward founding the company when he took over Diaghilev's contract in Monte Carlo. He provided dancers for the opera season, and called upon George Balanchine, already a distinguished choreographer with Diaghilev, to stage a sufficient repertoire for the season of ballet which the contract called for in the spring. Balanchine brought him two beautiful ballets, and two beautiful baby ballerinas, Tamara Toumanova and Irina Baronova, fresh out of ballet schools in Paris; he also re-staged some of the classics.

Basil then joined forces with Blum and there was a season that summer of 1932 at the Théâtre des Champs Elysées in Paris, where

187

I saw them and signed a contract to bring them to the United States. Still struggling for a foothold, Basil took the young company on tour in buses and trucks to the Netherlands, to the Scandinavian countries. Balanchine left to form his own company, taking Toumanova with him.

Meanwhile Leonide Massine had come to Paris. This protégé of Diaghilev, discovered when he was studying acting in Moscow and groomed by the great man as Nijinsky's successor, had left Diaghilev and gone to America, where the unforgettable Roxy offered him security for fifty-two weeks of the year and a free hand to stage his ballets and dance in them. Now Massine wanted to organize his own ballet company. With Ray Goetz he bought up the entire Diaghilev repertoire, dating back to 1910. He caught up with Basil on tour, and they pooled their resources.

There was another Monte Carlo season, a season at the Chatelet in Paris, and then a London season at the Alhambra, which was extended from four weeks to twelve. By this time Leon Woizikovsky had joined the company, a Pole and a veteran of both the Diaghilev and Pavlova companies. Tatiana Riabouchinska, another baby ballerina, had been snatched out of Balieff's *Chauve-Souris*. David Lichine, an athletic youngster who had served his apprenticeship with Pavlova, was with them. Toumanova had returned from Balanchine's *Ballets 1933*. In London they found Alexandra Danilova, young Diaghilev ballerina, who had been dancing in popular revues.

The company, composed so largely of youngsters, was given stability by Diaghilev's solemn six-foot *regisseur*, Sergei Leoniditch Grigoriev, whose stern discipline stemmed from the old school of St. Petersburg, and whose memory for every step in a ballet was more reliable even than that of the choreographer who had composed it.

Grigoriev brought with him his wife, Lubov Tchernicheva, the famous Cleopatra, Miller's wife (in *Three-Cornered Hat*) and Zobéide (in *Schéhérazade*) of Diaghilev days, and his son, young Grigoriev, whose wife Tamara was a soloist in the company and an extraordinarily beautiful girl.

The company had in Diaghilev's repertoire the classics of Russian ballet: *Prince Igor, Petrouchka, Schéhérazade* with the original settings and costumes, Bakst's stunning colors now somewhat faded but still, to an old-fashioned balletomane like myself, eternally beautiful. There were ballets from Diaghilev's later Parisian period too, very French, very modern, like *Jeux d'Enfants* with Joan Miró's decor, and the chic *Beach* of Raoul Dufy in which young Lichine as the Swimmer in sun-tan body makeup dove head-first from the stage into the wings and drew gasps from all the lady spectators. And many, many more.

Then there were the two Balanchine ballets, *La Concurrence* with Dérain's decor and a French provincial wit, and the lovely dream-like *Cotillon*. There were Massine's superb *Three-Cornered Hat, Boutique Fantasque* and *Les Matelots* from Diaghilev days, his *Scuola di Ballo, Les Femmes de Bonne Humeur, Snegouroutchka, Cimarosiana*. And Massine had outdone himself at opposite ends of his choreographic range with the Tchaikowsky *Les Présages*, the first of his symphonic ballets, and the effervescent *Beau Danube*.

Altogether an exciting repertoire, an exciting company. The one uncertain element was the American public, but that was uncertain as the very devil.

How to Launch a Ballet

Staggering difficulties in the sheer transportation of the company from the farther shore of the Atlantic to the hither one threatened to smother the project at the very start. The inventory of scenery and costumes alone, necessary for the posting of the bond with the customs in New York, was a major operation. We had passports of every description to clear through our immigration, including both the Nansen (held by the Russian émigrés) and the Soviet varieties.

And besides the precious dancers, each of whom presented an individual immigration problem, we had to open the reluctant portals of America to eleven Mamas, four Papas, three cats and two monkeys!

Cables flew back and forth from London that summer with the staccato frequency of notations on a stock ticker. Finally one morning I threw up my hands and turned to Mae Frohman. Diplomat, efficiency expert, trouble shooter without peer, she packed a bag on the spot and sailed, as I recall, the same night. She traveled from London to the English provinces with the company, hurdled language obstacles, soothed temperament, untangled passports, counted by hand every costume and every prop.

Here, meanwhile, we were wooing the American public, which had not seen ballet since Pavlova's departure in 1926.

Earlier still, there had been two successive seasons of Serge Diaghilev's Ballets Russes in this country, fathered by Otto H. Kahn and the Metropolitan Opera Association. In 1915-16 they came to the Century Theatre first, later to the Metropolitan Opera House. The incredible Diaghilev himself made the journey that year, but not his great protégé Nijinsky. The fatal quarrel between them, stemming from Nijinsky's marriage to the ardent Hungarian girl Romola, was already far advanced. But Adolph Bolm came, an able and all-around dancer, ballet-master and choreographer, and an executive as well. He carried virtually the whole burden of the tour, so well that Kahn later invited him to the Metropolitan, where he revived *Coq d'Or* and *Petrouchka*.

Massine came, a youth with enormous solemn eyes in a spiritual face, and made his debut as a choreographer in *The Legend of Joseph*. And the vivacious Lydia Lopokova came, with whom Heywood Broun fell head over heels in love, and who is today the unaffectedly gracious wife of the British economist Lord Maynard Keynes.

The following year Nijinsky was persuaded to come, while Diaghilev stayed behind. They played at the Metropolitan and toured the principal cities to California, Stravinsky and Bakst going ahead as envoys extraordinary of the company in its lordly progress.

The Diaghilev productions, brought over complete from Paris, were a revelation to the Americans who saw them. Such lavishness, such collaborations of great composers, great painters, great dancers had not been seen in this country. America was dazzled, a dazzlement which cost $25 an orchestra seat. And when it was over, Mr. Kahn paid a bill of nearly a half million dollars for America's balletic education.

In 1933 we inherited this glamorous tradition (though not, I hoped, its costliness) and the danger of invidious comparison as well. We were to discover how many New Yorkers and Chicagoans remembered Nijinsky. At $25 a head they should have been more than enough to pay Mr. Kahn's bill. The Diaghilev fans and the Pavlova fans were, however, our ready-made audience.

There were also the artists, the musicians and the art and music lovers. The names of the French moderns who had designed decors and composed music for the ballets would attract them, whether to admire or to sneer.

In September the office suddenly bloomed with old Diaghilev programs, with photographs of Nijinsky in *Spectre de la Rose*, with color reproductions of Bakst and Benois decors. All the Nijinsky legends were exhumed and revived. The anticipated ballet season was given a lavish Diaghilev setting.

Through no fault of ours, two books had been published and a Constitutional amendment repealed for our benefit. The repeal of Prohibition was a happy augury for us. Champagne and the Ballet, the perfect mates, were returning to America together. Out of our press office flowed reams of stories welcoming back the glittering gilded days. The fact that the country was still in the pit of the Depression was no deterrent to a press agent's imagination.

Tamara Karsavina's book, *Theatre Street*, and Romola Nijinsky's memoirs of her husband were our additional good fortune. *Nijinsky* attained a good circulation, and some of its revelations were sensational. *Theatre Street* became at once the Bible and the encyclopedia of the press department, which distilled out of it the essence of ballet in old St. Petersburg and spread an aura of nostalgia for ballet thickly over New York.

It troubled the press department not at all that the ballerinas of the new company had never seen Theatre Street (except for Danilova, who had, but only after the Revolution). They promptly seized upon the fact that the prima ballerinas who were mentioned in the book, Kshessinskaya, Egorova, Trefilova and Preobrajenska, had moved to Paris with the Revolution and established schools which carried on the traditions of the Imperial Ballet, and that it was these schools, chiefly Preobrajenska's, which had produced our "baby ballerinas."

The "baby ballerinas" proved to be sensational copy, long before they posed in their worn little-girl clothes for the ship-news photographers at Quarantine, their faces innocent of makeup, and not a crossed knee in the lot of them, although there were plenty of pretty knees among them to cross.

As I think back on it, that campaign to make America ballet-conscious was something of a sensation itself. We got up a Sponsors' Committee headed by the Grand Duchess Marie, with Mrs. Otto H. Kahn prominently featured and all the titles in the Russian and French set in New York. Prince Serge Obolensky was a constant help, and the Sponsors' Committee broke the newspaper society columns every time we looked around.

As New York goes, so go the capital cities. Boston, Chicago,

San Francisco fell in line and began printing copy on the elegant world, the champagne-in-a-slipper world that was coming back with the Ballet.

San Francisco is an amazing city. There never was a time when San Francisco did not follow closely in the footsteps of New York in the recognition of any of our artists, however novel or exotic. A city of three-quarters of a million population, in a class with Pittsburgh rather than New York or Chicago, it nevertheless supports its own opera, symphony and art museum, and offers eager welcome to the theatre, the ballet, and all visiting artists. It is the only city in the United States whose citizens allow themselves to be taxed to defray part of the orchestra's annual expenses. Its War Memorial Opera House is one of the most beautiful opera houses in the world. It has its Museum of Modern Art modeled after that in New York. It has its Art Commission, a municipal board, to watch over this rich municipal art life.

As New York went, so went the others. We had signed for the St. James Theatre on 44th Street, and prepared a tour. At last the day came and we went down the Bay to meet our ballet company.

Bread, Salt and Billing

I have a tender affection for the memory of that meeting on shipboard on a chilly morning in December, 1933. Toumanova with her incomparable Mamushka, young Eglevsky with his Mama, Baronova's well-scrubbed face between both Mama and Papa, Tanya Riabouchinska also with her Mama and looking underfed and gamine, David Lichine not very well shaven and with the hungry grin of an *apache*, gray-eyed Nina Verchinina, exuberant Genia Delarova, tall and willowy Lubov Rostova—there they stood, in their shabby and not very warm winter coats, their cheap Paris stockings and snub-nosed French shoes, their hair pulled tight under berets, kerchiefs or any kind of hat. Only Tchernicheva and Danilova looked worldly, chic. Perhaps I should say that only these two looked like ballerinas.

The very next year they all wore fur coats, bought with their American earnings, and nice silk stockings and high-heeled shoes, and they had their faces made up for the newspaper cameras they had learned to expect at every stopping place in America.

But that first time they were little girls still, full of the unlimited "ice creams" of the voyage; they had never heard of cheesecake photography or the Hollywood meaning of the word glamour. I must say they learned quickly. Before many weeks had passed they were puzzling soda-fountain clerks by asking, like David Lichine, for "Coca-Cola-vidoutice."

For the newspaper men, and to satisfy my own undying homesickness for Russia, we had a tray of bread wrapped in a white napkin and a little dish of salt, and on the pier I presented Colonel de Basil with the bread and salt of a Russian welcome. He smiled happily, and in the very next breath declared that he would like to see the theatre.

We left the company manager, long-suffering David Libidins, to shepherd the flock to various inexpensive hotels in the theatre district, and taxied uptown to the St. James.

The Colonel looked around and then reached in his pocket and took out a sheaf of papers.

"Pour le programme," he said. It was his complete biography.

Here was an impasse. How explain to him that the New York Theatre Program accepts only such copy, beyond the program itself, as it has space for, that only the briefest biographies of the actual performers find their way into those exclusive pages, that to get his life story printed in the program was an utter impossibility, supposing it was even desirable to do so? I tried in Russian, my press agent tried in French, we both tried in English. The Colonel was a man of granite. My press agent took the sheaf of papers and stuck it in his pocket, muttering.

The next encounter was the press agent's. As he left the theatre, a small wiry man leaped at him with poised fist. It was Woizikovsky, in a roaring Polish rage. He had seen Lichine's picture, full length, on the front of the theatre. Where was his? Only a little head, crowded among the other heads in a frame. What was the meaning of this?

The P.A. did his best to explain that no slight was intended, that he had been sent from Paris a very fine picture of Lichine, full length, but none so fine of Woizikovsky. Woizikovsky gave him a deadline: if his picture, exactly the same size as Lichine's to the last centimeter, was not up in front of the theatre by such and such a time, he would not dance.

Some time later, at a rehearsal, Lichine in his turn drew me aside and began to whisper mysteriously. I was sure the secret concerned his picture, the size of his billing, but I was wrong.

David had an invention. He had invented a flying machine.

David cannot complain that he wasn't listened to. I listened to him, and the publicity department listened to him, and at last we sent him up to New York University's School of Aeronautics to see if he could get an expert opinion on the value of his invention. The hitch came when David asked the professors to finance the building of a model. The flying machine is still, so far as I know, only a gleam in its papa's eye.

Champagne Out of a Slipper

We opened on December 21st. The program was La Concurrence, Les Présages and Beau Danube. I shall never forget Toumanova flitting about alone on the little French street of Dérain's set, or Woizikovsky's itching, wriggling shuffle as the Tramp. I shall never forget Baronova and Lichine walking downstage together in the slow movement of the Tchaikowsky symphony. I shall never forget the fiery high-spirited Mazurka as Massine and

195

Riabouchinska danced it in *Beau Danube*, or Massine and Danilova in the romantic Blue Danube waltz.

The audience liked it too. When the corps de ballet appeared in ballet skirts, there were audible sighs, even sobs in the house. As for the critics, they did very well by us next day. Conservative John Martin expressed some reservations in the *Times*, but on the whole the reception was fine.

I gave an opening night party at the Savoy-Plaza. Our Sponsors' Committee turned out for it, and Otto H. Kahn and Paul Cravath inaugurated the new era of sparkle and elegance by sipping champagne out of a slipper especially fashioned for the occasion by one of New York's finest bootmakers.

Our baby ballerinas looked as though they should have been put to bed in the nursery instead of staying out late drinking champagne. (Actually they had not yet learned to drink it—they ordered milk!) New York made pets of them on the spot.

Then began a feast for feature writers. Every backstage detail became picturesque, glamorous, important. How a ballerina put on her slippers, her *tutu*, what she ate for breakfast, her opinion of the American hotdog—the newspaper and magazine writers went away filled to overflowing with the delectable little items. They were especially impressed with the fact that there was a class on the stage every morning, because no ballerina, not even Markova, omits her class.

Every night backstage we stumbled over photographers unaware of booms being lowered onto their heads while they studied an angle; artists with their sketchbooks cluttered the wings so that the dancers could hardly get on and off the stage. The newspapers and magazines had a field day.

Toumanova, with her camellia face already breathtakingly beautiful, was photographed and photographed, until the whole company began to whisper about how Mr. Hurok was in love with Tamara. The story of her birth became a matter of national im-

Artur Rubinstein

Uday Shan-Kar

Alicia Markova

(Gjon Mili)

Alicia Markova and Anton Dolin

Queue for tickets for the Ballet in London

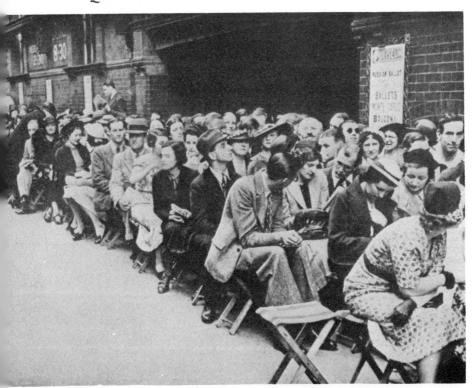

Irina Baronova and Anton Dolin in *Bluebeard*

Tamara Toumanova and S. Hurok

(Constantine Photo)

Luncheon for ballerinas (left to right: Janet Reed, Nana Gollner, S. Hurok, Nora Kaye, J. Alden Talbot, Alicia Markova)

René Blum greets Leonide Massine in make-up for *Gaité Parisienne*

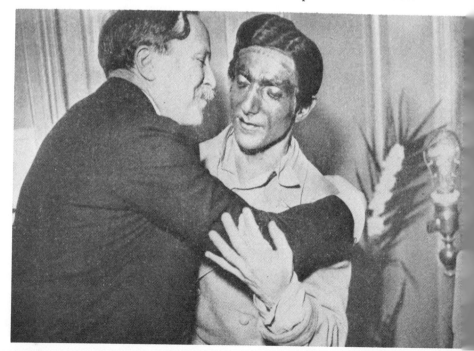

Georges Auric, Mme. Etienne de Beaumont and Salvador Dali

S. Hurok in *Petrouchka*

Leonard Bernstein and Jerome Robbins discuss their Ballet *Fancy Free* with S. Hurok

Ballet rehearsal: Janet Reed and John Kriza

Mr. and Mrs. Hurok

(Cosmo

Katherine Dunham and S. Hurok
dance the Conga

Jan and Alice Peerce

Jarmila Novotna

Patrice Munsel affixes her signature to her $120,000 contract with S. Hurok

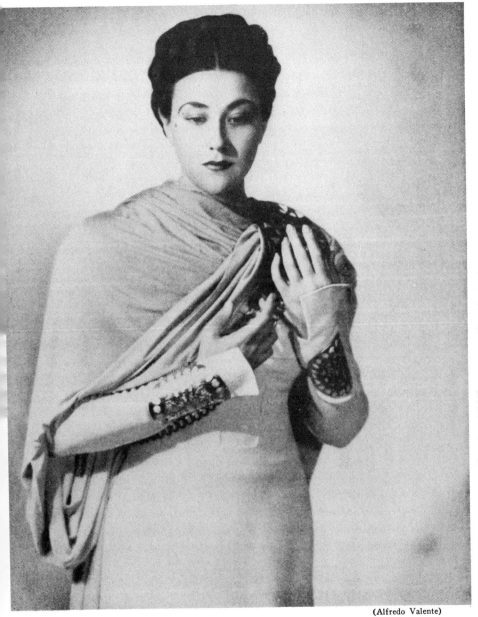

(Alfredo Valente)

Blanche Thebom

Isaac Stern

portance. So many clippings came in headlined "Born in a Box Car" that it presently became a distinction for a ballerina to have been born in any of the more usual settings.

With all this gratifying attention, I was merrily losing money at the box office. The St. James, indeed any house in New York, except the Metropolitan, is not for ballet. Aside from its narrow, shallow stage which had the corps de ballet bumping the scenery or each other at every step, the house could not make a profit for me even if we played to capacity at every performance. There were just not enough seats.

Ballet expenses are always high. Furthermore, we had put on a promotion campaign whose cost was out of all proportion to any possible income during the first two seasons.

So it was no surprise to me that I was not making money at the St. James. We had a tour, we would play in opera houses out of town, and prospects were good.

And then I ran head-on into a stop clause.

The Stop Clause That Would Not Stop

The stop clause is one of the neater Broadway inventions for torturing managers. There are several ways to engage a theatre on Broadway. One is to take the "four walls," that is to pay a rental for the theatre and manage the whole matter oneself. Another, the more usual way, is a sharing arrangement in which the theatre management divides with the producer both the income at the box office and the expenses, according to an agreed sharing percentage.

In this arrangement there is a clause which provides that if the box-office receipts fall below a certain figure for two successive weeks, the show must move, either to another theatre or to the warehouse, unless the producer makes up the difference. Conversely, if the box office is above, the show stays.

197

Bringing the Ballet to New York was attended by so many uncertainties that when we came to consider the stop clause in the theatre contract, we had no way of making a decision. There are not many large theatres on Broadway, and even in 1933, a depression year, we had trouble getting one for the ballet. We decided to accept the theatre's terms and worry about the stop clause when the time came.

Now the time had come. We were ready to embark on our tour. And there was the stop clause.

We were definitely not playing to capacity. But neither were we playing below the stop clause. We saw, too late, that the stop clause was too low, and the theatre management was determined to keep us in the theatre, as was their right. Until the box office fell below the clause, we were not going to be released.

Ballet Divided by Two

There was only one thing to do, and we did it. We divided the company in two, sent one troupe on the road and kept the other playing in New York.

Our first out-of-town date was in Reading, Pennsylvania, on January 29th. We sent Massine, Toumanova, Danilova, the larger part of the corps de ballet, and all the repertoire except three ballets.

At the St. James we kept Baronova, Riabouchinska, Lichine and Woizikovsky, augmented the corps de ballet with some local dancers and we gave the same three ballets for every performance. Night after night and two matinees weekly they danced *Les Sylphides*, *Petrouchka* and *Prince Igor*. New York liked it well enough, so that we stayed several weeks more until we fell below the stop clause, and the company was joined again in Chicago for a very successful season at the old Auditorium Theatre.

The road, too, was satisfied, and there I did not lose money.

198

That half company was better than a good many full companies I have seen, both here and abroad. Toumanova, Danilova and Massine carried ballet to America that season, and they did it superbly. They were welcomed everywhere by eager near-capacity audiences, and they gave a show.

On March 9th they came back to New York and we played the full company for the rest of that month. In April the entire company went to Chicago for a second season except for Grigoriev and a troupe which went to fulfill the Colonel's contract with Blum in Monte Carlo. Wonderful Chicago! Long before New York became a ballet town, Chicago was running London a close second in its devotion to ballet.

Ballet at the Met

In due time the company embarked for Europe to play in Paris and at Covent Garden in London. New productions and revivals of old ones were meanwhile made ready, and back they came again the following fall.

We still had no proper home for the Ballet in New York. I took them directly to Mexico City, to open the new Palacio des Bellas Artes. Again I sent Mae Frohman to straighten out a dozen problems. From Mexico I brought them by boat to New York, unloaded and loaded them again on trains and shipped them to Toronto, first stop on a coast-to-coast tour. In New York we took the Majestic Theatre for a limited engagement—five performances—and did not sell out. The Majestic, like the St. James, is a big house for Broadway, but we still suffered from a cramped stage, and a lack of illusion because the audience was too close. And we still could not make money at the box office.

It was not until the third season, the fall of 1935, that we brought the Ballet into the Metropolitan Opera House. Now for the first time New York really saw the Ballet. This was a house of the proper size to create illusion. The stage was a dream of spaciousness, big enough and wide enough and high enough to give a ballet company room to breathe.

And there is the atmosphere of the glamorous old house itself, the faded gilt and red plush, the monumental chandelier, the diamond horseshoe of boxes with their little three-leaved clovers of lights dimming long after the house lights have gone out. There are the big lobbies and the foyers. And there is Sherry's, where a proper Continental custom can be observed with a drink in the entr'acte.

And there was the incidentally pleasant fact that with a capacity of 3,300 seats and standing room, I no longer needed to pay for the New York season, and pay and pay.

With the Ballet at the Met, we went to town. New York embraced us at last, and the road, which had been doing nicely enough by us until now, went overboard. This was the first of the Ballet's brilliant tours.

My associations with the Metropolitan have always been happy. I loved the house when as a boy I stood two hours in line for the privilege of standing another five hours through Parsifal.

Since the Ballet has become a semi-annual visitor to the Met, my association with the management has become closer than ever, and I cherish that great old house as I cherish my home.

Fifty-Dollar Scream

That spring we cut loose with a publicity campaign on the theme that the Ballet had become a solvent institution, in a class with the Ziegfeld Follies or the Circus. We announced that the coast-to-coast season had grossed one million dollars.

That million was a touch of wishful thinking; it was not yet true. But it was true the next season.

We introduced the famous Nijinsky ballet, Afternoon of a

200

Faun, during the spring season at the Metropolitan. There was a nice bit of scandal surrounding the ballet. At its first performance in New York, at the Metropolitan, in fact, by the Diaghilev company the police had intervened and carried the Faun off to jail for an improper display. Romola Nijinsky, in her book, had given the ballet a sort of aura of sinfulness.

All this was recalled in the newspapers when the premiere was announced. The ballet went off in due course, David Lichine made an attractive Faun, and as the curtain came down on the Faun caressing the Nymph's scarf, a woman in the audience screamed.

The attachés at the Metropolitan are still talking about that scream. Certainly until now nobody but the woman herself has known that we hired her for the sum of $50.

By the fourth season, the season that the million-dollar gross came true, things were not running smoothly within the Ballet Russe de Monte Carlo. Massine was not getting on with Basil.

For my part, I had not got on with him too well either, and I was inclined to sympathize with Massine when he brought Julius Fleischmann on the scene.

Fleischmann was a cultured and sensitive millionaire who lived on his beautiful estate outside Cincinnati while Standard Brands went on earning money for him out of Fleischmann's yeast, Chase and Sanborn coffee, Black and White whisky, and other useful commodities. This accommodating business required no attention from him. For him an interest in the Ballet had the promise of a fascinating new world.

With Fleischmann as his first backer, Massine soon found himself financed by a group of American millionaires which included a Ford (Edsel), a McCormick, and some other highly solvent names. The group incorporated as Universal Art, placed the able organizer and manager Serge Denham in the executive position, and gave Massine as its artistic director a free hand in the choosing of his company and repertoire.

201

He engaged Alicia Markova, the fragile-looking English girl who was adored by her own countrymen, but scarcely heard of— be it said to our shame—in America. Nini Theilade was one of his discoveries, Frederic Franklin another. From Paris he planned to bring Serge Lifar, who had been more or less Massine's successor in the Diaghilev company, and who was, since Diaghilev's death, the *premier danseur* of the Paris Opera.

Some of Basil's own dancers were ready to leave him. Danilova was one. Another was Toumanova. By this time Toumanova and Baronova were no longer fourteen, and the competition between them as the glamour girls of the company had become steadily sharper.

Before the new company had been organized the attorney Halsey Malone had come to Boston to ask me to take it under my management when my contract with Basil was ended. There was a promise of ample funds for new productions. I was interested, provided the new company could buy from René Blum the name "Monte Carlo" and the basic repertoire.

I liked the shape of the new company. What I did not like at all was the prospect of two ballet companies cutting each other's throat. Why, I pleaded, can't you all just work together in one big ballet company, the biggest, the most wonderful the world has ever seen?

The Hamburger Merger

The reasons why were obvious, even to such an incurable optimist as myself. There were difficult financial problems, even more difficult clashes of personality. But I worked at it.

No one was more surprised than I when it began to look as though we were getting somewhere. Finally we reached the stage where the opposing attorneys of the two ballet organizations were drawing up an initial agreement. This had to be gone over clause by clause by both parties—and myself as manager of the One Big Ballet to be born.

We met for the final conference in the office of Washburn, Malone and Perkins, attorneys for Universal Art, Inc., at 36 West 44th Street.

At nine that night we were still there. Collars were wilting, tempers raveling and deadlocks sprang up gremlin-like out of every clause. Serge Obolensky labored to translate the legal phraseology to Basil, with an occasional assist from me.

Suddenly someone slapped the table and stood up. "What this conference needs is some food!" he shouted. I wish I could recall which of us had retained that much sense. I am usually the one in any group to remember the soothing value of food in a crisis. Whoever it was, Prince Obolensky and my attorney Elias Lieberman slapped hats on their heads and departed in search of nourishment.

They came back with an armful of brown paper bags containing hamburgers on rolls and pickles. Business stopped dead while we greedily unwrapped our hamburgers.

We had scarcely got our teeth into them when the last elevator man in the building knocked at the door. He was going off, he said. The building was about to be locked up for the night.

Obolensky took to the telephone and called up the Hotel St. Regis, of which he was an executive. Meanwhile, we all wrapped our hamburgers and pickles again, and went out and down to the street. The St. Regis doorman opened the doors of our taxis a few minutes later and looked frightened as we filed out, up the steps and through the lobby, each carrying a little greasy paper bag in his hand.

Obolensky led us to the conference room he had commandeered, and ordered coffee. We unwrapped our hamburgers for the second time and washed them down with coffee out of the St. Regis's handsome silver service. The conference continued.

To say that it went smoothly from then on would be a patent exaggeration. There were still stumbling blocks, not so much on the financial as on the personal side. The principal problem was the question of who was to have what authority.

At about four in the morning a verbal agreement was reached on most of the important points.

I walked out of the St. Regis feeling that I had the finest ballet company under my wing that had ever existed, finer even than Diaghilev, with his gift for retaining the best of everything and devil take the expense, had ever achieved. Basil departed, following his company to Berlin. From the boat, and from Europe, long cables and telephone calls continued, until the Colonel authorized his attorney to sign the agreement.

Filled with happiness, I embarked with Mrs. Hurok on the *Normandie*. The Fleischmanns and Washburn were also aboard. Together we drank to the future of the One Big Ballet.

My plans for launching the company began with a season in London at Covent Garden. I sent my press agent, Gerald Goode, directly to London to prepare for the great, the magnificent event.

Blow-Up in London

The great, magnificent event never took place. The wonderful merged company was the shortest-lived in ballet history. For when I stepped off the boat-train in London, I was met by my press agent and Germaine Sevastianov, Basil's suave and handsome young executive secretary, with the news that the merger was no more. Sevastianov is the same who eloped with Baronova, later was separated from her, and is now in the uniform of Uncle Sam. They have since married again.

In Berlin the Colonel had had time to think things over. In Monte Carlo, meanwhile, Massine, organizing the new company, had been informed that he must prepare to let some of his new

204

people go and join forces again with Basil. Confusion crept in, and resentments.

On the third or fourth day of our happy voyage aboard the *Normandie* I had received a hint that stormy weather was ahead for us. Fleischmann showed me a cable which hinted trouble. By the time I reached London the situation was irretrievable. Basil had in fact lost control of his company, which was taken over by Educational Ballets, Ltd. Baron d'Erlanger, who had a large interest in the company, called in Sevastianov and Victor Dandre, Pavlova's husband, to take charge. The Covent Garden season, which was to have been the debut of the merged company, was announced for the original company instead. It was as though Universal Art, and a merger reached in a New York hotel at four in the morning, had been a private hallucination of my own.

But it had not. Because Educational Ballets, Ltd., went just one step further and announced the Massine ballets in their repertoire —and Massine came to life with a bang. He engaged a solicitor and set about enjoining the corporation from giving *Symphonie Fantastique*, *Beau Danube*, *Three-Cornered Hat*, all of Massine's creations up to that time.

In short order the whole matter was in Temple Bar, where, before a white-wigged, impressively robed English judge, and an audience of delighted London ballet-lovers, critics and newspaper men, opposing solicitors also in white wigs and handsome robes courteously insulted each other in the curiously apologetic manner of an English court room, while they performed an autopsy on the dead body of my dream ballet company.

The case was not for damages or money of any kind. It was rather what we would call a hearing, a request for a declaratory judgment, to determine Massine's rights over the ballets of his creation.

English law on this matter, or indeed on any matter, is too complicated to go into here. The nub seemed to be whether

205

choreography is capable of being copyrighted, whether owner-ship rights can exist in dance design.

London was in a state of hysterical excitement over the pro-ceedings. The greatest ballet town outside of Russia had a field day. Not only did spectators jam the court room but the twenty-odd London newspapers carried full stories every day. The after-noon papers printed the proceedings of that day, and the morning papers summarized them the following morning. Any amusing exchange between opposing attorneys promptly made the front page. As each ballet came under discussion in court the papers took it up and ran elaborate critical and descriptive analyses of it—which was scarcely necessary, for the London public knew ballet by heart. Massine's ballets in particular are adored there, and Massine himself has great prestige in the English capital.

But the hearing which Massine had originated ended by throw-ing him for an almost complete loss. The court decided that owner-ship rights in choreography did in fact exist, that Colonel de Basil by dint of having presented the ballets had the right to continue presenting them, and Massine could not prevent him from so doing. He could re-stage for himself or any company only three of his many ballets: *Three-Cornered Hat, Boutique Fantasque* and *Beau Danube.* As to the others, he could re-stage them only after five years.

Two Ballets and a Police Station

So my dream of a ballet super-company had blown up in my face. My original contract with Universal Art was now in force.

I had stipulated from the beginning that the new company had to have the trademark "Monte Carlo" which at that time was still synonymous with ballet to the American public.

This was more easily arranged than seemed possible. Some time previously, in 1936, Basil had broken with René Blum; my successful American tours left him no time to fulfill the obligation to Monte Carlo.

Blum organized his own Ballets de Monte Carlo, with Fokine as his choreographer. He had a season in London at the Coliseum and traveled to South Africa.

Universal Art bought for Massine not only the right to use the two magic words, *Monte Carlo*, but also all of Blum's productions, including Fokine's *Don Juan* and *L'Epreuve d'Amour*, and the classic repertoire which is the nucleus of any ballet company.

So long as it bore the name, the new Monte Carlo Ballet Russe was thenceforth obligated to give a ballet season every spring in Monte Carlo, with four new ballets presented each season. This arrangement, with the use of the excellent rehearsal rooms, carpentry shop, and tryout facilities in that jewel-like Riviera city, had been one of the assets of the Diaghilev company, of the Blum and Basil companies. Now a new Monte Carlo ballet company has been organized since the war, availing itself of the patronage of the Prince of Monaco in the same way as had the others, and I hear very good reports of it.

That was the end of Blum's various Monte Carlo ballet companies although he continued until the war to hold his contract with the Prince of Monaco. I saw him in New York in 1939, when he came here in connection with the New York World's Fair. He went back to Paris, and when we last heard of him alive, this sensitive and cultured Frenchman was cleaning toilets in a Paris theatre, another victim of the Nazi sense of humor. He died in one of the murder camps in Poland.

There was still the London season to be managed. Covent Garden, historic home of opera and ballet, was lost to us. But there was the Drury Lane Theatre, equally historic, beautiful, enormous, and with two bars; Covent Garden has three. The Drury Lane dates from the Sheridan-Goldsmith period of the

English theatre, and my thoroughly American press agent found himself installed in a beautiful large room in the theatre, seated at a long refectory table in the chair in which Sheridan wrote *The School for Scandal*, waited upon by lackeys in white wigs, red coats, silk hose and shiny pumps with buckles who brought him tea in the morning and afternoon.

Welcoming him with all this eighteenth-century hospitality, England with the other hand denied him the right to work on its soil. I engaged an English publicity man to work under his direction.

We opened at the Drury Lane. Two short blocks away—so short that the genuine London balletomanes could buy tickets for both for the same performance and see the ballets of their choice on each program—the rival company was offering glamorous Baronova, piquant Riabouchinska, Lichine, the classic *premier danseur* Paul Petroff, and Sir Thomas Beecham as guest conductor. They had a new Fokine ballet, *Cinderella*, a tremendous success in London because it was a typical English pageant, although in New York we were never able to offer it except as a matinee ballet. Also London was seeing *Coq d'Or*, one of Fokine's most successful Russian spectacles with the delightful Rimsky-Korsakoff music.

We had a few aces in our hand, though. We had Massine. We had Toumanova. We had Danilova. We had Alicia Markova, the queen of English ballet. We had Serge Lifar, the darling of Paris. We had Efrem Kurtz as our permanent conductor. We had four new Massine ballets: the tenderly pious *St. Francis* with Hindemith's music, the modern expressing with such unexpected perfection a medieval holy man's story; Beethoven's *Seventh Symphony*, an exalted drama of the story of man; the inimitable *Gaité Parisienne* of Offenbach, and *Bogatyri*, a Russian spectacle to Borodin's music.

We revived *Giselle* for Markova, with Lifar as the traitorous lover of the tragic maiden, and *Coppelia* for Danilova.

We had enough beauty, enough talent, and enough in the way of new and interesting productions to be confident that we would hold our own against Covent Garden. We did.

Both houses played to utter capacity at every performance. During the intermissions the audiences of both would mingle on the two short blocks and exchange comments. The newspapers, which had given the London public a steady diet of ballet throughout the court hearing, continued the same with unabated interest. They made a running gag of the fact that the two theatres were separated by the Bow Street Police Station, very handy in case the devotees of the rival companies should come to blows.

At the Savoy I had my customary table in the Grill. This is the rendezvous in London for theatre folk after theatre. It is as though Sardi's and Lindy's merged and moved into the grand ballroom of the Waldorf-Astoria, with a steady flow of champagne to make the talk sparkle. There was scarcely a night when I had fewer than twenty guests coming and going at my table.

Lunch for ballet folk was at Gennaro's in Soho. This good Italian restaurateur—he was interned for a while during the acute stages of the war with Italy—made a custom of presenting every lady who was his guest with a single tea rose. A pitcher of his punch, a spécialité of the house, was on every table. Here the dancers of both companies regularly met, and, far from glaring at each other, fell into each other's arms and exchanged gossip until the air was thick with it as well as with the savory odors of spaghetti marinara and calves' liver Veneziana. Everybody connected with the ballet was too happy about everything to carry any grudges. That was a summer of summers in London.

While I lived in this happy cosmopolitan world, poor Basil hid like a recluse in a tiny house in Shepherd's Lane, a doll house like some of those still squeezed between apartment houses in our own Greenwich Village. He had won in effect a Pyrrhic victory. He had been forced out of the company, which was left under

209

the direction of Gerry Sevastianov and Victor Dandré, Pavlova's husband. I was his guest at dinner one evening in that little house, and I tried once more to bring the two companies together. It was hopeless; they were as far apart as New York and Tokyo. But between the Colonel and me there were no hard feelings.

Bad Boy from Paris

Our *Gaité* and *St. Francis*, complete opposites, were equally tremendous successes. Our ballerinas were worshiped. Lifar was our bad boy.

The handsome, black-browed boy from Kiev whom Diaghilev had made his protégé a decade before had grown into a very spoiled artist. He had appeared in the United States only once, and then probably at his worst, with a small concert ensemble, a batch of thrown-together sets and, if I remember correctly, two pianos in the orchestra pit. The unfortunate auspices of the tour did not help his celebrated temper, and the tour ended unhappily in Chicago.

With us he at first behaved impeccably. He staged *Icare* for us, an interesting if slight modern ballet about Icarus, the first aviator. But with every performance of *Giselle* the strain on his good manners became worse.

It happened regularly the same way. Markova and Toumanova alternated in the role. The London audience loved *Giselle*, and shared its love between the two ballerinas. The shouts of "Brava, brava!" brought curtain call after curtain call. Markova or Toumanova came out to take her bow, and, clutching her hand until he all but broke her fingers, Lifar came out with her.

The London audience soon caught on, and one night continued with increasing insistence to demand Markova, Markova and only Markova. The performance was stalled; the evening was running out. Finally in desperation the stage manager seized Lifar by the elbows and held on. Markova went out for her bow alone, the audience was satisfied, and the performance continued. But Lifar never forgave Markova. The sequel to this story came in New York.

Royalty attended both ballets with gratifying regularity, and according to the custom, no publicity was permitted until after the event. The young Princesses Elizabeth and Margaret Rose came to the matinees.

The stunning *Seventh Symphony* gave us two new male dancers. Frederic Franklin, who came to us from the Markova-Dolin company, had shown to advantage in a light romantic role in *Gaité*. Now he displayed a new power as the spirit of creation in the first movement of Beethoven. Igor Youskevitch in the Olympian scene became a symbol of beautiful flight. His full-length figure in godlike costume with the wings of Mercury on his cap was the trademark of our three-sheets and advertisements in coming seasons.

In time the beautiful ballet summer wore into the dog days of August, when the temperature reaches seventy-two degrees and all London collapses. Covent Garden closed; two weeks later we brought our Drury Lane season to an end. The old company went to Australia, while we embarked for New York and the Metropolitan.

Basil had gone to Paris before the season ended. I had luncheons and breakfasts with him. When Paris was blacked out he came to my hotel and we sat in a black-curtained room until four in the morning, writing contracts for a future season. He drove us to the station—taxicabs were not to be had—and helped us with our bags. Then he left for Australia, where he proceeded to have two very fine seasons indeed, and to become quite a figure in Melbourne and Sydney. Incidentally, he brought back with him two excellent ballets: Lichine's delicious *Graduation Ball* and *Paganini*. Antal Dorati, who had served as Kurtz's assistant conductor in the original Basil ballet, went with him as conductor.

One additional business matter was settled in London. Since

the merger was off, my contract with Universal Art had to be re-negotiated in the face of the new situation. We all met most agreeably at the Carlton Hotel for a series of conferences. The final conference lasted until after the London curfew had closed the bar. A bottle of champagne after hours cost some thirty dollars, and there were a lot of bottles of champagne.

I like to eat and drink, but I don't get drunk. I took one glass of champagne, then a second, and then I called a halt. The re-negotiation went through.

Through the golden haze of Ballet, we were all aware of the bleak night just over the horizon. That was the summer of Munich. Chamberlain was still a hero, and London was full of parading Nazis. The sight of those swaggering supermen struck a chill in our hearts.

Gala Performance

The opening of the new Monte Carlo Ballet Russe, the Massine Monte Carlo, at the Metropolitan in New York was a premiere of premieres. It was London all over again—the glittering audience, the Paris evening gowns and on the stage a performance of ballet to equal the greatest days of ballet history.

But there was a difference from London: with no Covent Garden two blocks away, keeping the company on its best behavior, the rivalries that always burn backstage at the ballet flickered up once or twice, and as usual it was the innocent who were singed.

Before the curtain ever went up, a ballerina's beau marched into Massine's dressing room and demanded to know why his favorite was not dancing on the opening night. Massine had planned carefully for this opening night, which was of the utmost importance to him, which must be perfect in every detail.

The angry visitor aimed his fist and struck. Fortunately he missed Massine's face and struck him in the chest, but it hurt.

Massine put a hand over the spot, murmured mournfully, "That this should happen in the world of art!" and went on making up for the performance. There was no change in the program. Markova triumphed that night in *Giselle* as she had in London. For the exquisite English girl it was not only a triumph. It was also a vindication. She had made her great name only in her own country, and her countrymen might have been forgiven if their appreciation of her gifts had been a little inflated by pride in a native ballerina.

For New Yorkers there was no such patriotic association. On the stage of the Metropolitan that night she stood strictly on her own merits. She met the ordeal, and New York lay beside London at her feet.

Exit Lifar, Storming

The next evening Markova found in her dressing room an anonymous note saying, in effect, "Do not dare to dance *Giselle* tonight or else—" Considering the fistic episode of the night before, and the accident which came later, the origin of the note remains a mystery to this day. Alicia tossed it aside and put on her makeup for the first act of *Giselle*.

The first act went off smoothly as far as anyone could see. But as the curtain came down on the death of Giselle, Alicia had to be helped to her feet. She was white under her makeup. Somewhere in the *pas de deux* with Lifar she had hurt her foot, and badly. She had danced the mad scene, one of the great emotional scenes in ballet, and had carried on to the curtain. But she could not stand, much less dance the uncompromising virtuosity of the second act. Slavenska was frantically hooked into her costume and the ballet continued to the curtain. There were no curtain calls.

The doctor who was hastily called carried Alicia off at once for an X-ray of her foot. The injury was not serious, except that it

213

would keep her out for three weeks, the entire New York season. This was a heartbreaking accident for a ballerina who had made a personal triumph on opening night.

No one accused Lifar of dropping her. But there were some who suggested that a partner has many opportunities to set a ballerina down hard, on her pointed toe. From the audience, even from the stage, none would notice.

Lifar was apparently determined on his own destruction. His next complaint, once Markova was out of the way, was against a variation in *Swan Lake*. In the version we were offering, the Prince's Friend dances a solo which is far and away more brilliant than anything the choreographer designed for the Prince himself. The American dancer Roland Guerard did it superbly and won an ovation for his performance. This the Prince, in the person of Lifar, could not abide.

He demanded that the variation be eliminated. Massine declined. Lifar challenged Massine to a duel. Massine again declined, pointing out that he had enough to do putting on a ballet and had no time for pistols in the sheep meadow in Central Park at dawn or any other hour.

I met Lifar storming out of Massine's dressing room in that backstage corridor of the Metropolitan where the life of the ballet seems to hit its most volcanic temperatures.

"My boy, you can do one of two things," I told him. "You can go home and take an aspirin—or you can take the next boat back to Paris. The *Champlain* is sailing on Saturday."

The next day the newspapers had a lovely time, tossing the duel around. They kept it in the air until Saturday, when they interviewed Lifar for the last time. The scene was aboard the *Champlain*.

"My honor," he told the reporters obscurely, "has been satisfied."

And that was the last we saw of Serge Lifar, brilliant dancer and bad actor. Reliable sources inform me that he enjoyed the poison fruits of friendship with the Nazis. I am told that he was Hitler's personal guide on a tour of the Paris Opéra, that he danced at the Opéra during the occupation, was flown to Berlin to dance, and even to Kiev, to entertain the Nazi butchers after a busy day of burning and massacring the people of his native city. When last heard of, he was exiled from France, sunning himself in Monte Carlo and asking the Soviet Government to let him come home.

Near-Corpses de Ballet

Violence in the Ballet can be no surprise to the public which has come to expect a certain amount of backstage uproar from a company of volatile artists from all parts of the world.

In a sense the people of the United States have been cheated of the fun. There has been a good deal more violence in the Ballet than ever reached the newspapers, and I myself have been guilty of keeping some of the juiciest items from them. The recent mystery novel, *Corpse de Ballet*, is several shades more plausible than most fiction of its kind. There have been several near-corpses de Ballet, though so far no actual fatalities.

One night in Chicago, in the second season of Ballet, I was awakened out of a deep and dreamless sleep in the Auditorium Hotel by a wildly hysterical hotel manager.

A man had been found lying in the hotel corridor, bleeding his life away through a knife wound in his back. The man was the handsome Dane, Paul Petroff.

Paul, who is now Nana Gollner's husband, seems too gentle a fellow to have become involved with a knife. Who stabbed him, and why, must remain his secret, but as a bachelor, he was no more immune to romantic intrigue than any other good-looking young man in a ballet company would be. The fact that he was also successful is proved by his rival's resort to the knife. When Paul emerged from the hospital some weeks later, he found that his prestige with the company had risen perceptibly.

But on that night we were not thinking of Paul's prestige. We got a doctor who tied him up and carried him off to the hospital. And then began the real work of the night.

I wanted no scandal, no investigation, no police probing for Paul's assailant. The Ballet was too new in America to stand up under such a sensation. If the news leaked out it might mean the end of the tour, perhaps the end of Ballet for years to come.

After the ambulance had left, I went back to my suite and sat down at the piano. I sat there, picking out "Liebestraum" with one finger, calling "Come in" as one visitor after another knocked at my door. It was only after the long night was over that I realized I had been sitting there in my pajamas, with a black overcoat on, and my top hat on my head, through all the conversations which followed.

I talked to a number of people that night, and all my conversations were more or less expensive. I have never reckoned the cost of Paul's little intrigue to me, but it must have been considerable.

How well I succeeded is borne out by the record. Not one word of the story appeared in any newspaper until some ten days later, when the New York Daily Mirror carried a story about a stick long. It said that a dancer was in a Chicago hospital as a result of a quarrel. No names, no places, no dates. I felt fine.

Jealousies run high in the Ballet. The peak of a dancer's life is so brief that she must fight to get there as soon as she can and stay there as long as she can. Every potential rival holds a knife at her throat. Choreographers also have their pangs of jealousy, and managers too.

Toumanova complained that during the last season she spent under Basil's wing, when it was known that she was leaving with Massine, people were constantly trying to trip her. She vowed, on the box car in which she was born, that one night a hand came out under the canvas backdrop and caught her ankle, to make her fall as she was about to step forward. She managed, she said, to disentangle herself just in time.

Broken hearts cause ructions in the Ballet every day. One would think American girls are too smart to cut their wrists, or take overdoses of sleeping potions, or jump out of hotel windows because of a man. But they run away to get married, and they run away to get divorced. The only difference is that they run away by plane instead of train. Ballerinas have done all these things in the decade-plus-one of my life with the Ballet. I am glad to report that all recovered nicely, without so much as a scar on their hearts.

The First Raid

There was in the company that year an obscure but very pretty soloist, dancing such roles as one of Florestan's sisters in *Aurora's Wedding*, the Can-Can dancer in *Boutique Fantasque*, now and then the Street Dancer in *Beau Danube*. The name on her passport was Brigitta Hartwig, but Basil had rechristened her Vera Zorina.

Zorina set the pattern for all future raids on our ballet personnel by Broadway and Hollywood. She left us to go into the London company of *On Your Toes*, where she enjoyed a fine success. She made her Broadway début in *I Married an Angel*, and then was taken up by Sam Goldwyn for a whirl in Hollywood.

She came back—they all come back. But as guest stars, which is considerably more expensive. Still, they bring something back with them. They bring a glamour, and a following, and nice big type in the newspapers.

Zorina came back to us in the spring season of the Ballet Theatre in 1943. She made a beautiful Helen in *Helen of Troy*, danced the Puppet Ballerina in *Petrouchka*, and appeared in revivals of her husband George Balanchine's *Apollo* and *Errante*. She showed

217

an earnestness and devotion to the hard work of Ballet which we somehow had not expected in a girl whose name had been in lights on Broadway and movie-house marquees. The more credit to her that we liked her as guest star no less than as modest soloist. I began my own career as a ballet artist in the first Massine season. I have every reason to be very modest about my talents as a performer, except at my own parties, when good food, good wine and good company give the host license to get away with anything. My imitations of Wigman, Escudero, Shan-Kar, and even my ballet *arabesques* and *entrechats* have been much admired, or at least so I judge by the laughter they arouse.

Nobody has ever caught me backstage, however, like my gaunt and long-legged friend Colonel de Basil, demonstrating to a ballerina the right way to strike an *attitude.*

But when the New York season of 1938-39 drew to a close I was at last willing to give my "talents" to the public. In the last performance, when I was sure my appearance could do no possible damage at the box office, I went into *Petrouchka* as the bear trainer. I have repeated this role at the last performance of every season since.

Once my name was on the program for a real part. I was going to replace Rex Cooper as the Bartender in that delight of ballets, *Fancy Free.* Jerry Robbins took pains to express his confidence in my artistic ability, but at the last moment I relinquished the golden opportunity to prove my merits. I found I would rather see *Fancy Free* once more than be in it, and who that has seen it can blame me?

Surrealist Ballet

Basil brought his company back from Australia the next winter. I had been talking for weeks about a longing to see Baronova in *Coq d'Or* once more. I brought the company to the Hollywood

Theatre in New York for eight weeks. I had my wish. It cost me $70,000.

But I also saw *Graduation Ball* for the first time, and along with all of New York I loved it. It is still the best of Lichine's ballets; I enjoyed it again when he and Riachoubinska came back as guest stars with the Ballet Theatre in the fall season of 1944. It has been a healthy addition to the repertoire.

That season of 1939-40 was notable for some interesting collaborations. Massine gave us the first Shostakovitch symphony in the ballet, *Rouge et Noir*, an abstract reminiscent of the theme of his first symphonic effort, *Les Présages*. Henri Matisse provided the decor and costumes.

Richard Rodgers made his bow in the ballet world that season with *Ghost Town*, a ballet of the American Gold Rush. The young red-headed Marc Platoff, who was born Marcel LePlat in Seattle and became Marc Platt when he left us for Broadway (notably *Oklahoma!*) performed his first choreographic stint in that ballet.

Dick Rodgers had long been one of Ballet's most faithful followers. He conducted his music for *Ghost Town*, and I shall always remember how, at the final rehearsal, the composer who has had some of the liveliest and longest-lived successes on Broadway became suddenly frightened of the awesome combination of Ballet and Metropolitan, and tried to persuade us that it would be better if someone else conducted. We made him go through with it, and he did himself proud. It is one of my nicest recollections, that memory of Dick Rodgers suffering from a case of ballet-fright, and walking down to the conductor's room on opening night like a little boy going to the dentist.

The first surrealist ballet was unveiled that season. Salvador Dali and Massine together concocted *Bacchanale*, and while the Wagnerites may have writhed at such use of the Venusberg music from *Tannhäuser*, the ballet was an instant success.

In his extraordinary book, *The Secret Life of Salvador Dali*—

219

"extraordinary" is the sheerest understatement about anything Dali touches—he tells how he and Mlle. Chanel worked on the costumes in Paris. She used, he says, real ermine, real jewels, and the gloves to be worn by the mad Bavarian king, Louis II, were "so heavily embroidered that we felt some anxiety as to whether the dancer would be able to dance with them on."

The question of the gloves was never answered, for the war came and the company left Paris in a frantic hurry and without the gloves. They spent that summer in Paris, rehearsing for Covent Garden and the American season. When the war broke at last, I struggled to get them aboard ship before they were marooned hopelessly in Europe. By great good luck they all arrived, some of them trickling across the ocean weeks later.

Salvador Dali had endeared himself to the New York public the winter before by breaking a plate-glass window in Bonwit Teller's on Fifth Avenue. I say he endeared himself, because I don't believe anyone has not at some time or another felt an impulse to break a window. Dali did it for all of us, and in grand style.

The slight man with the waxed mustaches of a hairdresser has a mind as agile as his body, and an inflexible will. He had returned to New York to find that surrealism had invaded the windows of all the shops up and down Fifth Avenue. So that when Bonwit's, a store whose windows are always exceptional, asked him to do a genuine surrealist window, he accepted.

He planned two scenes, "Day" and "Night." In a warehouse he exhumed some dreadful wax manikins of another generation of window display, with impossible human faces, real hair and forty years of dust and cobwebs on their waxen limbs. In "Day" one of these creatures was to step into a fur-lined bathtub filled with water. In "Night" the other was to lie asleep on a bed of live coals.

Dali worked on the display until six in the morning, and then went home to bed. It was not until afternoon that he saw it again;

the bed was gone, and the dusty wax manikins. The fur-lined bathtub in the frame of quilted satin and mirrors was all that was left.

One can hardly blame Bonwit's. The crush of window shoppers looking at the Dali display in the morning had blocked traffic on Fifth Avenue and threatened the window itself with accident. But Dali was beside himself. He got into the window with the intention of upsetting the bathtub, which was filled with water. Instead it crashed through the plate-glass window, and he walked out after it. He spent the night in jail, paid his fine in the morning and went calmly home.

At the World's Fair there were even bigger plate-glass windows in his pavilion, the "Dream of Venus," but they remained intact though his eager admirers waited hopefully for a crash. There were live mermaids swimming through a Daliesque undersea landscape, and a taxi with rain raining inside it.

Bacchanale, with its Venus in long flaxen hair stepping out of a Botticelli seashell, with its gnomes knitting red wool socks on the stage and the flock of umbrellas springing open at the hero's death, was thus not a complete surprise to the New York public at its world premiere on November 9, 1939. Even that part of the public which never stepped inside an art gallery had already had a taste of the Dali imagination.

At its premiere we very nearly came to grief, and because of the costumes. Mlle. Chanel's executions of Dali's designs were war casualties. Barbara Karinska, herself rather a fabulous person, was engaged to do them. Dali himself was in Europe.

On the opening night the curtain had already gone up on the first ballet—Bacchanale was the second on the program—and Karinska's costumes were not finished. People were frantically telephoning, finally jumping into taxis and going over to her workshop. Then a fleet of taxis began to arrive, each carrying costumes and pieces of costumes. Each load would be dumped on the floor outside the dressing rooms, and the dancers would dive into the heap, in a mad scramble for their own. Karinska herself stood in the dressing-room corridor, pinning the dancers in with safety pins.

Some of the costumes never arrived that night at all, and the girls had to go on the stage clad only in their full-length tights, which no one noticed.

While all this was going on the intermission stretched out for forty-five minutes. But from the moment the curtain went up, the boredom of the outrageous intermission was forgotten, and I heard people in the audience say, as the curtain fell and the applause quieted, that they would gladly sit through the ballet again that very night.

Surprisingly, it was a success on tour as well, and it was no more difficult to travel, for all the apparent elaborateness of the decor and costumes, than any other ballet. Nini Theilade, who wore the skin tights and long yellow hair of Venus, had some difficulty with the stagehands, who had to lift her up on the platform behind the scene from which she stepped out in her seashell. The skin tights were equally embarrassing to the stagehands and to her, until she hit upon the simple device of wearing a dressing gown until she was safely on the platform, and then dropping it off. Her small, delicately formed figure made her apparent nudity on the stage almost abstract. There was no naughtiness about the display at all.

At every performance the technical staff stood in the wings, making bets on whether the umbrellas would open at the cue, or too soon, or not at all. They were worked by springs from the wings, and they were more temperamental than any ballet dancer in the company.

Dali's program notes for Bacchanale had to be printed exactly as he had written them, an utter mystification to most of the public, an opportunity for gags to the critics. Since the whole ballet was taken in a spirit of good fun, this was no hardship.

The notes are an interesting bit of Dali-ism, but it is futile for Dali to think he can make himself clear in a couple of hundred words. He needs at least a book. Here are some excerpts:

The TANNHÄUSER BACCHANALE *here is shown through the deliriously confused brain of Louis II of Bavaria, who "lived" all of Wagner's myths with such profound visual hyperesthesia as to verge on madness. As the real protagonist of the ballet, he identifies himself with those legendary heroes, and the plot represents the hallucinations and emotions he was prey to.*

The opening chords of the overture evoke the departure of the pilgrims, and Louis in the form of Tannhäuser approaches Venus. Blinded by the effulgent image, Louis flounders in the darkness of the most obscure of myths—Tobie and the Angel. Venus is metamorphosed into a fish, and the fish into a dragon. Louis lifts Lohengrin's sword and skewers the dragon. But this heroism proves a boomerang, for the entrails touch his eyelid and his sight is further darkened by hiphagogical visions. At the supreme moment, wearing Lohengrin's helmet, Louis dies, his last vision that of Leda tenderly embracing the swan (classical symbol of heterosexual love). The object and subject of Louis' real death are present when his body is discovered; a parasol and the image of Lola Montez, both scintillating like real skulls . . .

Geological Foundations of Venusberg

I am writing this text in the shadow of the light of a little forest in Siberia, something similar to an illuminated clearing. It is Gala (Galouchkinetta).

Perhaps, and without perhaps, every passing day makes me feel myself, so to say, and this is the moment to state, nailed to my own geology . . .

223

If Wagner is the most difficult mountain to be observed distinctly, not only due to the lyric vapor in which he so often drowns, but also because of his non-prehensible morphology, the contours of Venusberg, one of the last mountains to be ascended by Wagner, are much more difficult to delimit. For it was in the Venusberg that Wagner made a meeting for himself with the unique, real and substantial Bacchanale of the imagination.

For all these reasons I have chosen the Venusberg as the summit of my first theatrical ascension.

You will see there what is seen in all other ballets: love, death, vice, virtue . . . all the usual and common happenings, etc.

You will also see the road passing through the grotto of Venusberg, the one which proves that all roads not only lead to Rome, but also serve for the return.

You will see Louis II, Venus, Leda, the Swan, Sacher Masoch and his wife, Lola Montez . . . etc. You will see the Nordic and hunchbacked foresters, worth their weight in gold, since their humps are filled with real gold. Finally, you will see the Three Graces, with so many graces attached to their anatomies that it is incredible.

And all this and many other things will you see lighted by the rising sun of the latest particular sciences of our epoch, especially psychoanalysis. Thus, if I exalt and render actual Wagner's genius on the one side, I consider that on the other, I pay my tribute to Freud, who has permitted me to see Wagner.

SALVADOR DALI

The parasol Dali mentions turned into the dozen or so black umbrellas which sprang open at, after, and sometimes before King Louis' death. Incidentally, the subtitle of *Bacchanale* in the program for the premiere reads "First Paranoiac Performance." Dali himself called the turn.

Some time later we had another delightful encounter with this remarkable artist, whom we found the more remarkable because he really functions on a sensible level in his day-to-day dealings with ordinary folk like ourselves. He designed the decor for his fellow-Spaniard, Argentinita, when she produced Garcia Lorca's *El Café de Chinitas*. Garcia Lorca, the patriot poet-composer of Spain, had been a friend of Dali's, and his martyr's death in the Civil War moved the painter deeply.

He designed a "graveyard of guitars," hundreds of guitars of every size hanging on an enormously high wall. The second scene showed the torso of a woman dancer, her hands upstretched in an attitude which might be Spanish dance or might be crucifixion, and where she held her castanets her hands dripped blood as though they had been pierced. This, he explained, was his representation of the crucifixion of his country by civil war.

He was prompt for a meeting with newspaper photographers at Dunkel's studio, where his scene was being painted, and when Madame Argentinita was delayed for several hours he accepted the news with perfect calm. He picked up a brush and spent the time adding his own touches to the canvas, while talking to Mr. Dunkel's painters in some artist's Esperanto which they all seem to understand.

When Madame finally arrived, and the photographer posed him with her in front of the guitar wall, Dali startled the poor photographer out of several years' growth by whipping out of his pocket a dead-white human hand. It took a few minutes to explain that it was only a plaster hand which Mr. Dunkel had given him—"Interesting, is it not?" The photographer mopped his forehead and took his pictures.

And Now—Ballet Theatre

By the end of the second season, deterioration had already begun in the new company as it had in the old. There was an actual lack of artistic freshness in the productions. And friction had begun between personalities.

It was a pity, for Massine had given all his great talent and immense toil to making this a fine company. As artistic director he had used not only his own gifts but his rich contacts with artists and composers in Europe. As principal dancer he had set a standard of performance for the entire company. He had brought Markova to this country, had restored Danilova to us, had built a fresh young company. Delightful, shrewd Genia Delarova, the then Mrs. Massine, shared his hours of planning and endless work.

The company had sprung into existence on a high peak of excellence, but when the initial momentum ran down the weaknesses of its organization began to creak. Colonel de Basil had been in some ways a difficult man, but he brought long artistic experience and a capacity for hard work to his managing task. The management of Universal Art were then only cutting their ballet eyeteeth, by comparison.

Consequently the emergence of Ballet Theatre was of acute interest to me. It had its roots in the Mordkin Ballet Russe, which had been giving sporadic performances, mostly on week-ends, and making an occasional short tour. By the time the organization achieved its three-weeks' season at the Center Theatre, Mordkin had left, and it had a new name—Ballet Theatre—as well as a new managing director.

When Ballet Theatre came under my management it had a nucleus of talented American girls: Lucia Chase, Nora Kaye, Nana Gollner, Janet Reed, Alicia Alonso.

Karen Conrad and Annabelle Lyon, who have since retired from ballet, were in that company. And Antony Tudor, who had already given Lilac Garden to the American public, but was to prove his genius with Pillar of Fire, Romeo and Juliet, Dim Lustre and Undertow in the seasons to come. Agnes de Mille had given them Three Virgins and a Devil.

Hugh Laing was another English contribution to the company. Now Markova signified her willingness to leave the disunited Monte Carlo and join Ballet Theatre.

By great good fortune, Anton Dolin, who had been on his way through New York en route to Australia, had become interested in the Ballet Theatre and had stayed to restage *Giselle*, *Swan Lake* and his delicately satiric *Pas de Quatre*. He did *Princess Aurora* under my regime.

This witty and charming Englishman, whose friends call him Patrick for the good reason that that is his name, had already performed in New York once before. In 1929, after the death of his sponsor, Serge Diaghilev, Dolin had appeared here in Lew Leslie's ill-starred *International Revue*. Gertrude Lawrence was in the show, and Argentinita, and in fact, enough wonderful talent to make twenty good shows.

Like Markova, Pat Dolin had devoted the years that intervened between the death of Diaghilev and the re-birth of ballet on the grand scale in this country to keep the art alive in his own land. Once with Nemchinova, another time with Markova, he headed his own company and toured the English provinces. He danced in the then struggling English companies in and around London. He danced in the music halls when necessary, too.

A really cosmopolitan person, he turned out to be a sound theatre person as well, hard-working, realistic.

With my understanding, Gerry Sevastianov joined the company as managing director. With him he brought his beautiful wife Irina Baronova and a contingent of talent: Sono Osato, Rosella Hightower, George Skibine, Yura Lazovsky, and many other gifted girls and boys. He engaged Fokine, and later Massine as choreographers.

Fokine began to prepare *Bluebeard*, which developed into one of his merriest comedies and became a perfect vehicle for Dolin

227

and Baronova. With *Giselle* and the other classics of the repertoire, we were able to plan a season.

In the fall of 1941 the Monte Carlo company played at the Metropolitan and went on tour. We took the Ballet Theatre to Mexico City and brought them back to the 44th Street Theatre on November 12th.

December 7, 1941, came in the middle of the season. On Pearl Harbor night we took in just $400 at the box office.

Business fell off sharply everywhere. A hundred and thirty million Americans hung on their radios, devoured their newspapers. With the long-expected cataclysm upon us, the launching of a new ballet company was a triviality so minuscule as to be all but unnoticed.

Still, we had made our plans, the dancers' livelihood came only from dancing, and there was no thought of not going forward. Nothing, not even the most terrible invasion in the world's history, had caused the Soviet ballet companies to miss a beat. On the contrary, they had doubled their efforts to bring joy and relaxation to the hard-pressed people, to the men in the front lines. Lepeshinskaya danced her Princess Aurora in full costume at an advanced air base, her stage the wing of a bomber. We could do no less than carry on, here in America.

We took the company on tour to Boston, Philadelphia, Canada, Chicago. The name Ballet Theatre had little meaning for the American public, conditioned as it was to Russian Ballet. I was forced to insert the words "Russian Ballet" in the billing. With little help at the box office, that launching cost me $60,000.

But I had the loyal co-operation of Ballet Theatre's supporters, who faced the problems of building a first-rate ballet company with vision and imagination. Sevastianov showed himself to be able as well as good-looking.

That spring, and again in the fall of 1942, we presented both companies successively in the Metropolitan season. People were buying, not ballet companies, but repertoire in those days, and I doubt whether the public knew or cared during those seasons which company they were seeing. They asked at the box office for *Giselle* or *Bluebeard*, for Agnes de Mille's wonderful *Rodeo* or *Schéhérazade*. The combined seasons went off very well indeed.

In the summer that intervened, the Ballet Theatre company went again to Mexico City as the guests of the Mexican Government, housed in the splendid Palacio des Bellas Artes, surrounded by courtesies and rejoicing in the excellent modern technical appointments of the new opera house.

Leonide Massine spent most of the season with them, working on *Don Domingo* and *Aleko*. *Don Domingo*, born of a worthy impulse to make a bow to the picturesque land which was his host, was one of his less successful efforts, rather overweight as to costumes and properties and light on creative imagination.

Aleko has come to rank as one of his fine works. The Alexander Pushkin poem of a city boy who joins a band of gypsies and falls victim to a fatal love for a gypsy maid, and the beautiful music of the Tchaikowsky Trio inspired both Massine and the great surrealist painter Marc Chagall to a deeply satisfying collaboration. Like all good work, the ballet has grown in beauty and in the favor of the public steadily since it was first presented.

Fokine was in Mexico too, working on his *Petrouchka*, *Carnaval*, and the new comedy, *Helen of Troy*, derived, of course, from Offenbach's opera bouffe, *La Belle Hélène*. It was a natural successor to *Bluebeard*, which had proved a sensational hit.

Alas, the great artist was no longer well. He returned from Mexico, leaving *Helen* unfinished, and shortly after his return he was dead, a tragic loss to Ballet and to his friends, among whom I was proud to count myself.

The future of *Helen* was in doubt for a while. It had promised too much, and too much had already been spent on it, to pack it off to storage. We called in David Lichine, who finished the ballet. When Vera Zorina rejoined us as a guest star the following spring, her husband Balanchine revised the role of Helen for her, and in the end, though three pairs of hands had shaped it, the ballet turned out to be a good comedy, bright and witty, a lively success. It was a good vehicle for Zorina, and has since shown off Baronova, Nana Gollner and others to our and the audience's satisfaction. André Eglevsky makes a virile and exciting Paris.

Not the least charm of *Helen* has been Jerry Robbins' performance as Hermes, the only Olympian to my knowledge who ever came from Weehawken, New Jersey. He chews gum, eats an apple, counts the house, and chaperons the amours of Helen and Paris by putting on spectacles and knitting a homely red sock.

An event of the fall season was the Russian War Relief benefit we gave with Ballet Theatre. Fokine's *Russian Soldier* was a moving experience of the evening. Marian Anderson, Jan Peerce and Mischa Elman shared the program.

Ambassador Litvinoff sat in a box with Mrs. Litvinoff. He saw Markova dance for the first time, was touched by *Russian Soldier*, but the ballet he fell in love with was *Bluebeard*. He wrote me about it afterward.

I sent a check for $7,000 to Russian War Relief next day as the entire proceeds of that single performance. The expenses of company, orchestra, stage and incidentals were my contribution.

At the close of the fall season we kissed the Monte Carlo and Universal Art good-bye. Denhaus and I both made farewell speeches backstage. It is always painful for me to part with a company for whose success I have labored. I did not like to say good-bye to those nice boys and girls. I visit them backstage when they are in town.

Bigger and Better Ballet

Ballet has grown steadily in America in these dozen years and in the past two years it has taken giant strides in popularity. The million-dollar gross, which looked so large to us in 1938, has been forging toward a million and a half, and I believe we shall see the day when the American public will spend as much as two million dollars a year to see ballet performances.

New York has at last fulfilled its promise and become one of the ballet cities of the world. Two years ago, in the spring of 1943, we scheduled a four weeks' season, and extended it to seven. That was the first season in which we began to offer guest artists— Zorina, Massine, Argentinita, and Igor Stravinsky to conduct his own works.

The following spring the Monte Carlo played at the City Center during part of my Metropolitan season with Ballet Theatre. New York filled both houses to capacity, as London had filled Covent Garden and the Drury Lane in that other twin ballet season, and kept us running at the Metropolitan an extra three weeks to boot.

For the past several summers we have taken the loss of Europe to the Ballet, as well as to our other artists, in stride, with summer seasons at the Hollywood Bowl, in San Francisco's War Memorial Opera House, in Seattle and Portland to keep them working. New dancers have emerged out of this yeasty, fertile American ballet world; despite the old adage of an aristocratic world that ballet dancers must be nurtured in a hothouse atmosphere, despite the nun-like existence which was considered essential to the development of a ballerina, our American democracy seems able to produce ballerinas in the grand style as well as it turns out low-price automobiles.

Our boys too have developed amazingly. When Tamara

231

Toumanova last season took young Johnny Kriza in hand and made a classic partner out of him, he responded in a way to make Tamara as proud as a mother hen with her first brood of chicks. Johnny has always been a beautiful dancer in the company. If he is willing to apply himself, he may one day be one of the great classic dancers.

Tamara joined the company as a guest star under the most trying auspices—a prima ballerina who had been out of Ballet for several years, who had spent one of those strange interludes in Hollywood which are supposed to change people so that their best friends no longer know them. The baby ballerina of a few years ago came back a film star, married to one of the really talented and successful men in the film industry. Little wonder that many, including in some cases the critics, assumed she was spoiled, her head turned, and that she had not so much as looked at a bar, much less worked at it.

But the management and the company soon learned quite otherwise. Tamara since her marriage to Casey Robinson, and with the hard work of a dramatic film behind her, was more mature, more businesslike, perhaps, in the sense that she was a grown-up artist of the theatre now, no longer a breathless little girl. But there was and is still the same voluble, gay charm, the same ready warmth, the same eagerness to be liked and accepted by the people with whom she works.

The company, so largely American, quickly responded to her in kind. They not only liked her, but respected her as an artist. No one could have blamed them if they had stood in the wings, watching for the glamour girl from Hollywood to make a misstep. I have no doubt that they watched, but when she made no misstep, but on the contrary showed them a dazzling perfection of technique, they gave her their honest admiration.

And again we had Mamushka, bustling around her Tamara, bustling around every young dancer in the company, encompassing them all in her round, warm, motherly embrace. She watches lest a shoe ribbon come untied, lest a thread hang from a gauze skirt. Wise in the ballet world as only a ballerina's mama can be, she hovers and gives advice in her wonderful Russian English, and they all love her.

But while America has been prodigal in supplying ballet with dancers, it has not been so rich in ballet creators. Except for Agnes de Mille, Jerome Robbins, Michael Kidd, we have a startling lack of American choreographers for ballet.

As I write these lines, the war has ended in Europe, and I am waiting for the first plane or boat to take me abroad, to re-establish those lines of communication which are life lines to music and ballet. I hope to find in London at least, perhaps elsewhere in Europe where the war has not destroyed art along with lives and cities, choreographers who will bring new ideas and new talents to refresh our ballet scene. England has already given us Tudor and Dolin, and England through the war has maintained its ballet life. Our De Milles and our Robbinses have just begun—from the long view of a full creative life—and we cannot burden them with the whole responsibility of infusing new life into the choreographic scene.

I hope also, now that the guns in Europe are stilled, to realize a dream of my life, and take our new kind of ballet, American ballet, to the land where ballet as we have known it was born. I hope to bring Soviet ballet here, the wonderful, grand-style, lavish ballet which the Soviet Government has kept alive through the war years.

When Walter Terry, who left the dance critic's desk on the *Herald Tribune* to join the Air Force, returned recently on furlough from the Near East, he told me how jealous our boys were when the Russians got their ballet performances, great prodigal shows with full companies and full orchestras, complete with costumes and stage sets.

233

Full evening ballets of four acts are the usual program in Moscow. There is the four-act *Swan Lake*, the four-act *Sleeping Beauty* from which we take our *Princess Aurora*. There is the *Hunchback Horse* with Pugni's music and Minkus's *Don Quixote*, and I don't know how many others, all full evening ballets.

It was Diaghilev who first established the custom of three or four short ballets on an evening's program, and we continued the custom during the decade or so in which we had to educate the American public to Ballet. Now I think this country's appetite is hearty and discriminating enough to enjoy the full-length ballets. I have been preaching this, and wanting this, and one day I shall do it.

Half a Romeo

One story remains to be told of all the ballet stories I could still tell. That is the story of the half-Romeo.

It was, as a matter of record, considerably more than half a *Romeo and Juliet* which we presented to a sold-out Metropolitan on that Tuesday evening, April 6, 1943. Less than ten minutes of the forty-five minute ballet was unfinished.

For once it was not Karinska's fault. Put it down to war-time transportation. I know of my own knowledge that Antony Tudor, the most earnest and painstaking of choreographers, had been working on the ballet for half a year. What he needed was time with the dancers, and time is what the railroads, by being late, by missing connections, by changing schedules as is inevitable in a war emergency, had taken from him.

More often than not, a train which on the timetable was to arrive at noon, leaving a whole afternoon for rehearsal, got the company to the evening performance by the skin of their teeth. Some performances they never got to at all. One performance began at eleven o'clock at night. The audience had come to see a ballet performance, and stayed until the company arrived to give it. Until the night before the world premiere of Romeo and Juliet was to take place, Tudor thought he could be ready. And then he told us he could not.

We spent most of that night showing him how it was impossible —with a sold-out house, with no way of announcing the postponement at such a late hour—to postpone Romeo. At last he agreed to give as much of it as was finished, with an announcement from the stage.

He made the announcement himself, and it was no small ordeal to step out before that expectant house, with standees to the limit the Fire Department allows, and tell them they were going to see an unfinished ballet. I had tried to spare him that ordeal, suggesting that Dolin, who carried no burden of guilt, could do it more easily.

The half-Romeo the audience saw that night was not only better than none; it was better than a good many complete Romeos that have been perpetrated on the public in the legitimate theatre. When the curtain fell on Markova being arrayed in the golden gown for Juliet's marriage to Paris, there was a stillness in the house, like a sigh, and then a burst of applause.

Tudor unexpectedly stepped out before the curtain at that moment, put his hand up to quiet the applause, and offered his apologetic, his humble thanks. The exalted poetic mood created by lovely Markova and ardent Hugh Laing collapsed, and one could almost hear the thought going through that packed house: "Oh, yes, that's right, they gave us only half a ballet, what a trick!" Sixty-four customers came to the box office and demanded seats for the first performance of the finished ballet.

Antony Tudor is a sincere creative artist, but he should have listened to a hard-boiled showman that night. If he had let Romeo stand on its own feet and not apologized after the curtain, not one person in that house would have gone away unsatisfied.

Both Romeo and Tudor have redeemed themselves a hundred times over since then, and no one has ever held it against either the man or the ballet. It is one of the great ballets of any repertoire.

Still, could there ever be a premiere of half a play, or half a motion picture? There's no doubt about it, Ballet is different. Some day I am going to write a book about it.

CHAPTER EIGHT

"Once in a Hundred Years..."

*M*RS. HUROK and I were strolling on the Champs-Elysées. It was one of those tender Paris evenings which are as much a part of our memories of the beloved city as the gaiety and the elegance, the good food and the good talk, the giddy chatter of the salons and the art galleries and the decorum of the Opéra.

The green of the chestnut trees was softly grayed; the Place de la Concorde swam in an enchanted twilight haze. Even the feminine shrieks which pass for automobile horns on the Paris taxis were muted. It was an evening for sitting at a table in a sidewalk café with one's friends, for drinking in the easy leisure of Paris over a slowly emptying glass.

We were only a few steps from our table when I saw on a pillar an *affiche*, half hidden, advertising a concert that night by "an American contralto." I stopped and read it.

"I think I'll just look in," I said to Mrs. Hurok.

"Oh, you! You're always 'just looking in' at something. I think I'll sit here and talk with our friends while you look in."

"I won't be long," I promised. I left her comfortably settled at a table with the others, and went to the Salle Gaveau.

The concert hall was not the biggest in Paris, but it was full. I found a seat and waited.

A tall, handsome Negro girl came out and walked with the grace of a queen to the curve of the piano. Her accompanist sat down; she nodded to him, closed her eyes and sang.

Chills danced up my spine and my palms were wet.

You who go to hear Marian Anderson today go prepared for an exalting experience. But I had gone in cold, and I was shaken to my very shoes. Ten years ago her voice was not the finished, the polished instrument it is today. But the same great heart was behind it, the same deep love and understanding for music as a language of the human spirit. Marian has added breadth and scope to her musicianship as she has refined her vocal technique. She has never ceased to grow in her art, and she never will. But anyone who had ears to hear her then could hear the great future already present.

The more was the wonder, therefore, that she had been singing obscurely in her own land for seven years since she had won a hearing with the New York Philharmonic Orchestra at the Lewisohn Stadium.

As soon as the group of songs was ended and I could decently leave my seat, I hurried up the aisle, and down the corridor that led backstage.

Marian was talking in her velvety voice to her accompanist, Finnish Kosti Vehaanen, when I came in. I introduced myself, and her eyes opened wide.

"Of course I've heard of Mr. Hurok," she said.

I wasted no time. "I want to present you in your own country," I announced.

"But I have an American manager," she protested.

I knew her American manager well. His is still, has been for many many years, one of the most respected names in the music business.

"Have you a contract with him now?"

And then it came out that she had a contract, which she had been carrying about in her trunk for more than a year—unsigned.

The story of her seven lean years in her own country had ended with a contract so disappointing that she had not been able to bring herself to sign it.

Since she had won the competition for that Stadium concert in 1926, Marian had been plodding a discouraging uphill road. Her manager had continued to book her with the same organizations for which she had sung before. She had had one Carnegie Hall recital in all the years.

Once, in all this time, he had gone to hear her. She was singing a concert for an important organization, sharing the program with the Hall-Johnson Choir. She is not certain to this day whether her manager had come to hear her or the choir.

He came backstage that time, glowing enthusiastically. "I had no idea you were giving such programs," he confessed. From then on, he said, things would be very different for her. Her fee would go up at once; she was to be promoted from the "recital" class of artists under his management to the big-time "concert" group. He described the new contract he was going to write for her.

When the conference took place she was stunned with disappointment. Something—or rather somebody—had changed his mind. He had under his management a well-known contralto, a star whose power was something to be reckoned with. Marian won the promotion into the concert class, but nothing else in the contract was as he had promised.

Disheartened with this becalmed career, she went to him at last and announced she was going abroad for study.

He countered with another suggestion. He would make an appointment for her with Madame ——, the celebrated contralto; Marian would sing for Madame, and Madame would decide whether Marian was not, perhaps, a soprano after all.

This curious proposal Marian declined, with the courteous firmness which I have come to know so well, and from which, as I also know, there is no appeal. She was determined, she said, to go abroad, and under the circumstances it scarcely mattered whether Madame thought her voice a soprano or a contralto.

Her manager made no effort to hide his displeasure. "You are only going to satisfy your own vanity," he told her stingingly.

"Well, then, let's say that is the reason," she replied.

He gave her a card of introduction to a European manager and, as his farewell blessing, the announcement that she must pay him ten per cent of everything she earned in Europe.

She had $750 in American Express checks, the fellowship the Rosenwald Foundation had granted her. With this she planned to buy the services of famous European teachers.

The Berlin manager to whom she presented her letter of introduction had a small concert business. He arranged for some recordings—these were later sold in Macy's for 59 cents, some for 29 cents each. He arranged a concert in Berlin which took $500 of her little fund. He sent her to Scandinavia for a series of six concerts arranged in pairs, the second concert of each pair to take place only if the first was successful.

Of that first Scandinavian tour, begun with such managerial caution, she made a march of triumph. The six dates swelled to fourteen before she left the peninsula.

The next season she placed her fortunes in the hands of another European manager and continued the triumphant progress across Europe for two wonderful years, ending with the concert at the Mozarteum in Salzburg in August, 1935, where Arturo Toscanini said to her, "A voice like yours is heard once in a hundred years."

Homecoming

But that was later, after I had signed the contract that would bring Marian Anderson home to sing to her countrymen's hearts as she had sung to mine in the Salle Gaveau.

We talked only briefly that night in the artists' room backstage.

Though she had no signed contract with her American manager, she felt she could not discuss a contract with me until he released her.

"Cable him," I urged her. I was impressed with her concern for perfect correctness in her relations with a manager whom she had in effect already left.

We met the next day in the office of the Paris manager, Fritz Horwitz. She sat across the desk from me, looking frightened. Her voice, one of the most beautiful speaking voices I have ever heard, was a little breathless. Her answers came slowly, but with certainty.

As Marian remembers it, I sat leaning with bent elbows on my cane which I had laid across the top of Horwitz's desk, and I looked, she says, twice as big as natural. Kosti, who sat quietly in a corner throughout the discussion, took her arm as they left the office and whistled a great sigh of relief. "Whew! I need a drink!"

I had no idea I was having such a steam-roller effect. There was, I confess, a single thought in my mind, and that was to present this girl to her own land as she should be presented.

Her manager did not answer her cable, nor two letters. Finally, there was a letter from a member of his staff. They would be sorry to lose her, he said, but they could not offer her a guarantee.

A guarantee was just what I had proposed, a specified number of concerts and a specified sum which she could count on in advance as her earnings for the American season. Security is a hard enough commodity to come by in any profession. In the early years of an artist's career it is utterly out of reach unless a rich patron provides it. The least a manager can do is offer a minimum guarantee to a young artist in whose talent he has faith.

We signed a contract in which I guaranteed her a season of fifteen concerts. Fifteen! Only a few years later she was to sing ninety-six in the United States alone in a single winter season. She still sings no fewer than fifty, and she could sing fifty more if there were twice as many weeks in the year. This in addition to the uncounted concerts she gives in the training camps and hospitals, for various causes and the bond and fund campaigns, and especially in the schools, which she visits whenever her schedule allows her time in a city.

When she arrived for her first concert late in December we had booked only six of the fifteen dates. But I was not troubled. I knew I would have no difficulty filling her schedule after she had sung in Town Hall.

I was not troubled until her boat docked. Then I thought she would sing no concerts at all that season. She limped down the gangplank with her ankle strapped. The next day an X-ray told the alarming truth—an unlucky misstep on a steep companionway, the last night on shipboard, had fractured a bone in her foot.

Visions of a concert artist singing from a wheelchair made my blood run cold. But I underestimated the indomitable spirit which had carried Marian Anderson through the thousand doors that are closed to a penniless Negro girl. Marian meant to sing at Town Hall on December 30th, and sing she did.

The audience was startled to see the curtains drawn on the stage. They were even more startled to see the curtains part and reveal the artist already standing, tall and straight, in the curve of the piano, her concert gown flowing into a rippled pool of green and gold lamé around her feet.

They would have been startled out of their seats to know that the gracefully draped train concealed a foot in a cast, held an inch off the floor, and that the singer held her balance throughout the concert only by leaning imperceptibly against the piano.

The curtains were drawn after each group of songs, when the artist normally walks off the stage to rest, and the attendant hurried to Marian with a chair. When the intermission ended the curtains opened again, and again she stood there, ready to sing.

It was only after half the concert was over that she explained to the audience the reason for the curious procedure. Then the house, already adoring, burst into abandoned applause in tribute to her courage. She took this, too, calmly, and continued the concert with the devoted concentration on the music which is always characteristic of her when she sings, and which wins the same single-minded attention from her audience.

The notices after that concert were not without reservations. They hedged: "In some respects a remarkable voice . . ." "Interestingly sung . . ." But Howard Taubman in the *New York Times* threw reservations to the wind and welcomed her with a ringing tribute to her voice, her musicianship, her deep feeling. He used such words as "stunning," "transcending," and called her singing "music-making that probed too deep for words." He began his notice: "Marian Anderson has returned to her native land one of the great singers of our time . . ." He ended it: "It is time for her own country to honor her."

And Olin Downes, the *Times'* senior critic, hurried over during an intermission of the opera which he was covering and inserted a paragraph in his opera review, seconding everything Taubman said. These two men of the *Times* had not long to wait before the other critics had joined unreservedly in the growing chorus of superlatives.

I lost not a day in arranging a next concert, in Carnegie Hall this time, over Miss Anderson's modest objections. I departed for the Coast, leaving that concert in the able hands of my secretary and boss, Mae Frohman.

When Mae phoned me, reporting that the January 30th concert in Carnegie was an even greater success than Town Hall, I told her: "Get another Carnegie Hall date immediately." That one too, on March 9th, sold out.

The fifteen concerts for the season, and more, came off as scheduled, and after two weeks of rest with her mother in Philadelphia, Marian went back to Europe. She toured the Scandinavian countries again, Russia, Southern France, Italy, Spain. She rested briefly on the Riviera, and then she was singing in her own country once more.

This was the pattern of her life until the war came. Constantly the demand grew for Marian Anderson in America, until the number of her concerts multiplied by geometrical progression, and she had less and less time left for her European tours. In the season 1933-34 she had given 112 concerts in the Scandinavian countries. There were weeks when she sang eight concerts in nine days, something a singer should not do. But that was at the beginning, and who can blame her if in those years she succumbed to the pleas of the people who first responded to her great gift?

Soon, however, we began to realize that it was our job not to seek dates for Marian, but to winnow out the most attractive ones each season. No human being could meet the demand that came clamoring to our doors. Marian knows what we have done when she goes to a town where she has not been before, and the local manager greets her with the complaint, "We have been trying to get you for so long!"

Marian had been with me for three or four seasons when I met her original American manager in an elevator one day. It was a priceless opportunity to taunt a rival, and I was human enough to make the most of it.

We were getting a fee in four figures that season, though it wasn't quite the figure I used to impress him. But Marian has never let me down. We reached that fee the very next season.

People Have Been Kind—and Not Kind

When Marian Anderson, after her long patient climb, saw spreading out before her her first European success, she wrote to her mother in Philadelphia. Wasn't there something, she asked, something her mother had wanted for a long time, that she could bring her from Europe, now that the good things of life were at last within reach?

Mrs. Anderson wrote back at once. All she wanted, she said, was that God would hold Marian Anderson "in the hollow of His hand and raise up the people to be kind."

People have been kind to Marian Anderson. The little girl who scrubbed the doorsteps of Philadelphia houses to earn four dollars for a violin—her first musical yearning—has grown up into one of those fairy-tale princesses who live happily ever after. Surely the tale-spinners were thinking of her when they created that immortal heroine whose goodness brought her through countless tribulations to find happiness at last.

The good people of the church at Martin and Fitzwater Streets in Philadelphia, who raised a fund of nickels and dimes for Marian's first singing lessons, did not dream that she would one day sing for the King and Queen of England in the White House. Or perhaps they did; they had the faith that moves mountains.

The first time that Marian was invited to sing at the White House—this time for the President and Mrs. Roosevelt—she sat waiting in a sitting room, nervous, rehearsing a little speech she had prepared for the great moment of meeting the President.

Mr. Roosevelt came in, reached for her hand, said cheerily, "Oh, hello, Miss Anderson, you look just like your pictures, don't you?" And she forgot all about her speech.

She herself tells the story of how she was presented to their Britannic Majesties. She curtseyed to the Queen but when she reached Mrs. Roosevelt in the receiving line, the First Lady greeted her and handed her on to His Majesty so naturally that Marian forgot to curtsey and forgot to speak to King George at all!

Marian tells these stories on herself. I have seen her in all sorts of awesome situations. I have seen her tremulous, even moved to tears by the honors that have come to her. But I have never seen her flustered. There is about Marian a poise even under the stress of great emotion, a dignity and a beauty of speech and manner that are unshakable because they come from within.

She has been honored with the Spingarn Medal, which Mrs. Roosevelt presented to her; with Doctorates of Music from Temple University, Howard University and Smith College. The Bok Award of $10,000, presented to the individual who has done most for Philadelphia, drew from her a speech of thanks so touchingly sincere that the audience was no less choked with emotion than she herself when she had finished.

She has been received by kings and princes, by the great of the world, and by the great in her own world of music. But she is after all a princess in her own right, though her father sold ice and coal and her widowed mother took in washing to keep the family of three little girls together.

The kernel of Marian Anderson's character was most truly, though unconsciously, expressed by herself not long ago, when she answered an interviewer's routine question.

"What was the greatest moment in your life?" she was asked.

Marian had so many great moments to choose from. Was it the moment when Toscanini took her hand and told her hers was the voice of a century? Was it when Constantin Stanislavsky, the theatre genius of Russia, came to her laden with white lilacs in Moscow's bitter midwinter, and begged her to stay and be Carmen in his Moscow Art Theatre production?

Was it in the white and gold salon of Jan Sibelius' villa, in the forested heart of the North, when the great Finnish composer waited for the last note of her song to end and said gravely, "My roof is too low for your voice." And then turned to call to his wife, "Not coffee, champagne for Miss Anderson!"

Was it when she first sang in the White House? Or when she went again to the White House to sing for the King and Queen? Was it when her own city of Philadelphia paid her its noblest tribute with the Bok Award? Was it the moment of winning the Spingarn Medal, or any of the honorary degrees?

Was it that Easter Sunday afternoon, when she stood beneath the massive, tenderly brooding figure of Lincoln, with Cabinet members, Supreme Court justices, Senators and national leaders on the platform behind her, with 75,000 faces upturned before her, and sang in the city where a group of intransigeant women of antediluvian minds had barred her from their concert hall?

It was none of these.

"Why," said Marian, hardly hesitating, "it was the day I went home and told my mother she wouldn't need to take work home any more."

Happily Ever After

As success came to Marian Anderson, life in the little house on South Martin Street acquired the unpretentious graces a patient mother had long wished for her daughters. First came security. Marian bought the frame house that had always meant home to her. Mrs. Anderson and Marian's two sisters live there, and the small nephew on whom Marian dotes.

They might have moved away from that modest neighborhood when fame and fortune came to Marian. They might have surrounded themselves with the world's goods and lived in sumptuous style. But it is like this little family—most of all it is like the gentle, motherly little woman from whom Marian learned her integrity and inward strength—that they stayed among their friends and clung to the simple way of life they had created for themselves.

Not far away is the Union Baptist Church, where Marian's voice was first heard, and where, when necessary, she substituted for any absent member of the choir from soprano to bass. Not far away, too, is the school to which as a little girl she walked every day with her sisters. This has been quite literally home to Marian; here she came, shining with the happiness of recognition, trailing new clouds of glory from Moscow, from Buenos Aires, from Mexico City, from Honolulu—and, what meant most to her, from the concert halls of her own land.

The neighbors came in to say hello to Marian and spend an evening hearing about the wonderful world they were discovering through her eyes. But if I know Marian, I know she did not do the talking. She asked questions—about this absent friend or that one, about this one's new baby and that one's graduation and another's recent wedding. I know, because this is the girl who, backstage in Moscow after one of the wildest ovations of her career, found her way to me past the generals and the ambassadors, past the world-renowned theatre folk and half the Soviet Government who had come to do her honor, to ask me how things were in Philadelphia.

She still telephones her mother from wherever she is, daily if it is possible, and the conversation still ends with Mrs. Anderson asking, "And when are you coming home?" When there is a concert within a hundred miles, or an honor to be conferred on her daughter, Mrs. Anderson packs her little bag and goes along because Marian wants her there.

She sits in the audience, a small figure in neat black, her worn hands quiet in her lap, enjoying the unique happiness that must be hers. I like her story of the excited dowager sitting beside her at a concert who turned, her own frantically applauding hands in mid-air, to whisper fiercely, "Good heavens, woman, how can you sit there like a bump on a log? Don't you know a great artist when you hear one?"

A few years ago Marian acquired her Connecticut farm, Marianna, where she now lives with her genial architect husband, Orpheus Fisher. He designed the alteration of the white-shingled Victorian farmhouse with a nice concern for its wide, welcoming porches from which a heart-lifting view of the valley spreads below, and for its low-ceilinged, friendly rooms. Its slip covers and draperies are made by Marian's own hand.

Marian calls herself a plain dirt farmer. Strictly a city person myself, I have no confidence that she will emerge from colloquies with her two very large and self-assertive lady pigs, Phyllis and Pontiac (sic!) all in one piece. I am also inclined to regard Marian's cozy conferences with her prize Jersey cow with misgivings, despite the mild look in the animal's eye.

But at the dinner table I am in full accord with her farm program. In the matter of food I am not infrequently described as an expert, and if the good things on her table are the product of her farming—and she assures me that they are—then she is a fine farmer.

My own taste leads me away from Marian's barn, down the lane to the brook that chortles through the shady rock garden, down to the naturalistic swimming pool with its fringe of tender green grass. This pool was my ally, that first summer Marian spent in her Connecticut paradise, her first vacation in six years. I could never have tempted her away to sing two concerts for me that summer, if it had not been "for the benefit of the swimming pool."

I am more interested in the house that stands on its edge. This is the studio artfully designed by her husband, where, with sturdy Franz Rupp at the piano, Marian polishes and perfects her programs for each new season. Here she sings new songs into her recording machine, playing them back and listening to herself with a sharp ear for possible improvement. It is a lovely cool room, furnished with grass matting and bamboo furniture which she brought from Honolulu, just the year before Pearl Harbor.

I think that, of all Marian's friends, I as her manager can understand most profoundly what Marianna means to her. The good people of Ishpeming, Michigan, and Laporte, Indiana, of Seattle and San Francisco and Chicago, see her on the concert stage, looking beautiful and queenly. They see her at her happiest moment, when she is giving them her song and receiving their vociferous gratitude. They do not stop to think—nor should they—of the many months in a concert artist's life during which her only home is the drawing room of a train, her most intimate horizon the impersonal plains and mountains of America speeding past the window, her human relationships the fleeting handclasp of a welcoming committee, the ministrations of a hostess in the few hours between train and concert, between concert and train.

The rewards of the artist are well publicized, but we rarely speak of the cost of those months of touring, the cost in peace and privacy, in comfort, and in personal happiness. What woman in Marian Anderson's audiences would like to make her home for six or eight months of every year in a train?

Marian has her own quaint way of carrying home along with her. She travels with fifteen pieces of luggage—and only one of them contains clothes. In the others are her phonograph and her recording machine, for work and study; her sewing machine, together with the materials and patterns for a new set of slip covers and draperies for the snug sitting room at Marianna, or for a new gardening wardrobe to wear at Marianna next.summer—surely the half-hour she snatches to stitch away at these brings Marianna closer—a nest of cooking pots, by means of which she varies the monotony of dining-car and hotel menus; and in a hatbox, her electric iron, with which she likes to press out her concert gown before a performance. Once she yielded to the persuasions of her friends and took a maid traveling with her. She finds it more like home to do things herself, as she always has.

Still, she would not change her life. And there is always Marianna, the simple and serene corner of Connecticut which she has fashioned to her own taste, to come home to.

Voice of a Race

"The voice of a race," Howard Taubman called Marian Anderson in a study he wrote of her for the *New York Times*. And this sensitive writer was speaking of her not only as a singer.

The Negro people can thank what Providence watches over the oppressed that it was given to them to offer Marian to the world. She is no militant fighter. She makes no complaint, creates no issues, offers no angry protest at the indignities that have been visited upon her because of her color.

When a taxi driver refused to carry her to the concert hall, she has made no answer, only shrunk into herself and stood patiently on the curb until another taxi driver came along who would take her. When a hotel would not have her, she has found shelter in the Negro quarter and traveled the long distance to the auditorium for rehearsal and performance.

She has gone her quiet way, singing in the South and the North, asking only that when she sang there should be no segregation in the concert hall. If she has been hurt, she has not shown it. Only once she said, without bitterness, "The Lord surely has no prejudice, since he gave this gift to a Negro."

She has been herself, strong in her inner integrity. And by being herself she has won citadels that never have been breached by doughtier warriors.

When we sent Marian out on her first tour, she was going to sing in regular concert halls, making a tour that was normal for any artist.

"You're sending her out to sing in those places, with a white accompanist? She'll be stoned," we were warned. Marian sang, and her audiences fell at her feet.

She made her first Southern tour the next season, without inci-

251

dent except that a local committee woman pointedly refused to shake hands with her.

Of such small slights there have been any number, petty and painful. There was the local manager who, on Marian's first visit, did not meet her at the train, did not call upon her at her hotel, did not see her at all until the moment before her concert, when he went backstage, bade her a cool good evening and did not shake hands. I suppose he went backstage at all only to make sure she was there all in one piece and his concert would go as scheduled.

The second time Marian arrived in that city, the local manager met her at the station in his own car. He shook hands with her when she stepped off the train, escorted her himself to her hotel. He fetched her to the auditorium for her rehearsal, and drove her up and down the streets of his city that afternoon, showing her the local sights. He drove her to the concert in the evening. And the next morning he drove her in his own car to the next stop on her itinerary, which happened to be a neighboring town.

"She's such a lady!" he exclaimed.

There was the time in another city in the deep South. The committee woman here drew our traveling manager, Isaac Jofe, aside before the concert.

"I understand that she has a habit of taking the hand of her accompanist when she takes a bow with him," said she. "She can't take a white man's hand—you must tell her we can't have that sort of thing here."

The devoted Jofe retorted that what Miss Anderson did on the stage was her own business, and he would tell her no such thing.

"I warn you, there will be a riot!" the woman fumed.

Marian sang, took her bow with Franz Rupp as she was accustomed to, and there was a riot—of applause.

It does not matter whether one local manager or one committee woman learns a lesson in democracy. What matters is that audiences are learning. Backstage, after any concert of Marian's, North or South, there is a milling mass of admirers yearning to speak one word to her, to shake her hand, get her autograph—or merely look at her close up. There are Negroes, and there are white people, and they stand one behind another on line. There is no segregation backstage. In the South, it is true, there are not many white people of the older generation on that line of admirers. But there are many, many white boys and girls, young persons in their teens and early twenties. In their hands lies the future of Democracy.

It was in Jackson, Mississippi, in 1942, with a temperature of 93 degrees, that the audience would not go home. Marian sang five encores, and still of those 4,000 listeners not one stirred to leave the concert hall.

She went out for a sixth encore and sang "Swanee River." When she came to the beginning of the second verse she said, "Won't you sing with me?"

The entire audience, Negro and white, rose and sang "Swanee River" with her.

Next day there were editorials on that community sing in both the Jackson papers. Said one: "Sometimes the human soul rises above itself, above racial prejudices."

And then there were backslidings. One season in a medium-sized city Marian sang before an audience of 7,800, about thirty per cent Negro. The next time she was scheduled to sing there, the Negroes were refused orchestra seats. At Marian's request we cancelled the concert.

Drops of water, says Marian, wear away a stone. But there are times when others are moved to be militant in her behalf.

When she could not find hotels to accommodate her in certain cities, a letter went out from our office to the local managers warning them that if they did not find decent hotel accommodations for Miss Anderson in the center of the town, convenient to the concert hall, we would not only not send Miss Anderson to those cities, we would deprive them of other of our very desirable attractions. Hotel accommodations were found.

In New York City itself there was for years a shocking situation which we were helpless to correct. When she came to New York from the little house in Philadelphia to sing at Carnegie Hall, there was nowhere for Marian to stay in the center of town.

We tried every hotel, to no avail. In the end the Hotel Algonquin, stamping ground of Alexander Woollcott, Franklin P. Adams, and the witty, knowing, literary and theatre folk of their set, welcomed her.

A long-time resident, an admirer of Marian's though not a personal friend, invited Miss Anderson to occupy her suite as her guest. Since then, Marian has enjoyed the hospitality of that gracious hostelry and the thoughtfulness of manager Frank Case and Mrs. Case, whenever she must be in New York.

Marianna, her Connecticut retreat, was not found without heartache. I cannot tell how many farms were flatly refused her, how many times the price unaccountably soared as soon as it was known that the prospective purchaser was Marian Anderson. I suppose the sudden leap in price was sometimes caused by a desire to get what the traffic would bear; Marian, after all, is known to be one of the five top-income artists in the musical field. But all too often the attitude was that if a Negro woman wanted to buy the place she would have to pay heavily for it.

When I am optimistically assured that democracy is making giant strides in America, that soon there will be no race prejudice, I remember the meannesses, the affronts, that this great woman has suffered, and still on occasion suffers, and I am not altogether convinced.

Easter Sunday, 1939

Once it was given to us to be part of a great, a dramatic demonstration of protest. After the constantly recurring offenses, from unwilling cab drivers up to segregated concert halls, it was almost a relief when the Daughters of the American Revolution presented Marian's friends with an issue big enough to bring out into the open.

The *cause célèbre* which came to its climax at the Lincoln Memorial on Easter Sunday in 1939 began with a perfectly routine request from Howard University in Washington, D.C., for a concert by Marian Anderson under the University's auspices. Arrangements were made in June, 1938, for a concert to take place in Washington the next season. When we were scheduling Marian's tour the date we gave the University was April 9th.

Early in January, 1939, the manager of Howard University's concert series applied to Fred E. Hand, manager of Constitution Hall, to reserve the auditorium for a performance on April 9th. Constitution Hall is the largest auditorium in Washington and the only one suitable for a concert by a leading musical artist. It is the auditorium in which all top-ranking concert performers regularly appear. It is owned, tax free, by the Daughters of the American Revolution.

Mr. Hand replied to the University's manager that a clause in the rental contract of Constitution Hall prohibits the presentation of Negro artists.

Mr. V. D. Johnston, treasurer of Howard University, wrote an open letter disclosing this information, and at once there was a small stir of protest. *The Washington Herald* wrote editorially: "Prejudice rules to make the capital of the Nation ridiculous in the eyes of all cultured people and to comfort Fuehrer Hitler and the members of our Nazibund."

When the University informed us of the clause, we wrote to Mr. Hand, asking him if it would be possible to waive the restriction in the case of Miss Anderson, so as not to deny to the people of Washington a great musical experience.

Back came the reply from Mr. Hand: "I beg to advise you that Constitution Hall is not available on April 9th, 1939, because of prior commitments." In the matter of policy, he advised us to communicate with Mrs. Henry M. Robert, Jr., President General of the National Society, Daughters of the American Revolution.

I wrote Mrs. Robert. Meanwhile Kirsten Flagstad wired the National Association for the Advancement of Colored People: "As a foreigner in America, I have always been impressed by the freedom and democracy in this country. I therefore am greatly surprised to learn from you that the use of Constitution Hall in Washington has been refused for a concert to my fellow-artist, Marian Anderson."

Lawrence Tibbett, not only a Metropolitan star but President of the American Guild of Musical Artists, wired: "Surely the Daughters of those who fought for the establishment of this great democracy would not wish to perpetuate such an obviously undemocratic and unAmerican rule as one which bars the appearance of any artist of whatever race, creed or color."

Mrs. Robert replied to my letter: "At the time that the Chairman of the Howard University Concert Series approached the Manager of Constitution Hall, the Hall had already been engaged for Sunday, April 9th, by another musical organization."

No mention of the discriminatory clause. Now it was our move to ask for another date.

Marks Levine, my good friend, of National Concert and Artists Corporation, wrote to Mr. Hand at about this time asking for available dates for a concert by Ignaz Paderewski in Constitution Hall. Hand replied with a list of dates which did not include the 9th, but did mention the 8th and 10th as open. I wired the University's concert manager that the 8th and 10th were open and he promptly applied to Hand for either date.

The answer came back: "The Hall is not available for a concert by Miss Anderson."

Now the facts were clear. The 9th might very well be closed, but neither was any other date open to Marian Anderson at Constitution Hall. Indignation began to sizzle.

Jascha Heifetz played a concert in the Hall and admitted to interviewers afterward that he felt "really uncomfortable" on that platform. "To think that this very hall in which I played today has been barred to a great singer because of her race made me feel ashamed," he said.

Dr. Walter Damrosch remembered an encounter with the restrictive clause when he brought his production of *O Captain, My Captain* to Washington and had to substitute a white choir for the Hampton Institute singers. "This lady," he added, "is one of the greatest artists of song that we have."

A side issue meanwhile had developed. The University, seeking frantically for an auditorium, applied to the Board of Education of Washington for use of the Central High School auditorium. Superintendent of Schools Dr. F. W. Ballou refused. A Marian Anderson Protest Committee sprang up and picketed the Board of Education. A petition bearing thousands of signatures was sent to the Board. A steering committee was formed by representatives of twenty-four national and local organizations.

Protesting telegrams continued to pour into the office of the DAR. Newspaper editorial pages bristled with editorials, crackled with letters to the editors.

And on February 27th Mrs. Roosevelt resigned from the DAR.

She announced her resignation in her column, "My Day." The front page of her paper in New York, the *World-Telegram*, carried it. Next morning the front pages of the *Times* and the *Herald Tribune* featured it, and every other paper in New York ran the story. They ran as well editorials, statements by celebrities; the columnists devoted their columns to the story.

Prominent Daughters from coast to coast were besieged by their local newspapers and the press associations for statements. Five of them declared they trusted the national leaders, would not comment on Mrs. Roosevelt's resignation. A California Daughter resigned; Mrs. Giuseppe Boghetti, whose husband had been Marian's teacher, resigned. The DAR's secretary declared that she had not received Mrs. Roosevelt's resignation.

Protests filled the newspapers from musicians, actors, Hollywood stars, music critics and Mayor LaGuardia. Only Westbrook Pegler raised his voice to protest against the persecution of the Daughters of the American Revolution, a minority group, by various persons on behalf of "a hitherto obscure Negro singer named Marian Anderson." Perhaps that was merely an example of Mr. Pegler's unique wit.

The Board of Education, reconsidering its refusal of the high-school auditorium, finally agreed to allow Marian to sing there—before a white audience. The dual school system in Washington was its explanation. The Daughters also had "explained" their restrictive clause on the basis of existing conditions in Washington. A resolution asking for an investigation of the Board's decision was presented to Congress.

On February 24th I had announced that Marian Anderson would sing in Washington, out of doors, within earshot of the Daughters and their Hall. I sent my press agent, Gerry Goode, to Washington with the intention of asking permission to use the Lincoln Memorial for the concert.

Walter White, the sparkplug president of the NAACP, was on his way to Washington too. Together they went to the Department of Interior, which has jurisdiction over the parks of the capital. Assistant Secretary Oscar L. Chapman listened, nodded, said, "Wait a minute," went into Secretary Ickes' office, and came back. In literally one minute the Secretary had granted permission for Miss Anderson to sing a concert at the Lincoln Memorial.

The Government did not, of course, sponsor the concert. But the list of sponsors reads like a Who's Who of Washington. Into Representative Caroline O'Day's office came acceptances of the invitation to sponsor the concert from Cabinet members, Supreme Court Justices, Senators, Representatives, and a host of persons whose names are the daily diet of the American newspaper reader.

As Marian Anderson's manager I had asked for the Lincoln Memorial for her concert. As her manager I paid the expense of printing, postage, telephones, telegrams, programs, invitations, announcements. The Department of Interior, as was its duty, provided park police to handle the crowd and prevent accident; there was a real danger, indeed, of that mass of good people, stirred to a peak of emotion and enthusiasm, rushing Marian and hurting either her or themselves. All this had to be anticipated.

Platform, public-address system, ropes to mark the aisles—all had to be provided. And the complicated business of the radio network, newsreel cameras, sound-recording devices had to be handled by an expert. My publicity staff was on hand to give the radio, newsreel and newspaper men the service they have come to expect in this highly organized modern world; they get it even from the War and Navy Departments when they are reporting the war.

We gave our services, we paid the incidental expenses, but this is one event I do not claim as a publicity stunt. Anyone who has read the record knows it was as nearly spontaneous an arising of men and women of good will in Washington as there can be in our times. Well managed, of course. No untoward events. No jarring notes.

Easter Sunday came closer. All the arrangements were made.

Everything was ready. For us the excitement mounted until it was almost unbearable.

And on Saturday, at about midnight, Marian telephoned from Philadelphia, "Must we really go through with this?"

For Marian it had been a difficult time. The denial of the Hall, then of the school auditorium, was a painful shock to begin with. And then the storm of protest that swirled about her innocent head, welcome as it was for the sake of principle, violated all her personal needs for privacy, serenity, peace. I have said it before and it bears repeating: Marian has not the instincts nor the temperament of a fighter. And when, through no fault of hers, the issue arose and the fight was on, she was as uncomfortable as one might well be at the center of a cyclone. Willingly as she did her part in the service of her people, she would far rather it had been some other, someone who could enjoy the fight.

And so on the eve of her greatest concert she telephoned in a state of actual fright to ask whether we really had to go through with it.

But when we took her from Union Station to Governor Pinchot's house, with the sirens of a police escort shrieking through the quiet Sunday-morning streets, she was calm and ready. At the Governor's, she changed to her concert gown and quietly glanced over her music once more, while the police captain stood on the sidewalk nervously counting the seconds ticking by. We drove to the Lincoln Memorial in a trance of hushed expectancy. As she walked beside me along the roped-off aisle and up the steps to the platform, where great men and women of America stood to honor her, the arm which I took to steady her was steadier than my own. She raised her eyes once to the great bronze figure with so much sorrow in the deeply lined face. Then she turned to the people who had come to hear her and to pledge by their presence there a faith in the rights of man.

There were 75,000 of them. To describe a crowd of 75,000 men and women—and children, too—standing with upturned faces, expectant, quiet, attentive, is beyond my powers. The effect of such a mass of human beings, their eyes and ears and very hearts fixed on one figure, is indescribable. Looking down at them, one feels a kind of buoyancy, as though one were floating on a sea— and it was a sea, with a tide of strong feeling flowing from them to the erect figure of a woman standing composed and ready by the piano on the platform.

When she opened her lips and sang, it was as though the tide flowed back again to them. She returned to them, with all the sincerity in her, the human goodness which they had offered her. We have come to expect of Marian and her singing not only the beautiful instrument beautifully used, but the truly great power of music. We listen, not only to be sung to, but to be exalted. On that Easter Sunday 75,000 Americans shared in that exaltation, and it shone in their faces.

A mural painting of that Easter Sunday afternoon, the work of Mitchell Jamieson, adorns a wall in the Department of Interior building. At the dedication in January, 1943, Secretary Ickes said, "Her voice and personality have come to be a symbol—a symbol of the willing acceptance of the immortal truth that 'all men are created free and equal.' "

To which Marian replied, "I am deeply touched that I can be in any way a symbol of democracy. Everyone present was a living witness to the ideals of freedom for which President Lincoln died. When I sang that day I was singing to the entire Nation."

CHAPTER NINE

Life Among the Stars

*W*HEN I BEGAN my career there was an unbreakable rule about tenors. A tenor could be either an Italian or an Irishman. If he was an operatic tenor, he had to be an Italian. If he had the misfortune to be born somewhere else, he had to sneak off to Italy, change his name, acquire an Italian birthplace, family and recipe for spaghetti as it is cooked in the region of his adopted "native" town. He could then return to New York with his brand-new personality for an operatic debut.

Thus it is a matter of constant astonishment to me that the greatest Italian tenor in America today, and probably in the world, was born, like Al Smith, on the East Side of New York.

I did not discover Jan Peerce. Jan discovered me. I don't know at what point in his remarkable progress he decided that my management was the one that would best help him to get where he wanted to go. With his own special brand of persistence—and there isn't a nicer kind—he proposed himself as a candidate for my concert list until I capitulated.

By temperament I am an optimist, eager to mark the rosy tint on the horizon for an artist with promise. I cannot now give any excuse for holding out in Jan's case, unless it was the old rule that a tenor must be an Italian. After all, a New York boy, singing five-a-day shows at the Music Hall—who could imagine him as the ardent Alfredo in *La Traviata*, as the gay duke in *Rigoletto*? Who

262

could see him alone on the stage of Carnegie Hall, facing the New York musical audience, than which there is no tougher, and the New York critical gentry?

Nothing in his record led me to believe he was equal to it. Nothing, that is, except his own determination, which shines through Peerce's whole history. He had supported himself through college as the leader of his own dance band, playing the violin and singing the vocals. After college he put away his violin, and concentrated on his voice. Expensive trips abroad to study with expensive teachers were not for him. He found his training right at home, picking and choosing among his teachers, taking tours and radio dates with dance bands to earn a living while his lovely, equally determined little wife Alice made ends meet.

He was singing and playing the violin on one of these occasional engagements, at a dinner in honor of Weber and Fields at the Hotel Astor, when S. L. Rothafel, the great "Roxy," first heard him. Roxy sent back his card, asking Jan to call on him at his office.

"Why do you play the violin?" Roxy asked him.

"Oh, I know I'll never be a Heifetz," Jan admitted, grinning, "but the fiddle helps to pay for my new baby."

Roxy began to paint a glowing future as a singer, a picture which made the youngster's heart swell. "Go home. Study. I'll call you for our first broadcast."

The first Music Hall broadcast, preceding the gala opening of the fabulous place, came and went, and no call from Roxy. Jan was in a panic. He had counted so much on Roxy, who had opened the door of the future and let him peer through the crack. A friend said, "He just forgot. Write him a letter." Jan wrote a letter.

Sure enough the call came. He went down and put himself in the hands of Roxy's program director, who gave him a song to learn, "Give Me One Hour" from *The White Eagle*. He learned it, rehearsed it, waited for the call to the second broadcast. Again no call.

On the third broadcast, at last he sang. Letters began to come in, asking who the new tenor was, where he came from. Peerce was in.

Preparations were going on for the gala premiere that would open to the public the doors of this unbelievable new motion-picture theatre with its two shows a day, reserved seats, waterfall, orchestra on an elevator, and a thousand other wonders. Jan was given a song, "Journey's End," and it almost proved to be journey's end for him.

On the day of the opening Roxy called him from rehearsal to his office in the Music Hall. "My boy, you're in show business now," Roxy told him. "You have to take the bad with the good." And he broke the news that Jan's number was cut out of the show.

It was no fault of Jan's; the show was too long. And even without Jan's number it was still too long, much too long, as those who saw it can remember. It was still going on at midnight.

Jan stood around in the wings during the show, knowing that Alice was out front waiting to hear him sing, and knowing she was going to be bitterly disappointed. He had not had the heart to tell her. Taylor Holmes stopped to speak encouragingly to Jan. Ray Bolger, coming off the stage after his number, put his hand on Jan's shoulder.

"Have you ever hit the tank towns?" Ray asked him with gruff sympathy. "Have you ever traveled with a circus? Have you ever played twenty shows a day? You're a trouper now. This is your first lesson."

But Roxy was ill, and nobody seemed to remember young Peerce.

He had a four weeks' contract, and each week he turned up to report to Bill Stern, the sports commentator, who was stage manager. One day the musical director asked him if he would like to earn his money. Jan said he would do anything, even sweep the floor.

He was given the assignment of singing into the microphone from backstage, while the new audience was coming into the house. By this time Roxy's impressive plan of a two-a-day movie house had been abandoned and the shows were continuous.

So Jan sang from backstage. No name in the program, no announcement, just a voice. And sometimes, like the time his brother brought a bunch of friends down to hear him, the mike went off, and even the voice was lost.

But H. B. Franklin, managing during Roxy's illness, heard him on the public-address system in his office, and sent for him. "Are you nervous? Are you afraid to walk out on the stage?" he asked.

"No—that's what they want me to do, sing backstage," he answered.

So Franklin put him in the pit of the Center Theatre, disguised as a member of the orchestra, and he sang his next assignment from there.

At last Roxy recovered and Jan was in the Music Hall show. When Roxy left, Jan loyally went with him, going on tour for Paramount with the troupe, coming back to sing in the Paramount Theatre in New York. The Music Hall invited him back, and after some months he returned. He was with the Music Hall, in all, about nine years.

Roxy opened more than one door to Jan. When he was sick in the hospital he asked John Royal of NBC to visit him there, and by planned accident, when he turned on the radio, there was Jan singing. Royal, impressed, gave Jan a sustaining program at NBC. His first commercial program came soon after.

Roxy would be proud of his protégé today. If he could walk down Broadway and hear Jan's voice coming from a jukebox, singing one of the exuberant Italian folksongs that Caruso used to sing, Roxy would smile. The great tenor voice has made the full circle, and now at his peak as an artist, Jan Peerce is more popular than the popular field could ever have made him.

It was while he was still at the Music Hall that Jan had his first champagne-and-caviar engagement. The Soviet Embassy in Washington invited him to sing at one of its elegant dinners. Mistaking his shyness for hesitation on political grounds (this was before the war) the emissary said, "Don't be disturbed. Another American will be there, in fact he will be the guest of honor. His name is Charles Evans Hughes."

The Radio City Music Hall paid Jan's bills, but did not feed his longings. He garnered a few concert dates, one of them at the Hollywood Bowl. He sang at labor festivals, benefits, rallies. I knew all this about him—and I did not see him in the role of concert artist or opera star.

For a year, it seems to me now, I kept meeting Jan Peerce. I walked past Carnegie Hall—and Jan Peerce came out. I sat in a barber chair being shaved—and Jan was in the next chair. He couldn't have planned all these meetings, but there he was.

Finally one of his teachers, the late Giuseppe Boghetti, who was also Marian Anderson's teacher, asked me to come to his studio to hear Jan. I had heard Jan, but I went.

I left the studio with a new concert artist, an Italian tenor who wasn't Italian. It was too late to book him for that season, but I had promised to do what I could for him.

It was later that season that Alice and Jan sat in my office and Alice said, "You don't believe in Jan, do you? And I don't blame you. You don't know what he can do."

Still later I was on the Coast when he came out to sing *La Traviata* at the Bowl; I knew then that I had a star.

I began talking about him at the Metropolitan, and finally I had an appointment for an audition. Jan sang six songs, and I said to him, "Go on out and have a cup of coffee. Everything is going to be all right."

He was unbelieving. "Are you kidding?" he asked me.

"No, I'm serious. It's going to be all right."

And it has been all right ever since.

That was five years ago. Each year Jan has grown in stature and achievement. Each year he has added another and another of the great operatic roles to his repertoire. Year before last it was Verdi's *Masked Ball*, which I have always loved. Last year he sang *La Bohème* for the first time at the Metropolitan.

Jan has the voice of the great tenors, but that is not all he has. He is sound, he is workmanlike, he is steady.

He has a professional attitude toward his work, which is rather a new thing in music. Theatre folk have always had it, and prided themselves on it. They call it being a good trouper. Our young American stars have brought it into the music world, and while we are likely to have less chewing of the scenery, and perhaps less picturesque memoirs, we'll have more and better music.

Jan's great voice and his admirable musicianship earned the most coveted tribute a musician could win, the attention of Arturo Toscanini. Jan tells charmingly the story of how he first sang for the Maestro, who was looking for a tenor for the Ninth Symphony.

Jan rang the bell of the Maestro's apartment in the Hotel Astor, and Toscanini opened the door himself. Jan is rarely caught without a word to say for himself, but in the unexpected presence of the man he admires most in the world of music, he was tongue-tied.

In the living room with the big piano to give him confidence, he found words to answer the questions the Maestro asked him. He had not brought any opera music, no, but he could sing a number of arias from memory. Good, approved the Maestro. He himself would accompany.

The strong, lined hands at the piano swung into the opening bars of "Una Furtiva Lagrima," that most difficult of tenor arias, from *Elisir d'Amour*. Jan wondered whether he dared open his mouth, whether any voice would come. Outside on Times Square it had begun to snow. He stood at the window, watching the snow, and, forgetting who his accompanist was, he sang.

So well has he sung for Toscanini, then and since, that the Maestro calls Jan his favorite tenor, and has summoned him again and again: to make the "Hymn of Nations" film with him for the Office of War Information, a thrilling morale film shown in liberated lands abroad; to sing the leading role in Toscanini's two-part broadcast production of Beethoven's *Fidelio*.

Jan knows his art, and he knows his business. By this I don't mean he is a business man. Alice is far the better business man of the two, and Jan is the first to admit it. There was the matter of the radio contract. A very good contract, a very good sponsor, but it would tie Jan up so that he could do nothing else. Alice said no. I said no. Jan said yes, and signed the contract.

And then the Metropolitan offer came through.

Alice got Jan out of his fix, and he has only recently finished paying off his penalty in radio appearances at the union scale. The funniest thing about this is Jan's willingness to confess that he got himself into that tight spot all by himself, with no help from anyone. No alibis, no complaints.

There aren't many artists like Jan, nor, for that matter, many human beings.

Either his three fine children or his career or the combination has made a suburbanite of Jan. Larry, who is fourteen, nine-year-old Joan and little Susan need plenty of space, and Papa needs space too. There are few apartment dwellers in New York who will listen to an opera tenor sing his scales.

So Jan is a commuter, a fact which surprises no one more than himself. He leaves his beautiful house, which he bought two years ago, in the morning and catches a bus to the New Rochelle station, going to his rehearsal for the Celanese hour (on which he has been a fixture for three years) or some other radio rehearsal, to his conferences, to his Victor recordings or his Metropolitan Opera rehearsals like any business man to his office.

Steady, sunny-tempered, smart as a whip, Jan has only one annual fling at temperament. As train time draws near each fall he is agonizedly certain he is catching a cold.

I don't hold it against him. Who could want to leave that nice family, anyway?

Most Civilized Man in the World

I count that day a happy one when Artur Rubinstein came to look upon me as a friend. I do not know exactly what day it was— the day in Paris when I succeeded at last in persuading him that it was time for him to return to America, or the night of his first performance in Carnegie Hall in this third and greatest Rubinstein epoch. Or perhaps it was the day I saw him off on the boat after our first season together, when he knew beyond a doubt that I had been right that afternoon in Paris, that America was in the palm of his hand from then on, and that we could look forward to a long and happy musical marriage.

Rubinstein's volcanic personality struck me no less than his colossal artistry at the piano when I first heard him in Carnegie Hall during the season of 1921-22. He was unique in every way: in his dynamic approach to his instrument, in the grandeur of his interpretations, in the charm which left a train of adorers wherever he passed by.

Even his appearance was extraordinary. In her book about the great who frequented her salon, Music at Midnight, Muriel Draper described him with an uninhibited ecstasy, speaking of his "beautiful head . . . Eyes pale with intensity seemed more like hieroglyphics of intelligence than eyes in a face and a somber Semitic nose carved with chastening Polish delicacy supported

269

them. Pale firmly-full lips smiled with nervous sadness, and only the chin was allowed to rest a little from the forward-moving pace of his vitality. It afforded a slight pause in the breathless race to take in the rest. The next minute you realized that its backward movement was controlled with a fierceness that could defeat a Napoleon. . . ."

Miss Draper's rhapsodics notwithstanding, I saw in Artur Rubinstein a man with the exciting individuality as artist and person which accompanies greatness. More than that, I liked him. I liked his grace, his elegance, his old-world courtliness, his lightning intelligence. I liked his burning, uncompromising patriotism. I liked his acid wit tempered with humanity, combined so oddly with a sturdy democracy of spirit, a child's tireless delight in living, and a prodigious energy for both work and pleasure which left ordinary folk panting in his wake.

I wooed him that season, borrowing him from his manager, R. E. Johnson, for concerts in Philadelphia and in the Brooklyn Academy of Music. But he was not happy in America.

He had been here before. In 1906, as a prodigy of sixteen, he had made a whirlwind tour of the country, playing seventy-five concerts in three months and arriving in San Francisco just in time to be caught by the earthquake and to see Caruso, as he recalls, "running like a rabbit in his nightshirt."

His coming to America had been preceded by a fanfare of wild excitement. A protégé of the great Joachim, who had conducted the orchestra for his debut in Berlin at the age of eleven, he had displayed his talents all over Europe, had been presented by Saint-Saëns to the Concert Society of Paris as "one of the greatest artists I know." He had been sent to pay a call on Paderewski, who persuaded him to stay three months. He was already, at sixteen, a fabulous person.

He was to become more and more fabulous. When American critics granted him "the intelligence of maturity and the wit of a 'boulevardier,' " but made certain reservations on the grounds of his "immaturity," he returned to Europe and disappeared from sight for four years. When he turned up in Berlin in 1910 he had emerged from a storm cloud compounded of love of music, love of country and love—a cataclysm which would have shattered a lesser spirit, but from which he rose triumphantly greater in soul.

Europe opened to him then. He toured the Continent with a passport from his native land bearing the inscription, "On a mission of art for Poland." In 1916 he went to Spain to give four recitals, and remained to play one hundred twenty. The Spaniards petted him like a matador, called him a "special Spaniard," and acclaimed him a master of their own greatest composers, Albeniz and De Falla.

From Spain he went to South America, then to the United States. After the 1922 season he did not return until 1927. Then he forswore this country forever.

His was the same experience as Chaliapin's. It is not infrequently the fate of great men to be first spurned, then worshiped. Their very uniqueness, the qualities which make them greatly memorable, frighten conservative folk away from them at first. Like Chaliapin, Rubinstein came to America trailing clouds of glory; the battle against conservatism in the New World—paradoxically, the New World has always been more conservative than the old in matters of art—was not to his taste, and he withdrew to the cities which knew how to value him, to London and Paris and Madrid, to Vienna and Warsaw.

But not to Berlin. He had spent his childhood there, had learned his art at the feet of Berlin's great teachers. He had been, during the First World War, in Paris, rebelliously using that gift of tongues which made him more valuable behind the lines, as a reader of secret German documents for the Allies. When, in Poland after that war, he saw the murder perpetrated by Ger-

271

many, he swore he would never play in that land again. And he has not.

From 1928 on, I pursued Rubinstein. To me his decision to remain away from the United States was not final. I talked to his European managers each time I went abroad, and at last one day in Paris I cajoled him into a conference. We talked an hour or more, and in the end I had convinced him that America was ready for him at last.

In November, 1937, he and his lovely wife stepped off the Queen Mary. His marriage to Nela Mlynarski, daughter of the famous Warsaw conductor and one of the celebrated beauties of Poland, had been a fairy-tale wedding in London in 1932. For years Rubinstein had coursed around the world, a world of end-less delight to him; he frolicked and drank champagne and protested that he was "99 per cent interested in women." To witness the end of that life and the beginning of the new life as Nela's husband, all the notables of Europe flocked to Lon-don. The Polish Ambassador was his best man; Ruth Draper gave the bride away; and seven Ambassadors, as well as the painters, musicians, statesmen and social dictators of Europe were there.

Dozens of his friends came that chilly November day to see them step off the boat, bundled in furs, onto the soil of America for the first time in ten years.

Characteristically, he had prefaced this arrival with a stupendous amount of journeying. Beginning in Europe the previous October, he had given seventy-two concerts on the Continent, had sailed for South America with Nela and the two babies, to stay three months and play sixty concerts; had flown with his family back over the Andes to take a boat for Boulogne; had paused in Paris long enough to see his family re-established in the converted cob-bler's shop of which he had made an enchanting home; had hur-ried to Amsterdam to catch a plane for Australia; had played

272

twenty-four concerts in two months there, flown back to Paris, and found time to rest before embarking for America in November. He arrived not even panting, although the mere recording of this prodigious race leaves me breathless.

His first concert was with the New York Philharmonic, John Barbirolli conducting. He played the Brahms B flat Major concerto brilliantly, but Daniel Gregory Mason's *Lincoln Symphony* had its first performance on the same program, and the critics devoted their principal attention to this event, giving the return of Artur Rubinstein to the American concert platform only passing notice.

I was disappointed, but not discouraged. That Sunday afternoon he played with the Philharmonic again, this time the Tchaikowsky concerto, and this concert was broadcast. Away out in Dallas, Texas, John Rosenfield of the *Dallas Morning News* listened at his radio and threw his hat in the air. Rubinstein was back!

He played seventeen concerts in those nine weeks, appearing with seven leading symphony orchestras. By the time he reached Carnegie Hall in January for his first of two solo performances the critics were writing of his "triumphant return," his "inflammatory" playing. Olin Downes wrote: "Mr. Rubinstein must have possessed six hands and thirty fingers on his person, perhaps an orchestra as well, concealed in the vicinity of his sounding-board." "Mr. Rubinstein left his audience cheering and his piano limp," wrote Louis Biancolli in the *World-Telegram*. "Galvanic," "powerful," "delicate and diaphanous"—the critics' hunt for new synonyms to describe his exciting pianism had begun. He played Stravinsky's *Petrouchka Suite*, arranged for piano and dedicated to Rubinstein, for the first time at that concert, and the audience cheered.

But the public in general had not yet caught the flash of a new and electric personality, and the receipts for the first season were not good. I had complete confidence, however, and presently the bookings that began to come in for the next season bore me out. It is no secret today what Rubinstein is. His tours are a record of sold-out houses. He races back and forth between California—his thirty-second "permanent" home—and New York two or three times a season, selling out consistently all over the country, breaking box-office records. He plays two or three times a season in Carnegie Hall in solo and with orchestra besides. He is a busy, happy man, fulfilling his artistic and his personal life in a seemingly endless round of study and concerts and people from early morning far into the night.

To see him greeting his friends and admirers in the artist's room at Carnegie Hall after a concert is to understand a little the great zest for living that is Rubinstein's. He stands at the end of the room, dynamic even in relaxation, wearing one of the many tailcoats with the satin cuffs—he calls them his "working clothes"—and a fresh collar replacing the one wilted by his exertions at the piano. His collar has wilted, but never himself; he looks fresh as the morning.

The door is opened and the room suddenly shrinks in size as the people pour in, always too many. One after another he greets them, remembering the name, the face, even the language of each, darting about among his seven tongues and delightedly at home in each, kissing the ladies' hands, reminiscing, dropping an encouraging word to a young pianist just beginning on the long road he knows so well—and all at lightning speed, his eloquent face and hands in constant motion, yet so graciously that not one in that room feels he has been hurried through his greeting, nor given less than his proper moment with his idol. Not all artists know the art of communicating with people. Rubinstein has made this art peculiarly his own.

He loves parties at least as much as I, and he and Nela are magnificent hosts. The Hollywood set embraced him at once as a kindred spirit, and the Basil Rathbones made him welcome with

274

the first of many parties in his honor, all duly reported by Hedda Hopper.

Elsa Maxwell began to recall the many times and places she had met him. The columnists from coast to coast began to recount stories of his prowess, like the one about how he smashed the Prince of Wales' piano (it had belonged to Queen Victoria, and at one chord of the powerful Rubinstein hands it collapsed on the floor), and to quote his *bon mots* ("A pianist should never go to another pianist's recital; if he plays badly it is irritating and if he plays well it is annoying!").

And always he has played superbly, magnetically, colossally. The critics have run out of words and begun again. An artist in the grand tradition, he has taken the hardships of touring with the perfect aplomb with which he takes everything. When a piano had not arrived in a small Midwestern town, he rode to the next town himself and came back on the truck with the piano.

Once he came from Baltimore the evening before a Philharmonic concert, with his face unbelievably swollen from some food poisoning. Dr. A. L. Garbat tried to help him but at the rehearsal the next morning he played with his face bandaged so that only his eyes showed. He looked as though he had just come out of an encounter with a ten-ton truck.

He played the rehearsal through, and went home to rest for the concert. I called Mrs. Rubinstein every hour, and every hour she reported that he still hoped to play the concert.

He played the concert. One of the critics mentioned to me that Rubinstein could lose a little weight.

"It's nothing," I said, "it's the light on the concert platform that makes his face look fat."

During the season of 1944-45 we twice scheduled afternoon broadcasts on the Sundays when he was playing solo concerts at Carnegie Hall in the evening. The first of these was in fact an appearance with Toscanini, no mean occasion in itself.

"I like it," he said. "It fills the time of waiting for the evening concert to begin. It is a warm-up."

Only a man of Rubinstein's prodigious vitality could quip that a Toscanini broadcast was a warm-up for a Carnegie concert. But it is true, he hates the time of waiting. He regularly arrives at the latest possible minute for his concert, throwing off his coat, flexing his hands, and standing ready in the wings at precisely the moment the concert is scheduled to begin. When he comes off the stage for the intermission the tension has gone out of him and he is again relaxed and merry. With all his charm and gaiety, with all his glamorous social life, he is never less than supremely serious about his art. Mrs. Rubinstein says it is easier for her to have a baby than for Artur to make up a program.

He is serious, too, about the world. When Mussolini passed the anti-Jewish decrees of 1938, Rubinstein at once sent back his decoration as Commander of the Order of the Italian Cross, with a telegram signed "Artur Rubinstein, Jewish pianist." Incidentally, he cancelled all his concerts in Italy and has not set foot in that country to this day. And of all the world, love of Poland is ever burning in his veins. He played in San Francisco during the United Nations Conference. Stepping out on the stage of the War Memorial Opera House, transformed into a world-conference room, he looked about at the flags, at the faces of the delegates. He saw the flags of nations which had fought and of nations which had not fought—but not the flag of Poland. He sat at the piano and played the Star-Spangled Banner. Then he rose, quite pale, and said, "Now I will play the anthem of my own country." He played the Polish anthem, and the conference hall full of delegates stood and cheered him for ten minutes.

To hear him tell an anecdote is an experience. His mimicry is scathing. Ambitious mothers of young aspirants to concert fame, pompous and false persons of every station are stripped bare by his wit. But I have never heard him say an unkind word to any

276

honest person, however lowly. To young artists—though not to their mothers—he is especially gentle and kind. He remembers their faces, remembers who sent them to him, remembers what they played for him and how they played it. They go away from a moment's encounter with Rubinstein walking on clouds.

With all the many shining facets of his full life, as devoted husband and father, as social luminary, as citizen of Poland and of the world, music is always and forever his mistress. The number of works dedicated to him by first-rate composers are more than enough to make a full-length concert program. It was he who called attention to the extraordinary Villa-Lobos, and the Brazilian composer returned the compliment by dedicating to him his "Rudepoema," which critics describe as a "ferocious" tonal portrait of Rubinstein.

All his life Rubinstein has fought the tendency of the critical fraternity to label him a "specialist" in the works of this or that composer. When he arrived here at the age of sixteen he was already a specialist in Chopin, Beethoven, Brahms and Liszt. On his second entry into America, after Spain had embraced him as her adopted son, he was hailed as a specialist in Spanish music. Now, in his third and greatest epoch, he has at last shaken off the shackles of "specialties," selecting his programs from the whole world of music.

Beyond his exquisite sympathy for the color and atmosphere of the music of Spain, beyond his prodigious power which prompted Olin Downes to look under the piano for a concealed orchestra, perhaps the contribution for which the world is most grateful to him is his new Chopin. His is not the languid, tubercular poet we knew, but a passionate, fiery, even heroic Pole. He played an all-Chopin program at Carnegie in the fall of last year, choosing predominantly the stirring and militant aspects of Chopin, and he amply proved his point.

His devotion to the best music brooks no compromise. He has had the courage to play "That Concerto," the Tchaikowsky work which band leader Freddy Martin snatched from the concert hall for the jukebox, playing it with such tender, fresh illumination that the critics no less than the audience of serious music lovers heard it as though for the first time.

This one-man rescue of Tchaikowsky from the jukebox was only an incident in a duel which Rubinstein has waged for several seasons. The first round occurred when the dance version appeared on discs, with a vocalist singing a mournful lyric. Suddenly the record shops were besieged by demands for the Rubinstein recording of the authentic concerto, and sales of the album made Victor history.

Seeking other dance treasures in the classical storehouse, the band leader next laid hands on Grieg's concerto, and the jukeboxes soon were wailing "Love in the Morning."

Again the record shops were besieged for the original work, and Victor Records relayed the demand to Mr. Rubinstein, who complied by making a recording with Ormandy and the Philadelphia Orchestra. More than 100,000 of the albums were sold in the first three months after its release.

Then came the playing of the Tchaikowsky concerto in concert, and it appeared Rubinstein had reclaimed the deathless music and won the duel. Or so it seemed, at least, until last summer, when a record crowd at the Lewisohn Stadium greeted him with the kind of squeals and swooning sighs normally reserved for Sinatra. Now it is a toss-up whether the bobby-sox have captured the concert hall, or Mr. Rubinstein has captured the bobby-sox. About one thing there is no doubt: great music is the victor in either case, an outcome which pleases Rubinstein to the tips of his magic fingers.

The Rubinsteins' third child was born in January of 1945. Such is the life of a concert artist, that Artur, en route from Los Angeles to New York, did not hear the news until six hours after the baby's arrival, and did not see his new daughter Alene until she was six weeks old.

Serious as he has always been about his music, he became even more earnest when he became a father. "I would not want Paul to be told some day, 'Too bad your father was so lazy,' " he says apologetically.

But it was Eva, who adores her father, who innocently dealt him the unkindest blow. She was tiny, just about walking, when he returned from a long tour. She ran to his arms, hugged him and begged, "Daddy, play for me!"

"I would play for that baby, how I would play!" he tells, recounting how he carried her, transported by anticipated delight, to the piano.

"No, no!" she protested, wriggling away from the piano bench, "Play the gramophone!"

Once in his lifetime, Rubinstein wants to play a concert without a printed program. He has played such concerts in other cities here and abroad, but never in New York. Several times he has been on the verge, but at the last moment he has retreated before the anxiety that it might be called a stunt.

Why does he want to do it? He has described eloquently the feelings of the concert artist, who must be at his best at the moment he sits down to his instrument before his expectant audience, not an hour before, nor the next morning, but only and exactly between the hours of eight-forty and ten-forty on the advertised date.

His program has been announced weeks before. Suppose at the hour of the concert he longs to play Brahms, not Beethoven, Stravinsky rather than Ravel?

Once, at least, he would like to break down the barriers of convention and tradition that stand between artist and audience, and play for his Carnegie Hall listeners exactly the program which pleases him most as he steps out of the wings onto the concert stage. And, being Rubinstein, he will do it.

Lady of Spain

If Lew Leslie did nothing else with his *International Revue*, he saved me the cost of a trip to Spain. Because it was in that production that I first saw Argentinita. She was smothered in inept staging; her essentially pure and simple art staggered under the burden of cumbersome elaboration. She did not receive good notices.

But to me she was a perfect jewel in a too-big, too-fancy setting, a chaste gem in a gaudy brooch. I wanted her as one of my concert artists.

I began to lay siege to her then, in 1930. It took me six years to persuade her that America would love her when she was properly presented, and another two years before she was ready to set foot again on the soil which had proved so chilly the first time.

Again and again I have found myself confronted with this difficulty. A great artist, who because of unfortunate auspices or infelicitous presentation has met with less than his due on his first entry into America, is naturally reluctant to try a second time. Why should he break his heart against the wall of American indifference when Europe clamors for him, South America welcomes him like a king, Australia kills the fatted calf whenever he chooses to make the long journey "down under"?

So I have developed a skill like that of the trainer urging a nervous and beautiful race horse over a hurdle which has once tripped him. After one miss, the hurdle looks twice as high as it did the first time, and the persuader needs all the art he can muster. If I had any tinge of uncertainty in my soul, I probably should not succeed. For artists have a superhuman scent for another's doubts and hesitations.

But I cannot imagine a half-hearted pursuit. When I have gone after artists, it is because I believe in them, and in my own ability to present them to their and my advantage. It must be that my confidence, my optimism without a chink in it, has won them over. In every case where I have persuaded a reluctant artist, I have been able to make good on my promises of cheering audiences and solvent tours.

So it was with Argentinita, who had been the adored queen of the dance in Spain and, whenever she ventured across the border, in Paris as well. An actress in Martinez Sierra's theatre in Madrid, a friend of the martyred Loyalist poet Garcia Lorca, she had followed the dance from end to end of the peninsula, into the mountains and even into the caves of Granada where the gypsies tread their *bulerias*. She had shown Spain's own great art of the dance to Spain itself, had earned the love and gratitude of her own people, and gone on to carry this subtle and delightful entertainment to Europe's capital.

With the Civil War, her ballet company denuded of its male dancers, she made her way to London where Anton Dolin and Lady Eleanor Smith sponsored her debut. London, too, was at her feet when I coaxed her at last to try America once more.

She danced at the Majestic Theatre on November 13th—the year was already 1938—and by November 14th she knew I had been right. The critics warmed at once to the diminutive black-haired figure on the stage, with the straight back and the proudly carried head, weaving through the intricacies of the highly complex dances of Spain, dancing and singing to herself as though the audience out front were not there at all.

"She dances to please herself," the European writers had discovered to their own astonishment, and the Americans not only accepted her curious self-absorption on the stage, but were enchanted with it.

Though you sat in a crowded theatre, elbow to elbow with your neighbors, you had the illusion that you were standing in a square in some old Spanish town on a day of fiesta, watching the best dancers of the countryside step out spontaneously into the cleared space to dance for their own pleasure and that of their neighbors.

So it was with Argentinita, with her sister Pilar Lopez and her partner of that season Antonio Triana, with the guitarist and the other members of the ensemble. But chiefly it was the dancing of Argentinita herself, who translated so perfectly to the theatre the pure dance of Spain that she brought with it the atmosphere of dancing for the joy of dancing itself.

Time Magazine echoed at the week-end the happy augury of the dailies, calling her "Spain's No. 1 Dancer" and described how "Manhattanites thronged the theatre, stamped and yelled, gaped at castanet playing that would have made Gene Krupa sit up, foot-work (*zapateado*) that would have made Bill Robinson's eyes pop."

So began a happy association with a great and lovely lady. Encarnacion Lopez—as she had never been called since her schoolmates named her "the little Argentinian" when she returned to Spain from her native Buenos Aires—was one of the most charming and chic women I have met in a lifetime of meeting women both charming and chic. The angle of a hat, the inflection of a greeting were details calling for perfection, just as the precision of a rhythm in the castanets was a vital detail in the perfection of her dance.

She had traveled to the remotest villages in Mexico and South America in search of dances, had had herself swung up in a basket to the highest Andes. Not only the *jotas* and *fandangos* of Spain but the simple and innocent dances of swamp and mountain Indian villages in Latin America had received from her this concentrated, this fanatic devotion to perfect detail. And the results showed in such exquisite fragments as "Los Viejitos," the "dance of the little old men" which she won in a trade of dances with the chieftain of a tribe in Mihoacan; or in the classic dignity of the Inca women in "El Huayno," which our critics called "the greatest dance of our generation."

There is a story some wit invented—could it have been my own press agent?—that archeologists with rifle and machete, cutting their way through virgin jungle in Central America, once met a tribe of natives who told them of a little dancing lady who traversed the area long before them, armed only with a pair of castanets.

The tale is more nearly fact than fiction. Argentinita did not follow the tourist route in the New World any more than she did in her own Spain, and the result was a constantly fresh, constantly surprising repertoire, so artfully reproduced from the first-hand viewing in its native setting, and so craftily designed for sophisticated audiences, that both art and craft vanished and the spectator was conscious only of the dance itself, perfect in its humor or melancholy, its simple candor or its sly subtlety.

Only by understanding the difference between blunt reproduction of folk art and its translation into our theatre terms can you grasp the genius of Argentinita. As mere copyist she would have been of little value on the stage. She would have done better to hunt her material with a motion-picture camera and present it to a museum.

But she was an artist, an actress and a showman. And one must be all three, to bring a folk art from its far-off villages to the sophisticated audience of the concert and theatre world.

Annually she crossed the country between ocean and ocean, making of her concert tour a triumphant journey. Each season I had gotten into the pleasant habit of engaging her and her ensemble as guest artists with the Ballet at the Metropolitan. She offered her own dances, her ballets *El Amor Brujo* which I produced for her, and the Garcia Lorca *Café de Chinitas*. She danced also with Massine in *Three-Cornered Hat,* or in *Capriccio Es-*

pagnol which was the product of their joint talents as choreographers. One season we presented her in a Spanish festival at the Metropolitan Opera House, with José Iturbi conducting members of the Philharmonic. *Café de Chinitas* had its premiere, with Salvador Dali's settings commissioned by the Marquis de Cuevas, perhaps the finest theatre work Dali has done to date. I have described it earlier in these pages.

Argentinita herself gave no hint in a casual meeting of her demonic energy in search of material, of her fanatic devotion to the true and the real. On the surface she was the chic and charming woman of the world. Yet, wherever she was, artists and composers and theatre folk gathered. She was a sort of peripatetic Spanish dance festival; any little supper party sooner or later turned into a fiesta of Spanish dancing, when Argentinita led the dance.

She died on September 24, 1945, an appalling loss to her thousands of friends, her millions of admirers, and to me. Her heartbroken sister, Pilar, who danced beside her across three continents, conveyed her home to be laid to rest in the Spanish earth.

Anthropologist on Broadway

It is a paradox of my life as an impresario in search of the exotic that possibly the most exotic artist I have presented is a girl from Chicago. I am speaking of that amazing and unpredictable young lady, Katherine Dunham.

When Miss Dunham came under my management she already had a company of Negro dancers superbly trained by herself, a repertoire of productions with ingeniously economical sets and costumes designed by her artist husband, John Pratt, and a record of performances which jockeyed back and forth unbelievably between the most serious concert halls and the rowdiest of night clubs. Such is the ambivalence of her art, that she performed her "Barrelhouse" number both in San Francisco's Art Museum and

284

in Chicago's Chez Paree, to the rousing applause of both audiences. The story of Katherine Dunham is one of the seven-day wonders of the American entertainment world. When the critics greeted her opening at the Martin Beck Theatre by declaring they "heard the scenery sizzle," and someone pointed out that this could scarcely be, since after all Miss Dunham was a Master of Arts in Anthropology who had lectured to the Anthropology Club of the Yale University Graduate School, someone else pointedly remarked, "Maybe, but there are lots of fine anthropologists at the American Museum of Natural History, and yet you don't see people lined up at the Museum as they are lining up at the box office of the Martin Beck!"

Katherine Dunham really is an anthropologist in good standing in her profession. To her, anthropology was the answer to conflicting desires in a brilliant young mind. She wanted to dance, and she wanted to understand the origins and impulses of her people's wonderfully rich dancing and music. With the great good fortune of a fine mind and a sinuous and athletic body, she has made herself both a scientist and an artist, and a remarkable entertainer to boot.

She was born in Joliet, and grew up in Chicago. While she studied anthropology at the University of Chicago she gathered a group of boys and girls and taught them dancing in an unheated barn.

A dance recital in an empty loft happened to have in its audience Mrs. Alfred Rosenwald Stern. At Mrs. Stern's insistence Katherine was invited to a committee meeting of the Rosenwald Foundation. When they asked her what study she would like them to finance for her, she answered, "It's difficult to describe. May I show you?" Whereupon she stripped off her trim tailored suit and stood revealed in rehearsal tights. She showed them first the kind of dancing which was taught in Chicago—simpering arabesques, pirouettes, the watered-down kind of classic ballet which, alas, constitutes dancing in many of the little studios through the country.

Then she threw off these restraints and gave them her version of an African tribal dance. "I want to learn something that will teach people about the Negro," she told the committee. "I want to go where they dance like that."

The West Indies was the laboratory she chose for her Rosenwald fellowship. She spent a year and a half there, while back in Chicago the committee gladly renewed her grant and extended the period of her studies. She danced in voodoo ceremonies in the jungles of Haiti and in the Beguine in Martinique. She was a spectator at illegal performances of the dangerous wrestling dance, l'ag'ya. She came back with a thesis for her master's degree, a book about the strange Maroon people of Jamaica, and numerous articles for scientific journals and some not so scientific. *Esquire*, which makes a policy of printing only articles from a masculine hand, published hers under the pseudonym "K. Dunn."

She also brought back dance material which had never been seen outside its native locale, and hunted out the boys and girls who had danced with her in a Negro Ballet she produced in 1931 for the Chicago Beaux Arts Ball.

Since then she had struggled mightily to keep her troupe together. The Federal Theatre gave her an opportunity to do a ballet. She came to New York with her group to dance Sunday nights in the 48th Street Theatre where the International Ladies' Garment Workers' revue, *Pins and Needles* was playing—a highly successful project—and stayed to give a series of concert performances—thirteen of them—at the Windsor Theatre on Sunday evenings.

In *Cabin in the Sky*, in which she had the acting role of Georgia Brown, she was an enormous success as actress, singer, dancer and dance director. Several spots in film musicals and a Technicolor short followed.

This was where we came in. She had shuttled between concert and night club with her troupe in the effort to keep the company together, for she held herself responsible for their livelihood, whether she had work for them or not. Our plan was to routine her repertoire, which was still for the most part new to New York, into a revue which would be acceptable both on Broadway and the road as a theatrical production, and which could be toured in the concert halls as well. We added a Cuban tenor, and a "hot" group of musicians recruited from among the famous "Dixieland Band" veterans.

Tropical Revue was the happy result. After the riotous opening-night notices, and the box-office lines which queued up at the Martin Beck the very next morning, I discarded all notions of taking her on tour after two weeks, rearranged the out-of-town bookings, and prayed with the theatre manager for the longest possible extension. He was able to give me two months until his next tenant was due, and we played to capacity houses the whole time.

For the last two weeks of the show's stay in town we moved to another theatre, and then we sent *Tropical Revue* on the road. The combination of theatrical and concert booking kept the show moving for two seasons, with a return engagement in New York last winter.

Last spring Miss Dunham announced her desire to go into theatrical production, and we have, for the time, parted company.

CHAPTER TEN

Things to Come

*L*IVING IN THE PAST is an unaccustomed role for me. While I like to serve up a yarn as well as anyone, it is not my way to look backward. Today and tomorrow are the normal boundaries of my thinking, and within those boundaries tomorrow is even more important than today.

I would delight in writing of Jarmila Novotna, the beautiful singing actress who is Czechoslovakia's gift to America; of the Spaniard Andrès Segovia who makes classic magic on his guitar, of the Russian Edmund Kurtz whose 'cello has charmed Toscanini and will charm thousands of Americans next year on his first concert tour. This office is a kind of artistic League of Nations, always has been.

But I am thinking now of tomorrow, of our young American artists, of their future and the future of music and ballet in a world grown wonderfully and frighteningly small, now that no part of the globe is more than sixty hours away from any other, and I can listen to music being played in Sydney, Australia, in my living room on Central Park West in New York.

I am thinking of Isaac Stern, of Blanche Thebom, of Patrice Munsel.

What could be more glamorous than the slender, graceful, seventeen-year-old youngster who walked into my office and signed a contract for three years of concertizing at a guarantee of $40,000 a year? Patrice Munsel had never appeared on any stage, concert or opera, had grown up in a good American middle-class home in the West, the daughter of a successful dentist and a sweet-faced woman who liked to play the piano. There was not a trace of *spaghetti pomodoro* in her history, nor any *crêpes suzettes*— just lamb chops and mashed potatoes and lots of healthy spinach. But her coloratura voice was none the less wonderful, and her capacity for work none the less impressive, and the critics, who were reluctant to accept her for what they thought she should be at her Metropolitan debut, are gradually coming around to recognizing her for the fresh and exciting young artist that she is.

Those who have accused us of bringing Patrice out too early do not guess how many motion-picture offers, radio engagements, concert dates we have refused. Several artists could live comfortably on the handsome sums we have declined, in order to give Patrice time for greater growth, for the study and preparation of a shining young talent before whom stretches a long, distinguished career. Her scope of opera roles increases each season, and it is a charming thing to see a Gilda, a Lucia, a Juliet, a Rosina who is in fact a lovely young girl, whom you can listen to with your eyes open.

There are still as many ways of achieving greatness as there are worthy aspirants, and each arrives in his or her own way. Isaac Stern's way has been to play his violin continuously, with the delight of a boy who loves his instrument and understands it, with the absorption of a true musician, and with a vitality that overrode all obstacles. He insists he was not a prodigy—he was all of eleven when he made his debut—and says he took to the violin only because a neighbor in San Francisco made such atrocious sounds on a fiddle that he grew morbidly curious and wanted to try it too. In California, Isaac points out, violinists grow on trees like oranges. That may be, but even California cannot grow more than one Isaac Stern.

Isaac Stern's way was not easy, nor was Blanche Thebom's. Perhaps the way to greatness is never really easy. Blanche put all dreams of a career in music out of her head and became a stenographer, recognizing, with the hard-headed realism of young America, that a steel-worker's daughter in Canton, Ohio, could not afford the privilege of study in New York.

But Fate has curious tricks up her sleeve. Blanche's father and mother had saved for years for one trip home to Sweden, and Blanche, as the only daughter and the youngest, went along. A ship's concert, a proud father's whisper to the captain that his daughter could sing, and the fortuitous presence of a fine musician who had been Marian Anderson's accompanist; by this roundabout means did Fate rescue a noble mezzo-soprano voice from obscurity.

With a letter from this pianist to Marian's teacher, Giuseppe Boghetti, Blanche could no longer ignore the summons. The modest business man for whom she had typed letters in Canton, Ohio, offered a modest stake, and Blanche presently was living in a tiny apartment in New York with another candidate for musical fame, doing her own dusting, cooking and laundry, and filling her days for three years with scales, languages, *Lieder* and opera scores.

I heard her sing in Boghetti's studio, and gave her a contract on the spot. I was to wait three years for her first New York concert in January of 1944, but it was worth waiting for. She bore out every word of my enthusiastic predictions to my friends at the Metropolitan, and her debut the next December as a radiant Fricka in *Die Walküre* threw—in the words of *Time Magazine*—the New York critics into "fits of excitement." She has moved steadily forward, adding Italian roles to the Wagnerian, encompassing a heavy concert schedule, appearing in a motion picture, recording for Victor, winning bids from the major broadcast programs.

Blanche's intelligence is no less remarkable than her artistry, and her good sense is equal to her striking beauty. Blanche needs no maestro to stand over her with a little rod, to beat her into working. She knows how to work, and she likes to work. Music to her is not a chore, but a life. The design of a costume is a matter for long research among period engravings in the library; an armlet for the part of Amneris may mean hours among the little jewelry shops of New York. She has assembled an amazing music library, just browsing among second-hand music stores, which she came to know well during the three years of her apprenticeship when she frequented them from necessity. No European star of the old days, rising from obscurity to the thrilling spotlight of fame, has a more inspiring story than this modest, poised, beautiful girl from Ohio.

There is a quality among our young American artists, a quality I have already mentioned in talking of the Ballet of today. They are honest, serious, workmanlike. They rely not at all on temperament, on flinging an inkwell where a few quiet, considered words will make the point. They do not trade on connections, on knowing the right people in the right places. They pit themselves and their realistic evaluations of their talents against the hazards of a very hazardous profession. And—as I think I said once before, but it bears repeating—their way will produce fewer memoirs, perhaps, but more and more and always more music.